THE

MECHANISM OF THE UNIVERSE,

AND ITS

PRIMARY EFFORT-EXERTING POWERS.

The nature of FORCES and the constitution of MATTER ; with remarks on the essence and attributes of the All-Intelligent.

TWENTY-FOUR PROPOSITIONS ON GRAVITATION.

ILLUSTRATED BY

FIVE LITHOGRAPHIC PLATES.

By AUGUSTUS FENDLER,

Corresponding Member of the Academies of Natural Sciences of Philadelphia and St. Louis.

WILMINGTON, DEL.:

PRINTED BY THE "COMMERCIAL PRINTING COMPANY."

1874.

PREFACE.

The following pages owe their existence to an earnest search after truth, especially to the desire of finding a rational explanation for the action of gravitation, to find out its true nature and cause. This was the main problem I undertook to solve first.

As in the midst of the sterner duties of life I went slowly along with the above task, one after another of the several topics of this work came up and claimed a share of my attention. The new ideas, as they rose to the mind's horizon, were jotted down with no premeditated design to favor or to disfavor any special doctrine or dogma now in vogue.

As no aid nor encouragements whatever, with the exception of those offered by my esteemed friend Mr. Julius Hutawa of St. Louis, who furnished gratis part of the lithographic plates, were extended to me in this undertaking, I was left at liberty to pursue my own chosen path independently, without being swayed by any influence or pressure from patronage, and thus not hampered in exposing what I conceive to be true.

Having arranged the different subjects somewhat systematically, I thought it not amiss to disseminate the germs of new ideas by publishing them in book-form, believing that not only the philosopher and physicist, but also minds of intelligence generally, will find in them abundance of material for reflection. May they incite to further inquiry and investigation, and stimulate to profound thinking, which is seldom exerted in vain!

These subjects are capable of being more fully elaborated and extended; yet not being a man of leisure, and not knowing how long my lease on life has to run, and uncertain whether some of the new ideas contained in this paper would ever hereafter suggest themselves to another, I herewith transmit them as they are, without further detention. A considerable part of the writer's life was spent in solitude in the State of Missouri, where the principal matter of this work was conceived and written. And although with respect to polish of style a secluded mode of life must be considered a disadvantage, such a life is, on the other hand, well calculated to bring to view in clearer light, during its calm and peaceful hours, some of the deeper truths generally believed to be inaccessible to man. When at the wane of day, midst soothing sceneries of rural life the glowing sun sinks out of sight, the inner light of mind is sure to rise—and as the twilight fades, our thoughts are apt to wing across sidereal space into the unknown depths of firmaments and meditate the motive powers of nature.

That the views contained in this essay will have to fight against prejudice on account of the many new ideas, is to be expected. In presenting a new view or theory it is certain to provoke opposition if not in consonance with the reader's preconceived ideas, for man always believes more readily that which he is familiar with,* and prefers it; he skips the more abstruse points for want of patience to investigate, "and there are some who reject even the light of experiment and observation;"—from sheer arrogance they resolve to maintain the greatest absurdities rather than to acknowledge a mistake; and another class shuns the depths of science from superstition.

It may also be remarked that the reader who attempts to peruse the book in a hurry and at one sitting, in hopes of thereby acquiring a thorough understanding of it, may perhaps be disappointed. It is not fruit to be in this manner gathered and devoured. Rather should it be tasted carefully, attentively, a little at a time. In this way partaken of, it may be thoroughly digested, and yield not only material profit but nourishment for the highest faculties of mind also.

With regard to the new terms introduced, I may say that new words are absolutely necessary to express new ideas, and that I could not do justice to the latter without employing the new terms to be found in this work.

The insufficiency of the different doctrines about the most primitive motions in nature hitherto advanced by the learned, and their contradictory views about the actions of matter and force, leave many of the most essential questions unanswered, many of the most important phenomena unexplained. To introduce a more consequent system based upon sound axioms of reasoning as well as upon the experience of science has been my present aim.

When we take into consideration, that the problem of the cause of gravitation has proved of such absorbent interest to some philosophers; that men of high attainments and intellect can be named who devoted thirty-five and even sixty-three years of their lives to its investigation and study; and that the problem of the nature and constitution of matter has been, from the days of the ancient Greek philosophers to the present time, a fertile field of speculation, and has even of late occupied more minds reflecting on this subject than ever before; the writer will not be thought preposterous to enter upon a similar path. Though high abstractions are rigorously discountenanced by the professed scientist, yet with regard to the problem of the constitution of matter it has been found that he is not averse to listen to such abstractions, and even takes refuge himself to some of the most improbable and strange ones, in hopes of gaining firmer ground to build upon.

To live in the memory of at least some of the good people of coming generations is a common desire very natural to man. But if I have to choose between two evils I would say: rather let the name of him who wrote these pages be forgotten forever, if only the truths and ideas laid down therein be saved and made use of, and not, on account of their weight, be allowed to sink into oblivion, before some mightier voice in more arousing accents can hold them up towards the light of day.

A. FENDLER.

WILMINGTON, DEL., *August*, 1874.

---

*While some persons who always have lived on the higher land of the interior of continents, and who are ignorant of the flow and ebb of the sea, cannot be made to believe that there are streams in the low lands of the sea-coast which alternately flow towards their sources as well as towards their mouths,—so have I seen persons who always used to live in regions where the tides of the ocean run alternately up as well as down the channel of streams, and who cannot be made to believe that there are rivers the waters of which should constantly be running towards their mouths only, and never run back towards their sources.

INTRODUCTION.

Precision in the use of Terms.

"The loose use of words serves men well enough in their ordinary discourses or affairs. But this is not sufficient for philosophical inquiries. Knowledge and reasoning require precise determinate ideas."—*Locke.*

1. Every attentive student of natural philosophy must feel somewhat disappointed on finding that, when philosophers have occasion to speak on abstruse general principles, and deep and fundamental entities which cannot be weighed and directly experimented upon, confusion, disagreement, and contradiction are frequently evident, leading to endless controversies, by which the difficulties are still multiplied, the subjects made doubly intricate, and the progress of science is retarded.

2. The main cause of all this is to be sought in the confounding of the meaning of words, originating in unclear ideas of obscure objects. Wrong or incomplete definitions have been given to them, and there is no sharp line of distinction drawn between different terms which now are taken as synonyms although originally they were made and meant for widely different ideas, lost or not recognized by succeeding writers. Hence their misapplication.

3. No wonder then, that men who use promiscuously different names for the same idea, or have different ideas under the same name, cannot understand each other, and in trying to explain phenomena add only to confuse them. This mixing of ideas might have gained the approbation of schoolmen and wrangling philosophers of the past centuries, and even of some of the present time, but will never satisfy an inquiring mind searching for truth. Thus the purity and simplicity of philosophical truths is destroyed by confounding the ideas they teach, and by taking real substantive quantities which have an existence in themselves for mere phenomena, and mere phenomena for substantive quantities. In this way is, for instance, the term "force" confounded with that of "motion."

4. The mistakes arising from the confounding of terms are, however, not always the fault of the author, but very frequently that of the reader or the audience, which have been accustomed repeatedly to join in their minds one and the same idea to two distinct terms, so as to substitute one for the other; and hence as long as they are under this false impression they are incapable of conviction, no matter what pains the writer or author may take to apply the terms properly and with precision. And thus the confusion of two different ideas fills the hearer's head with wrong views,

and his reasoning with false inferences. Hence it is absolutely necessary that when one uses a term he should use the same constantly in the same sense. An ability of drawing nice distinctions between similar yet not identical ideas is also necessary for the success of both parties.

5. Let us then in the first place try and follow the path wisely chosen by mathematicians, which is: to define accurately the terms they use, and to lay down as axioms certain self-evident propositions that allow of no doubt, and on which their reasoning is founded, in order to raise upon these a superstructure which may stand alike the tests of reason and experience.

DEFINITIONS.

6. (1.) **Power** [not force, but primitive active power of nature] is not a mere ability capable of acting, but it is a real acting ability,* an ability that continually and unremittingly *does exert* itself by effectually *acting upon* or *against something;* the word "exerting" contains already the idea of effort *for some purpose.* [v. §29 notes, and §47.]

Power Points. It is sometimes not only very convenient but even necessary to speak of the *unit* of power, or *power-point,* although in reality they are always either united—composing a substantive entity of extension—or they are *inherent* in such an entity of extension. Power-points can never exist singly and separately by themselves. Power-points not acting upon any other power-points are non-entities, cannot exist. A power-point in the abstract has [like the mathematical point] position but no extension.

(2.) **Primitive power** generally, as well as **power-points** [power in its least intensity] may be defined as an unremitted exercise of a kind of potent *will* or *effort* upon something to be acted upon; yet not a clear will or effort consciously directing with intellectual design, but a crude unconscious effort, steadily exerting itself and endeavoring to perform unswervingly its own peculiar function, and thus is immutable in its character.

(3.) **Lineït** (shortest line) is the most primitive and simple substantive of extension, determined by and consisting of two confronting and reciprocally operating power-points, permanently holding each other coupled in such a manner as to effectually *resist any change of distance* between them. The lineït has extension of only *one* dimension.

(4.) **Cosmolineæ** are the continuous force-lines of indefinite length traversing the universe, and are composed of lineïts joined end to end.

(5.) **Force** and **Force-unit.**—A lineït associated with and acted upon by a primitive power so as to be kept in *motion,* constitutes a *force-lineït,* or **force** in its possibly least quantity.—Forces, whether considered as units or in the aggregate, therefore, are lineïts *kept in motion* by a primitive power, as long as that power acts within or upon them.—Hence force is not mere motion, but motion of *a something* (the lineït) that is moving. It is a substantive something having an independent existence, it is an entity by itself.† [v. §9 (2)]

(6.) **Monit** (atom) is the minutest, most ultimate constituent of matter.

* Power is always active, not only in effort but also in exerting itself; if it seems to be inactive, it is only because its action is hidden. "A *power* is a thing so much of its own kind, and so simple in its nature as to admit of no logical definition."—*Reid.*

† Force associated with matter causes the matter to move.

It consists of a certain number of diverging lineïts, permanently joined with one of their ends in one common point, standing in the shape of rays or radii in every direction all around this point and rotating perpetually about an axis. The monit most effectually resists penetration as well as separation, and it cannot be divided without being destroyed in its very nature, [as explained in §106 (5).]

(7.) **Matter** is an aggregate of monits (atoms) considered merely as an aggregate without any definite figure and size.—All matter is ponderable, and whatever is ponderable is matter.

(8.) **Body** is a quantity of matter in some definite shape or outline.

(9.) **Motion** is nothing more than "change of distance between any two things."—*Locke.* It is a relation of things with regard to change either of place or position. It is not force. Nothing seems more absurd than that there should be motion without anything moved, or without anything doing the moving.

(10.) **Resistance** is counteraction.

(11.) **End-unition** (51) is the inner effort and power of lineïts to join each other end to end, so as to compose themselves into a continuous line as straight as possible, and to persist in this their natural linear arrangement, and to assume this arrangement again as often as it is disturbed.

(12.) **Synduction** (56.) Lineïts parallely connected and immovably fixed, so as to be absolutely without motion, have an endeavor and ability to make parallel to their own direction and position any isolated stray lineït which may happen to come in immediate proximity to them. This ability and effort we call the power of **Synduction.**

(13.) **Versatile Activity** (56.) The monits of matter and certain lineïts, called versatile lineïts (60), possess a restlessly stirring power endeavoring and being able to make the monits rotate, and the lineïts it dwells in to change position continually, not only rotatory but also vibratory. This power we call **Versatile Activity** (v. 56).

7. Of ultimate primitive powers we know only the three defined in §6 (11, 12, 13,) viz: End-unition, Versatile Activity, and Synduction.—Of forces or force-lineïts we have: heat-, velocity-, gravitation-, repelling-, and nerve-lineïts, or muscular energy, also lineïts of electricity and magnetism.

8. *The* THREE *great* POWERS, *End-unition, Synduction, and Versatile Activity, are inoriginate as well as indestructible; each remains with regard to its own peculiar mode of activity eternally the same; they are not convertible one into another; whereas the* FORCES *or* FORCE LINEÏTS *enumerated in* §7, *are convertible or changeable one into the other, though the substantative lineït itself of which all these forces are mere conversions is in its constituent existence as inoriginate and indestructible as the powers it harbors.* (v. 61–63.)

These two postulates §8 I especially wish to impress, here in the very beginning as very important ones, upon the reader's mind.

9. To give a few specimens of the confounding of terms, we will mention the following:

(1.) The words **power** and **force** are indiscriminately used from habit. The unit of force (the force-lineït), although frequently attached to and associated with matter and then called accessary force, can also exist separately *per se;* but the unit of power (the power-point) never can exist singly by itself. (v. Notes app.)

(2.) The words **motion** and **force**; while force is a real extended substantive entity capable of existing *per se*, a quantity capable of being added to and subtracted from matter,—motion is nothing else but a phenomenon, or a relation of things with regard to change of place or of position, nothing but a series of successive positions of a substantive entity in different points of space. Neither do we mean by *force* as some do, simply "the *tendency* of a body to pass from one place to another," for this would be admitting the existence of an occult quality in the body. *Motion* of a particle or body is only one of the effects which the force of attraction acting in or upon that body is capable of bringing about; another and very different effect of the same force is manifested in the holding tightly together particle to particle or body to body, causing them to *persist* in their respective places. Here force is to be found not in motion, but in fixedness. Hence force cannot be synonymous with motion. (v. Notes app.)

(3.) There is especially great confusion with the words **body** (matter) and **substance.** Substance or the substantive something is a term of a far higher and more general capacity than that of body; it includes not only matter and body, i. e. substrata of extension and resistance in *three* dimensions, but also substrata of extension and resistance in less than three dimensions, for instance the *lineït* [6(3)], which is a substratum of only *one* dimension.

Faraday justly remarks: "Substance consists in the energy of forces." Now, as the energy of force with regard to its action against other forces and objects can only be conceived as acting in *directions*, it is evident that we may conceive as easily of an energy of force in *one* dimension, i. e. of a substance of *one* dimension, as of a substance of *three* dimensions. The former is found in our lineït, the latter in body (matter). While the one is called *material substance*, the other must be called *immaterial substance.*

(4.) **Body** and **matter**; in using the term "matter" we have mainly in view that which is impenetrable and weighty, while "body" stands more for an extended and figured aggregate of matter defined in its outline and surface.

(5.) **Power** and **cause**; the ambiguity of these words tends to perplex. "Cause" may be taken as *efficient* cause in one sense equivalent to *power*, while in another sense "cause" means only some antecedent changes of which a phenomenon is the necessary consequence. In the latter sense I wish it to be taken in these pages.

(6.) **Being**, when there is assigned to it a more general and wider capacity (*esse*), is equivalent to entity or existence; while in a more restricted sense it is used for an organized thing, animal, etc.

(7.) **Annihilable,** i. e. liable of being changed into absolute nothing, is sometimes improperly substituted for the terms decomposable, demolishable, destructible. Only these latter terms and never the word "annihilable" ought to be made use of when speaking of a compound as being liable to be broken up into fractions, or into ultimate particles, or into its elements; never can anything existing be said to be annihilable or liable to be turned into nothing.

(8.) **Inertia.** Inertia is generally defined as the property of bodies by which they tend to retain their state of rest, and by which they continue to move if they are once put in motion; but how a property by and through which a body is *kept moving* could ever be called inertia, i. e. inactivity or indolence, can only be explained by the fact that in the Newtonian philosophy it is supposed, that the continuance of a body in a uniform rectilinear motion is *no* change, and consequently needs no active power but mere inertia or indolence to change; but we know that there is a change of place at every moment of the body's rectilinear motion, hence this supposition that no active power but mere inertia (indolence or inactivity) is needed for the continuance of a body's uniform rectilinear motion can not be true. And if on the other hand, the *vis inertia* is considered as an *active* power, as needs it must be, for *in*active powers there are none, what need is there for using it to *keep* a resting body at rest, especially as we know that by applying an active power to a body just balanced in equilibrio by counteracting powers, it will be disturbed in its rest and be moved.—The contrariety of the *vis inertia* is most perplexing and has always given rise to great confusion of ideas.

(9.) **Infinite.** This word is in common parlance frequently used in its loosest acceptation for the words immense, immeasurable, incomputable ; but in science we ought to have only one meaning for it, viz : *absolutely without limit*, without end.

(10.) **Gravity, Gravitation.** By *gravity* we mean the pressure which, by its own mass, a body exerts towards the centre of the earth upon any obstacle hindering it from going there. By *gravitation* we mean the phenomenon of one body approaching another according to certain laws first taught by Newton ; by gravitation we never mean the *power* or powers that *cause* the bodies to approach ; we do not consider gravitation as an inherent primary cause or quality.

AXIOMS.

10. Axiom I. The axiom of IDENTITY: Every thing is what it is (A is A, and B is B.)

Axiom II. The axiom concerning CONTRADICTION: Judgments opposed contradictorily to each other cannot both be true. [A is not B, and A is B, cannot both be true.] Cor. 1. Being is always being and cannot be non-being, which latter exists not. Cor. 2. It is impossible for the same thing to be and not to be.

Axiom III. The axiom of CAUSATION: Every thing or fact, which has a beginning, has a cause for its beginning.—If it has no beginning, it needs no cause. Or: Whatever begins to exist under a new shape, state or condition, or as a new product, compound, etc., must have a cause which produces this change of state, or the compound.*

Axiom IV. The axiom concerning ORIGIN: It is impossible for any thing, either matter, or power, or force, to proceed from absolute nothing.†

Axiom V. The axiom of CONSERVATION: It is impossible for anything, either matter, or power, or force, to vanish into absolute nothing, or to be annihilated.

Corol: From axioms IV and V it follows: that the whole quantum or sum total of the elements of matter, as well as the sum of power and force in the universe is constant, and can be neither increased nor diminished.

Axiom VI. The axiom of OPERATION: Every act or operation supposes an efficient power that acts.

Corol: And no power-point [6(2)] can act, and hence cannot exist, if it has no other power-point to *act upon*. For to act or to exercise a power on nothing is a contradiction.

Axiom VII. The axiom of IMMEDIATE OPERATION. Any thing capable of operating can without a medium operate in no other place but where it is at the time. Or: Neither power nor body can operate or act immediately where they are not.

---

*There cannot be any cause for the *most ultimate* and *most simple* principle in nature, viz: for the power-points and for their effort and action upon each other. For there is a certain real limit of causes in nature, "and it would argue levity and inexperience in a philosopher to require or imagine a cause for the last and positive power and law of nature, as much as it would" argue levity and inexperience "not to demand a cause in those" laws and phenomena "that are subordinate."—*Bacon.*

†Strictly speaking only the most simple ultimate things or entities [the lineïts and their power-points] are inoriginate, i. e. had no beginning, and as there is not a thing that can ever vanish into nothing, these simple inoriginate things are also imperish-

Axiom VII*a*. Without a medium nothing can be acted upon where the acting agent is not present.

Corol. 1. That things with any manifest distance between them should strike and repel one another without leaving their places and without making use of any intervening medium, is absolutely impossible.

Corol. 2. None of the efforts of any two or more things to approach one another can, without a proper medium, be executed over any greater than infinitesimal distances.

Axiom VIII. The axiom of MOTION : A body under the action of a force, and a lineït under the action of power may move; but either body or lineït, when under the action of *no* force and *no* power cannot move at all, whether uniformly or not uniformly.

Axiom IX. The axiom of NON-UBIQUITY : The same unit of matter, force, or power, cannot be in different places at the same time.

Axiom X. The axiom of QUALITY : Every quality supposes a subject to which it belongs. Or : "It is repugnant to our conceptions that modes and accidents should subsist by themselves." [*Locke.*]

SECTION 1.

"The motion of the hands of a watch may be called a phenomenon of art, but the case is similar with the phenomena of nature."—*Tyndall.*

11. Introductory remarks. The universe certainly has its mechanism, its store of force, and its effort-exerting powers acting unremittingly. The ultimate problem of physical science, then, is 1st, to reveal the mechanism of the universe; 2d, to discern its store of force; 3d, to find out the mighty effort-exerting powers that are everywhere unremittingly active; and 4th, to show how, according to eternal immutable laws, the interactions of the different powers and forces take place, and produce the phenomena that necessarily flow therefrom.

12. That it is not impossible to reduce to an intelligible system and in harmony with mechanical principles, the seemingly complicated operations of the known physical forces, is an opinion which has been held in all ages by some of the most prominent intellects, by men who delight to inquire into the laws of nature, and from scattered particular facts to infer the ultimate prime causes to which they are due.

13. The task to judge from a most *general* and *simple* point of view of the above operations of forces, and to conceive them as correlatives under one harmonious system, is by some supposed to offer insurmountable difficulties, and is considered a problem that proposes to comprehend the veritable soul of nature which lies concealed beneath the external phenomena —a problem which for centuries has been fixing the attention of the intellectual world. Visions of its solution loomed up from time to time either in deceptive colors or in a steadier light, yet as often evaded the grasping mind of man.

14. The more science in its progress discloses the laws of the material world, the more do we see the truth confirmed: that one of the grandest features of nature consists in the very *simplicity* of means by which not only the universe in all its vast expanse, but also every minutest part of the most complex organism, is alike balanced and regulated through all their different grades of phenomenal variation.

15. Acknowledging this truth, I too have ventured at an attempt of the solution of the great problem, and the exposition laid down in the following pages exhibits one more effort in this direction with a view not, indeed, to offer to science the new edifice in its complete and finished state, but merely to give the position, foundation and general outline of the structure.

16. In discussing the various topics I have as much as possible avoided all algebraic expressions. It is therefore believed that the different subjects will be accessible also to readers not initiated in the higher mathematical branches. But even if the subjects should require close application, and some special efforts should be necessary to comprehend them, it ought to be recollected that our aim is a lofty one, inviting to the sublimest contemplations of which the human mind is capable, and therefore worthy the efforts and earnest attention of every reflecting intellect. Profound meditation on the constitution of *matter* is especially calculated to present to the acute mind of the more philosophic of physicists new ideas of immaterial agents, and make them acquainted with real existing entities of power they had never before thought of.

Ever since the main features of this Mechanism first unveiled itself to my mind's eye, the words: "Felix qui potuit rerum cognoscere causas," have proved of most genuine stamp as far as the contented state of mind is concerned. They will, no doubt, prove so to other minds likewise, who can master and make the views contained in this little volume serviceable to themselves.

17. By far too many, even of the scientific readers are, now-a-days, partly from impatience and partly from scantiness of time, inclined to skim hastily over the surface and fish up what from its lightness the stream of intellect carries upon it, while they most generally permit to sink out of sight that which is solid and weighty. Let us not imitate this majority, but on the contrary let us carry our researches deep to gain a firm basis.

18. By striving perseveringly not only to become familiar with the peculiar ideas laid down in these pages, but also still further to extend them on his own account, the reader may at least be in better hopes than heretofore, of lifting the veil that screens the wheelwork of nature and hides the connection between cause and effect. Only after we have learned to decypher lineaments hitherto obscure, can we recognize in them traits of uniformity and unity which escaped us at first. Let us then look steadily at the great all-absorbing questions, and light will not fail to dawn upon them at last.

19. At all events we must prepare to rise above narrow conceptions and prejudices heretofore entertained, so as to have intellectual liberality enough "to concede whatever is highly probable, however new and uncommon the points of view may be."

20. A theory may at first appear forced and unintelligible to those who have not pursued the same path of thought with its author; and from predilection for some other preconceived theory these readers may offer to it a most stubborn opposition at the very outset. But just let us endeavor to be a little more tolerant, and try with patience to accommodate our thoughts and views to what we read, and we may become reconciled by and by, as soon as we have got fairly in the track of the new theory and have become more familiar with its new terms.

21. We shall be called upon not only to take a glance at some of the intricate movements going on in the minutest particles of matter, but also from an elevated position to take a general view of the gigantic motions, as for instance in gravitation and radiant heat, executed by numberless space-traversing force-lines,—to survey their coursing and intercoursing, their going to and fro, performed according to immutable laws, and to comprehend the causal connection of whole trains of natural phenomena.

22. We shall try to answer the important question that again and again is repeated by every attentive student inquiring into the economy of the universe, viz: what becomes of all the immense stores of heat continually sent out in every direction not only by our great luminary, the sun, but by millions upon millions of similar suns called fixed stars.

23. After the writer had begun to search for the cause of gravitation, the sole object of his inquiries at first, one by one of the various propositions contained in the following pages crowded upon him.

24. Most of these propositions are problems which neither empirical knowledge alone, nor *a priori* reasoning single-handed, can ever solve. It is only in combining both these methods of investigation that we may possibly obtain the desired result. All philosophical reasonings which reject the field of facts and objects and do not recognize the axioms established in natural science, become unintelligible and untenable—a fantastic play of words.

25. Hence we propose to follow here the inductive mode of research supported by analogy and empirical laws, as far as the subject admits of; and whenever these become insufficient, there is nothing left us but an appeal to the combining and discriminating powers of the intellect to tell of things invisible to sensual eyes. (v. Notes appended.)

26. Through our senses we take cognizance of the existence of the grosser kind of things. There must be, however, in the physical world things we cannot discern by way of our senses, since physicists entertain no doubts about the real existence of some of these things. They say, for instance, they have evidence of the existence of something like an *ethereal medium* filling all space of the universe, as they have also a conviction of the existence of ultimate particles of matter called *atoms*. Both of these they conceive through the exercise of their intellectual faculties by induction and inference, although the realities themselves lie beyond the reach of their external senses, and can make no direct impression upon them.

27. In elucidating the mechanism of the universe and its operation, we should always go according to the sure mechanical standard of the laws of motion. The laws of motion must have *universal* validity, they must be identically the same whether applied to celestial mechanics, or to our industrial machinery. Under such conditions only can we feel that we are treading on safe and solid ground in our physical investigations.

28. The value of a theory about objects of nature must be measured by the number of particular facts and phenomena that can successfully and satisfactorily be explained by it. The simpler it is, and at the same time the more harmonious with well established laws of nature, and the wider the field of its application, the greater will also be the claim of the theory upon us for its acceptance. Let it be confronted with experiment and observation as far as possible. The way to truth is but one, and is pointed out plainly enough by the stern law: to proceed from the knownto the unknown.

29. Argument.—Every fair-minded reader of these pages will, no doubt, 1st, admit that even if he denies the existence of everything else, he must at least be conscious of something existing in him which he calls *his power* or powers put into action by *his effort* in the overcoming of obstacles;—thinking* as well as mechanical motion, both denote and presuppose active power.—† 2d. He will likewise grant that out of nothing never

* "It is no less certain that the muscles of a horse are strained by a heavy load, than it is that the brain of Shakespeare undergoes molecular agitation, producing definite chemical results, in the sublime effort of imagination."

†*Effort* (or will) and *power* are two of those most elementary principles in obedience to which every living being acts and moves, unconsciously though it may be, which effort and power every one of us must acknowledge in himself, and which no intelligent sensible human being can disown. Although our own consciousness may be regarded as the first starting point of all true philosophy, we are not entitled to speak of the

can nor could have proceeded power—(when here we speak of power we always mean *active power*, and in speaking of power in general we include matter, because matter is only known by its power, by its power to resist, to attract, etc.,*) and as there is in nature nothing else known from which power could have proceeded which is not itself a power, he will 3dly, take as legitimate the inference: that therefore from eternity there must necessarily have existed one or more kinds of active power.

30. With our next step, which is to find out the peculiar nature and character of these most primitive powers in action which we proved never to have had a beginning, we are at once launched into the field of actual sensual experience; we have to observe and investigate closely the course of natural phenomena as they are enacted in the world around us, and when we perceive action or change of motion to take place outside of us, without any effort or exertion of power on our part, we naturally refer these actions to other powers existing outside of us, and conclude according to Axiom VII that these powers are in the very places where they act. And as the horizon of our knowledge becomes more and more extended, we are forced to acknowledge that the very thought or idea of the primitive power (or powers) implies both utmost generality and simplicity, and hence unity of all phenomenal action of the universe.

31. "Nature's foundations are plain and simple, yet her superstructure various and wonderful. Her causes few, her effects innumerable. Her course the easiest and shortest possible, and her means the fewest that can possibly bring about her ends. The sublimity and profundity, with the almost infinite variety, as well as constancy and uniformity, which we cannot but notice, lead us to look for causes and powers almost as diversified as the effects. It is found, however, that the more fully and deeply we enter into the inquiry, the more do we become satisfied, that the *simplicity of the first principles* is as much calculated to excite admiration as the infinity of the results."—*Exley*.

32. To conceive, to ascertain, and to enumerate these most universal powers in their ultimate utmost *simplicity of action* is our duty next. They must be of such a character that, without contradicting ourselves, we can show the high probability that from them do arise and have arisen all the great variety of motions known to us in nature, both of the present and of all past ages. That the acute mind of *Bacon* considered the solution of such a problem possible, is evident from the following sentence: "And assuredly, since the words or vocables of all languages in all their prodigious variety are compounded of a few simple characters, so, in like manner, are the agencies and powers of the universe composed of a few primary properties or original springs of motion. And disgraceful would it be to mankind to have studied with such pertinacious exactness the tinkle of their own utterance; but to have been in the tongue of nature unlearned." Therefore let us begin to learn the simple characters, the alphabet of nature, first.

"existence of consciousness" as the surest existing something, as some of the leading philosophers now do. Consciousness is nothing more than a peculiar condition or phenomenon dependent upon some active *power* to produce it, in a similar sense as *vibration* [that of a cord, for instance] is dependent upon some active power.

*Take away from matter all the power of resistance of solidity [i. e. the cause of impenetrability], the power of attraction, repulsion, gravitation, chemical affinity, and what will remain? Nothing. You may say substance, but pray what is substance? without power to resist or to bear up, it would not even serve us for a substratum.

Of matter said to exist *outside* of power, or what is the same, independent of power, we can never have any conception, because matter and its extension is essentially made up of power, viz.: each monit or smallest particle of matter is composed of a number of lineïts (§100), and each lineit is composed of two *power*-points. [83(1)].

33. What we must do by all means is: to find the *most simple units* in nature. If in our investigations we are able to set out from what is the *most simple, durable, eternally active,* and *universal,* i. e. everywhere present in nature, we may be confident of having opened "such broad paths to human power, as the thought of man can in the present state of things scarcely comprehend or figure to itself."

34. EFFORT-EXERTING POWER [6(1),29].—The great question sought to be solved by sages of all historic ages, viz.: what is the ultimate, most universal and primitive principle, on which the universe and its phenomena depend, philosophers have attempted to answer in many different ways. Some of the moderns say: it is the *The Unconscious.* But the words "the unconscious" give us nothing more than a bare negation which, without any positive qualification whatever, can lead to nothing. Other philosophers are a little more positive and substitute for the word "unconscious" the word "Will." But a will without action and without power, to achieve something, is with regard to the mechanism of the universe of no value whatever. Moreover, the idea of Will alone being too abstruse, vague, and incomplete, let us substitute the words: *Effort-exerting power,* which term already includes that of Will or volition.—*Goethe's* "Faust" searching for that which was in the beginning reads: in the beginning was the "Word;" but finding this not sufficiently deep, he substitutes "Sense" (reflection). Sense being thought, yet without any operative power, and by itself insufficient, he next substitutes "Power." The word Power simply by itself, however, only signifies ability, but does not necessarily include Effort or Will to act, and as such, power alone can make no universe. Faust at last substitutes "Action," "deed." This comes pretty near, yet not quite up to the mark; because such words as "action," "motion," "attraction," etc., express merely qualifications of different kinds of phenomena performed by ACTING EFFORT-EXERTING POWER. We well may say then: it is Effort-exerting power that had no beginning, that always IS, and never shall cease to be everywhere present in the universe, even in places void of ponderable matter. With regard to the universe we may rightly say: Effort-exerting power was not only at the bottom of all *in the beginning* of the phenomenal world, but it existed even *antecedent* to the latter, just as fundamentally to the then pre-phenomenal universe.

35. Whatever be the elementary principle or entity existing from eternity, and out of which matter and the phenomenal world assumed its present form, *it cannot be inactive,* can never have existed originally in a state of rest.

36. Just as every body and all material things are ultimately composed of the *most minute particles* i. e. of atoms, so every operation and motion in nature, when traced to its deepest source, is found to be brought about by the *most minute efforts,* hence let no one hope to discover or even to understand the mechanism of the universe unless he has properly studied and comprehended these minutest of efforts by having analyzed the more compound changes and the mighty, grand, and imposing energies of nature, which always will ultimately lead him to immaterial power-points of Effort-exertion [6(1)].

37. As with matter so also with regard to Effort-exerting power, are we obliged to admit that it allows of divisibility only to a certain limit and no further, for if you do not admit in abstracto of *ultimate* individual units of power (unextended), you can have no expression for the power's greater or less intensity. For instance, in making comparisons about the different intensities of power, if you say: a certain power is twenty times as intense as another, you have already involuntarily admitted some *unit* of power capable of being defined, or else if you admit no unit, it would be all the same (and would have no meaning) to call a power four times, thirty-, or two million-times more intense. You may say: I need no definite power-unit here, I can institute the comparison by the work it performs in a certain length of time. Very true, but does not the expression 'certain length of time' indicate that time itself is made up of units of time, and that in the same ratio of its units also must be considered the intensity of power? And in order to have a definite unit of power, we can have it by defining it to be *the possibly least amount of power in* nature, bearing the same relation to the most simple power-product [the lineït] that a geometrical end-point bears to the possibly shortest geometrical line that can be thought of between two points just escaping from vanishing into one.

38. *Omne ens est unum* has long since been received as an axiom in metaphysics; by which is meant that every being, thing, or entity that exists must be either one indivisible entity, or must be one composed of a determinate number of indivisible entities. Every thing, material as well as immaterial entity, is subiect to number. Number expresses both unit and plurality, and can be applied as well to intensity as to extension. By adding unit to unit we get the natural series of numbers.

39. It is the *unit* we need, as well in the case of the powers of the universe as we need it in the case of the numerical series; in the one case it is the ultimate unit of Effort-exerting power, in the other it is the unit of mere numbers. And as without units we can have no system of numbers, so without ultimate units of effort-exerting power we can have no system of the universe. If there were no ultimate units of power in the universe, there could be no unit whatever, even that of number not excepted.

40. These power-units considered as ultimate and indivisible, of which more by and by, I have called *power-points*, and in recommending them to the kind reader, it is fondly hoped that these pages may not share "the fate of Democrit's theory of atoms which was long neglected on account of its remoteness from common notions, was unsettled and nearly overthrown by the arguments of other philosophies which came nearer the vulgar comprehension."—(*Bacon*). Atom, however, is quite a different thing from power-point and although itself indivisible into smaller atoms, is rather a complex of these very power-points, as we shall hereafter endeavor to show.

41. But in order to analyze and decompose the complicated motions in nature into a few most simple motions, we must first know the most simple things that *are moved* as well as the most simple powers that *do* the moving, and then by legitimate inferences of the mind we may be able, from what we know by practical experience, to deduce what no empirical eye has yet seen or ever shall see.

42. The laws of thought are in general as immutable as any other law of nature. They are the same for the mind of the mathematician as they are for the mind of the physicist. It may in truth be said that even mathematics are founded upon actual tangible relations.

43. Let us, therefore, take advantage of the true distinctions of the different most elementary conceptions with regard to magnitudes already established by the sagacity of ancient geometricians, and let us apply them in physical science wherever we can, the more so, since most mathematicians are now convinced that mathematics belong more to the natural than to the speculative sciences.

44. Hitherto in going back to the most simple ultimate thing, or to the most simple substantive something, physicists always stopped short at the *atom.* It was the greatest drawback to a deeper analysis of nature that matter itself, i. e. the individual atom, was never conceived as a subject capable of any further analysis, or as a compound consisting of elements of extension more simple than the extension in *three* dimensions.

45. On taking a closer view we find that an atom has extension in *three* dimensions [or rather offers resistance in *three* dimensions] corresponding to that of a "solid" in geometry. The only difference between a geometrical solid and a physical solid (atom) is that the former has *ideal* extension in three dimensions, while the physical solid, i. e. the atom, has real extension *sustained by active resistance* in three dimensions. The word "three" in the definition of atom, however, indicates that certainly there must be something more simple, and we easily get at the idea of extension or resistance in *one* dimension, which directly leads to the conception of a line; in geometry to a mathematical line, and in physics to the physical line, which latter sustains its extension by *active resistance* in *one* dimension. As a line, however, may be divided into smaller ones, we have still to go back to the *most simple* line, which in physics can be no other but the possibly shortest physical line capable of existing between two power-points, and which by division would yield nothing but two power-points. This most simple couplet of two power points we propose to name **lineït**; and as an atom is considered a unit of *matter*, so is the lineit to be considered the unit of *force*, and power-point the unit of *power*.

46. A "point" in mathematics has position but no magnitude, and since more than one point may be in the same position, it is necessary to say that by the term "*another* point" we always mean a point having not the same but another position outside the first one spoken of. A *point* of *power* can have no existence singly by itself, because the word power as understood by us (§6(1)] contains the significance as being not a mere ability to act, but an ability that continually and unremittingly does exert itself by effectually acting *upon* or *against* some other most simple object; this other most simple object, however, can be nothing else but another power-point at infinitesimal distance. The power-point is therefore only found to be existing in reciprocal action with another point of power, either as *constituent* power-points determining each other so as to form an indissoluble couplet, or else as *accessory* power points dwelling in such a couplet, and acting upon one of its points.

47. But power-*exertion* cannot be conceived without having some tendency; the word "exerting" contains already the idea of effort for some *purpose*, aim or intention; hence there is not only exertion of one power-point to act upon another power-point, but a *determination to act in a particular manner*, which may be called its *determination* of action. The most universal tendency or determination, the one that is the condition of the constituent power-point's very existence, is: to join or *unite* to another power-point in mutual corroboration. (v. Notes app.)

48. In accordance with this tendency the power-points coupled in pairs make up the most primitive substantive something of stability, that is, the most elementary simple extension possible, of *one* dimension only, and being the minutest of all extended entities or things. This most simple entity which we have already (45) called the **lineït,** may thus be said to consist of two separate, and reciprocally operating power-points connected by their own most primitive and simple action in such a manner as to effectually resist any change of distance between them.*

---

*Two or more lineits may be connected so as to have one of their end-points in com-

49. Two things are necessary to action 1st, an active thing communicative, and 2d, a recipient. But as there can be no action without reaction, or in other words: as there can be nothing absolutely passive and without action, it follows that each of the aforesaid two power-points is *active* upon the other, while at the same time each power-point is also the *passive* recipient with reference to its companion.

50. The lineït then is the great desideratum which was felt by *Locke* when he said: "could the mind come to so small a part of *extension* or duration as *excluded divisibility*, that would be as it were, the indivisible unit or idea, by repetition of which it would make its more enlarged ideas extension and duration."

One power-point couples another power-point by reciprocally acting upon each other. This permanent combination or couplet—the lineït—maintains its permanency in its *one* dimension against all attacks, and this action is what is called *impenetrability* in this one dimension, i. e. in the longitude of the lineit. The idea of impenetrability, says Bacon "the vulgar school puerilely catches at with an easy grasp of words by making a canon of the *impossibility of two bodies occupying the same space*, overlooking the *power* that is the cause of all this, and how great a light would thence be thrown upon science."

51. Thus we have at last arrived at the most simple something of stability and of extension, or of *resistance* in ONE *dimension*, the **lineït**, that may serve as a kind of substratum to uphold power,* or as the most elementary object to be moved or acted upon by the most primary powers mentioned below. One of these powers we have already found in the *unition* of two mutually corroborating power-points, and the same power will also serve for joining and uniting the end or point of one lineit to the end or point of another lineït, without changing the direction of the latter. In this *particular determination* of the power-points, then, we have our first kind of primary power, and shall call it **End-unition.**†

52. Although by the action of End-unition two lineïts may be able to move and make each other approach when separated by exceedingly small distances, yet one lineït isolated by itself can not move itself from its place by its inherent power of End-unition.

---

mon while these lineïts' other end-points stand around the common one as around a centre; in this case the intensity of the central power-point's action is to be measured by the number of outside power-points upon which it acts, that is by the number of lineïts so connected, and there is no other measure of the intensity of a power-point, so that if the power-point is common to a thousand lineïts, its intensity is thousand, if it is common to ten, three, two, lineïts its intensity is ten, three, two; the intensity of each of the two power-points of a lineït is one, and that of a power-point supposed to belong to no lineït is nothing. In this sense only can we say that one power-point may have greater intensity of action than another, and this intensity is always in proportion to the number of lineïts of which it is the common end-point.

It may be said . two or more power-points can be conceived as being in one and the same point and acting upon each other, and yet it is evident that in this case no lineït could possibly result therefrom. To this we answer, that the assertion that two or more power-points may be in one and the same point acting upon each other, can apply only to the end-point of lineïts, and never to any other power-point that does not belong to a lineït, for the simple reason that there are no isolated power-points in existence.

*To meet the objections which may arise, that power, if it be no subject itself, cannot exist without a substratum in which it inheres, we answer: a *couplet* of power-points according to the preceding view is no mere quality or attribute, but a real entity which by mutually operating upon each other not only exist in, but constitute the very subject, in fact the *most simple* subject (the lineït), in which they may thus be said to inhere and to which, if you will, they may be attributed; and consequently power-points need no other subject to inhere in, or to be attributed to.

† *Unition*, the act or power of uniting. (Wisemann.)

53. Whatever other original powers besides the power of End-unition there may be, they can never exist by themselves. Hence the only way in which such original powers could exist at all would be by existing *upon* the lineït, as upon a substratum; for this reason such powers may be called *accessory* powers of the lineït. And as the lineït existed always, so these original accessory powers, if any such we find hereafter, must be as primary as End-unition itself, which latter for the sake of distinction we may call the lineït's *constituent* power.

54. Now let us see whether we can conceive of one or more original *accessory* powers. With regard to the most simple *modes of action* that can possibly be conceived to be performed between two lineïts we have two, 1.) of diminishing the distance between their confronting points, but leaving the direction of the lineïts unaltered [as in fig. 1'. between **a** and **b**.].—— 2.) of turning point **a** (fig. 2'.) away from **b**. leaving **c** at rest, that is of increasing the distance between their confronting points as well as of changing the direction between the two lineïts at the same time (as in fig. 2'.) by *one* simple motion of *one* point.

Fig 1'.

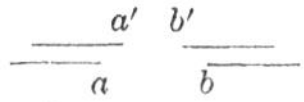

a' b'

a b

Fig. 2'.

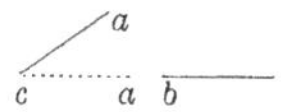

a

c a b

55. In these two actions are included three different motions of two confronting points, namely the *nearing* [(1)§54], the *removing*, and the *inclining* [2)§54]; and herein we find the first germs of the idea a) of attraction, b) of versatility or rotation [repulsion being merely the *result* of versatility, c) chemical affinity and structural inclination. In the above case numbered 1) we recognize the **action** to **bring together**, performed by the power of End-unition in endeavoring to **unite** the end-point of one lineït to the end-point of another lineït;—in the case numbered 2) we recognize the **action to turn away** [one point of a lineït out of its position, while the other point of the same lineït remains in its place]. Accordingly we are justified to assume besides End-unition another power of action, viz: that which does the *turning*. But we find also that this turning may be done either (a) to make parallel one lineït to another [fig. 5', §60], or (b) it may be done to destroy the parallelism already existing between lineïts [fig. 4', §60].

56. If no other primitive power existed but that of End-unition, all the lineïts in existence would be for ever at rest, united end to end in serial succession. But as we find *motion* every where in nature it follows that there must be besides the power of End-unition, one or more kinds of original powers very different from End-unition, and accessory or inherent to a great number of lineïts to act disturbingly upon such other lineïts as contain nothing but End-unition. Descending to the most simple modes of action of disturbance (54, 55), we find that the *turning* of the end-points of a lineït may be done either (a) to **make parallel** one lineït to another [fig. 5' : §60], or (b) it may be done to destroy the parallelism already existing between lineïts. Allowing for each of these two most simple motions an active power we call the one, acting in the first case (a), **Synduction**, that acting in case (b), **Versatile Activity.*** If the latter be of sufficient

---

*Versatile Activity, we may say, consists in an Effort-exerting power accessory to each of the two power-points composing the lineït, which power exerts itself to turn away or *flee* from its companion. From the very nature of the lineït, this *fleeing* motion cannot be more fully executed in any other way but in the turning of each point around the other.

Bacon has defined this versatile or rotatory motion of bodies in the following unique manner: "It seems to flow from a natural desire of the body which moves, only that it may move, and follow itself, and seek its own embraces, and excite its own nature, and enjoy it, and exercise itself in its proper operation."

energy and vigor so as to turn both end-points of a lineït, the one around the other in quick succession, then we have the *whirling* action. From its peculiar nature Synduction acts not upon the lineït it inheres in, but upon other lineïts adjacent to its own, and at inconceivably short distances, while Versatile Activity acts only upon the lineït it inheres in.

57. As already has been remarked, End-unition may be called the *constituent* power of the lineït, for without this power no existence of the lineït is possible, hence it is in every lineït without exception; while the two other powers, Synduction and Versatile Activity are inherent or resident powers, capable of being shifted from one lineït to another, and therefore they are *accessory* powers. Yet none of the primitive powers is convertible into anything else.

58. Although the primitive constituent power of End-unition cannot exist in the condition of separate isolated points by themselves, but can only exist coupled in pairs of points to compose, and in fact to constitute, the *lineït*, yet a clear distinction must always be maintained in abstracto between 1st, this resultant *substantive*, the lineït, as something capable of being moved, and which, with regard to motion from place to place, cannot be otherwise but *passive*—and 2d, the power-points (the constituents of the lineït) which are always *active*, not only in resisting their being separated, but also in doing the moving of other adjacent lineïts. So the lineït may in one view be considered as *passive*, while in another view it must be considered as *active*. The non-comprehension of such fundamental distinctions as these has for centuries caused innumerable vehement disputes and much confusion among philosophers, for instance about the atom of matter, which is subject to a very similar misapprehension, and which is declared by one party as inert, by another party as full of action; both parties are conditionally right, but being limited in their respective views, they cannot agree, because unable to see the other side of the question, and hence they persist in their own one-sided idea.

59. The above named three potencies or powers, End-unition, Synduction, and Versatile Activity, are, properly speaking not *forces* in the ordinary acceptation of the term. They do not belong to that class of forces to which we reckon: heat, gravitation, molecular force, dynamic eneregy, electricity, magnetism, cohesion, centrifugal force, etc.—End-unition, Synduction, and Versatile Activity are Effort-exerting powers*, not subject to the laws of

---

* The three primitive powers of nature are efforts, we might almost say, are some rudimentary analogues to a living being's will, an active, though unconsciously acting tendency exerted to some definite simple *purpose*. "I am not able to form a conception how power can be exerted without a will." (*Reid.*)—These powers strive to win their end not by means of a *free conscious* activity; it is in acting by *unconscious* will and effort that they realize their tendency.

These views and reflections lead not to materialism nor to spiritualism, but to *power-realism*, based on effort-exhibiting power—not, however, without having paid some regard also to idealism in as much as the word *effort-exertion* partakes of. From the effort-exertion of power-points in couplets, as the most primitive effort, and from the stability of these couplets (in the shape sf lineïts), we endeavor to deduce the world of phenomena. We thus confess to a kind of dualism.

Effort-exerting power—unreflecting, unreasoning power, exhibiting a stubborn though unconscious will exerted to some definite simple purpose—we take as the most primitive will-power, out of which afterwards all the *conscious* efforts and *intellects* of the universe proceeded, not only those of the versatile inclined lineïts (§210) but also that of the All-intelligent (§236). In its most simple form and aims, this most elementary effort or will can exhibit (as shown in §51–56) no more than three very distinct determinations, and hence we may say: we have no more than three kinds of primitive power.

convertibility, and rather the cause than the correlatives of the forces just enumerated; they are entirely distinct from them. (v. §7, 8.)

60. To recapitulate then, we have represented in fig. 3′ the lineïts **c, a, d,** possessed and influenced solely by the universal primitive power of End-unition*, yet destitute both of Versatile Activity and Synduction. Such lineïts we call *common* lineïts. In fig. 4′ the power of Versatile Activity permanently dwelling in lineït **a**, has turned one of the two points of **a** out of its position. This lineït **a** possessing only Versatile Activity besides End-unition we call **versatile** lineït; such as the heat-lineït, the polarized lineït, and the constituent lineït of the monit. Fig. 5′ indicates that lineït **a** of fig. 4′ has been turned back again, and made parallel to the fascicle of parallel lineïts **b b b** by the power of Synduction inherent in the immovable parallel lines **b b b.** Such lineïts **b b b** possessing only Synduction besides End-unition, we call **steady** lineïts. A lineït supposed to be possessed both of Versasatile Activity and Synduction besides End-unition, i. e. of all the three primitive powers, should be called **versatile inclined** lineït. (v. 208–218.)

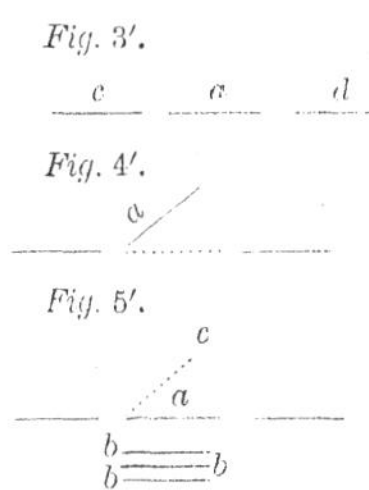

61. We are now in possession of three different kinds of primitive active powers and one kind of a most simple *substantive entity* of *extension* in ONE dimension, which latter may also serve as the very substrat, requisite for the upholding of either one or both of the two accessory primitive powers (57) that are ever unable to exist by themselves without a subject in which to inhere. More we do not need; while on the other hand fewer and more simple powers than these three cannot well be conceived, capable of serving as the fundemental ones, from which all the more complicated mechanical motions may be legitimately deduced. If they are properly understood by the reader and viewed in the same light that the writer beholds them, and their operations duly appreciated, the following assertion of *Bacon* may yet be verified: "For it is most unquestionable that in proportion as simpler notious are discovered, in the same proportion will the power of man be augmented, delivered from the trammel of using only specific and elaborated substances, and invigorated to strike out new lines of operation."

62. We have thus ascertained the four inoriginate *primitive* entities, viz: the three powers, End-unition, Versatile Activity, and Synduction, and the primary most simple substantive of extension, the **lineït,** the absolutely indivisible unit of extension. Of these lineïts we can say with *Locke:* "These least portions whereof we have clear and distinct ideas, may be perhaps fittest to be considered by us as simple ideas out of which our *complex* modes of space...... are made up."

62′. The whole energy in the universe consists in the three *acting powers* of bringing together, of turning away, and of making parallell; and all the numberless phenomena, all the various *motions* performed therein are brought about by the same three powers acting upon the most simple substantative entity of extension, the **lineït,** which latter they also make use of as their substratum.

63. From out of the three primitive powers and their bearer, the lineït, and by and through their varied interaction everything else that exists in the universe may be deduced and conceived as being a product or compound of them. The *most simple* and direct of such compounds will be, of course, the most important ones.

---

* Without which no lineït at all can exist.

63′. The lineït and the three Effort-exerting primitive powers are the true real Existent, the real *esse* of Parmenides; they can never have come "of what is not, for none can say or imagine how **Not-Is** becomes **Is**;" neither can they become nothing.—They themselves never become anything different from what they are, they are unchangeable in their constituent existence—yet by combining they not only have composed the imperishable monits of matter and the equally imperishable soul of the universe, but in co-operation with this cosmical soul and with the monits of matter they likewise have produced, do still, and shall hereafter produce all the innumerable different perishable products and compounds, and bring about all the fleeting, vanishing, ephemeral phenomena which of themselves have no enduring existence and which, in fact, consist in nothing but a successive motion and a continually shifting of the *really existing* entities, from place to place, under different inclinations and directions, under all modes and manners.

64. Having the *lineït* for a movable substantive on which the powers can and do act, and which moreover is the bearer of the powers, we get the following four *most simple extended* COMPOUNDS or productions in nature.

1. Action and reaction between End-unition and End-unition produces — — — — — — —, which we call **cosmolinea.**

2. Action and reaction between End-unition and Versatile Activity produces ✺, which we call **monit** (atom).*

3. Action and reaction between End-unition and Synduction produces ≡≡≡≡≡≡≡≡ **cosmo-velo.**

4. Action and reaction between End-unition and Synduction in spiral shapes produces ◎ , **convolution.** Besides these four most simple compounds of extension we have 5th. Action and reaction between Synduction and Versatile Activity begets the *faculty* of **intellect.**

65. With regard to the first of these products, viz: the cosmolineæ, we shall next endeavor to prove that they exist everywhere throughout the whole universe, except in the minutest particles of which matter is composed; and by another train of reasoning very different from the one in §48, etc., we hope to arrive at the same conviction: of the lineït's real existence.

66. Every clear and intelligent mind cannot but admit 1st, that everywhere, in all directions and in all distances, at least as far as the most powerful telescopic view does reach, there necessarily is extension; and 2d, that the most simple extension is extension in *one* dimension, i. e. in a straight line. But what is extension? Either it is something that exists extended as a substantive entity *per se*, and then this most simple extension can be found in our *cosmolinea* §6(4), as agreeing most completely with these requirements; or it is a power, or, as *Bacon* would have called it, a quality or character,† and then it cannot exist without a substantive something [of *one* dimension at least] in which it inheres and by which it is upheld or sustained (axiom X). So in either case are we obliged to admit for the most simple extension a substantive something of one dimension that must be considered as necessarily existing *per se* everywhere and in every direction, as far as light and gravitation betoken—substantially existing as the *most simple* extension, that is, in only *one* dimension and not in three dimensions [which would be a solid or matter], hence if it can not be

---

* The radii standing in every direction, form a globule.

† Extension, "The state of being extended."—(*Bacon*). "Quality=character."—(*Bacon.*)

matter it must be *immaterial.* The physical lines which go by the name of **cosmolineæ** [§6(4). 64(1). 97.] extend, we may venture to say, not only as far as the utmost limits from whence the rays of light proceed that strike the eye of the astronomer, but throughout the whole universe, in every place and direction we can think of. And as it is thus everywhere in the universe, it is best qualified to serve as a universal medium. " Even extension without solidity" [meaning extension in less than three dimensions] " may be substantial enough to *subsist by itself,* and to deserve the honor of the name of substance."—*Dr. Watts.*

67. If it should be asked: cannot extremely attenuated ponderable *matter,* such as physicists are wont to call "luminiferous ether," be the universal medium supplying all the requirements and do all the services of your cosmolineæ? I would say that we may easily conceive of places without matter; for the specific weight of a body being a measure of the comparative number of its ultimate particles, atoms or monits [not molecules] (§155, 156), and it being known that a cubic inch of pure hydrogen gas of a certain temperature weighs about 238,300 times, or nearly a quarter of a million times less than a cubic inch of gold, it follows that if the gold filling a certain measure, consisted of one million ultimate particles or atoms of matter, the same measure if filled with hydrogen of common density would possess only four such particles, and if a still lighter matter, for instance an assumed ether, be substituted for hydrogen, its (the ether's) ultimate particles would be still more widely separated. [With good reason do physicists discard and exclude all *imponderable matter.*]

68. Hence, to substitute an ether, itself composed of atoms, for the purpose of filling up the interspaces between grosser matter would be decidedly adverse to our aim, because it is a fact that the rarer the aeriform bodies are, the more susceptible are they of yielding to compression, thereby proving that they have still greater empty spaces between their atoms than the more dense bodies. This leads to the inference that within the measure of hydrogen, and still more so of the assumed ether there must certainly be interspaces *void* of *matter.*

69. And indeed, the interspaces between the atoms of ether are by physicists assumed larger in proportion to the size of these atoms than the interplanetary spaces are to the size of the planets. That atoms thus existing by themselves isolated and wholly without mutual contact, cannot act upon each other, except by means of an immaterial medium between them, is evident.*

70. We are perfectly convinced that in these interspaces thus proved to be void of matter, there must *necessarily* be extension, for even if the mind endeavors to remove from itself this idea of " extension" between two or more ultimate particles of matter (remote of each other as we are led to believe they must be) the mind will find it utterly beyond its power to do so.

71. Annihilation of *extension* cannot be conceived even in thought, because thought in its most *simple* operation namely: in thinking of two mathematical points successively, cannot do so without going or extending itself from one to the other. The supposition of non-existence of extension necessarily carries with it the supposition of non-existence of thought, be-

* With regard to the purely hypothetical "ether" so generally and confidently assumed as really existing, a recent writer says: "The purely hypothetical 'ether' (which is nothing but a clothes-horse for all the insoluble difficulties presented by the phenomena of sensible material existence—a fagot of occult qualities and *principia expressiva,* whose *role* in the material world at large is analogous to the part formerly played by the *aura vitalis,* and similar phantasms in the organic world.")—*Stallo.*

cause thought must cease to operate, i. e. cease to think, as soon as all extension is taken away. Therefore thought is obliged at all events to acknowledge the *necessary* REAL EXISTENCE of *extension*. "There can be no existence without extension."—(*Locke.*) That is to say: nothing can exist unless it either has extension itself, or inheres in something that has extension. Now, as nothing seems more absurd than that there should exist extension by itself without any subject or any thing extended,—the cosmolineæ readily offer themselves as representatives of the extended something thus required.

72. Some one, perhaps, may ask, why cannot "space" be considered as the substantia of extension you speak of? We answer: space and extension are widely different; we can properly speak of lines of extension but not of lines of space. Moreover, by *pure* and *simple space* is to be understood neither a substance nor a property, nothing else but the mere **possibility for extension,** it has no real existence *per se*. But if to "space" is given the meaning as expressed in the following sentence (72′,) then we may consider the term "space" equivalent to: the totality, the web and weft of the whole aggregate of the cosmolineæ.

72′. What is commonly called "space" is in fact nothing else but the complex mode in which the lineïts themselves, that is, the most simple extension of which we have any clear and distinct ideas, extend in all directions and in all places wherever imagination and the power of thought choose to look for space inside the universe. Independent of these lineïts there is no such thing existing as: "simple space" pure and void of everything, abstracted by itself.

73. How strange it seems that this something—this, no matter how it may be called, but which I have taken the liberty to term *cosmolinea*—should so long have been ignored; this substantive entity which is absolutely indispensable in our scientific and philosophical inquiries, and without which the science of dynamics and our conceptions about the constitution of matter will always remain incomplete and obscure.

74. This substantive entity of one dimension, this dynamical line or cosmolinea has, no doubt, been suggesting its own existence ever since men began philosophically to think and to reason about the essence of nature; and how it ever could have been allowed to escape the firm grasp of the physicist's mind, is really one of the strangest phases in the history of intellectual development. The conception of the dynamical line's existence is very apt to flash across the youthful mind with the first lessons in geometry, but the weight of pedantic authority smothers the vital spark as soon as it begins to scintillate.

74′. After the present little work in all its main features had been conceived and composed in retirement in the far West, without the aid from libraries, the latter at last became accessible to me in the fall of 1871. Of the many authors which since then I examined with regard to their views relative to the different points treated in my theory, I was agreeably surprised that with reference to a really existing something of only *one* dimension—hence not a corporeal (material) something of three dimensions—but an *immaterial*, though extended, real entity—I had found at least one man advocating similar views, and this no less a one than FARADAY. This illustrious physicist and philosopher in his experiments and observations had been forced to the conviction of the *existence* of force-lines, as entities physically subsisting *per se*, so that they may be substantial enough to be shaken by molecular power, and thus to serve (instead of the universal ether assumed by most physicists) as a vibrating medium, and that among these physical lines he recognized the lines of gravitating force. It was a kind of encouragement to me to see that I was not standing alone with regard to this unheard-of innovation; for this new conception is so much out of the beaten track of long ago adopted tenets and familiar notions that, on this account alone, very likely it would be laid aside without further examination, if no one else had ever reasoned upon it and had held it up to the scientific public.

75. "Two-thirds of the rays emitted by the sun" says Tyndall, "fail to arouse in the eye the sense of vision. The rays exist, but the visual organ requisite for their translation into light does not exist." Neither is it a delusive fancy to imagine through all the unfathomable depths of the firmament that surrounds us, rays continually darting in all directions, real physical lines, which to be recognized as the *cosmolineæ* in all their admirably simple operations "require but the development of our intellectual organs, to translate them into certain knowledge" unveiling to us mysteries never before thought of.

76. To believe in the existence of imponderable bodies or *imponderable matter* is absurd, because it is contradictory; but some philosophers emphatically deny the existence of *any thing imponderable*, whether it be matter or no matter, they deny that there can be any extended substantive entity whatever that is imponderable or immaterial.

77. And yet the same philosophers also assert the great truth that "Force cannot be annihilated." This, their assertion, however, already implies in the word "force" the EXISTENCE of *something* that is *not* matter, for if a thing does not exist, there is no need to assert that it cannot be annihilated. Thus they affirm in the first place the *existence* of force. If it exists, it must either have extension itself, or be inherent in something else having extension, (v. Axiom X,) for "there can be no existence without extension."

78. But it may be said: the same philosophers also define force as "a mode of motion, an affection appertaining to matter." They then mean to say by this in the above sentence "force cannot be annihilated," [setting the words "affection of matter" instead of the word "force"] that affection of matter cannot be annihilated. This affection or mode of motion belonging to matter is, however, by them supposed to travel by vibration, by transversal undulations, etc., "each *atom* taking up the motion of its neighbors, and sending it on to others," from particle to particle and from one body to another. Force being defined "an affection" can as such, according to one of the axioms, not exist *per se* nor travel *per se* without a subject in which it may exist or along which it may be travelling. Hence in travelling, it can do so only by proceeding along a *continuous* mass of particles of matter in actual contact with one another; or if matter is *not* continuous it (the mode of motion) must proceed along something else that is *not* matter, hence not ponderable yet having extension, and which must be supposed to *exist* in continuity between the particles of matter. Experiments have fully demonstrated that particles of ponderable matter never can touch one another and therefore cannot be continuous. Hence even if clinging to his doctrine of mode of motion, the philosopher would of necessity have to admit the existence of a substantive something having extension and being im*ponderable* and *continuous*, in its nature entirely different from matter. Or even if atoms of ether are supposed to fly to one another and thereby impart their motion, how are they to oscillate back again if their motion is thus spent, as it certainly must be.

79. Moreover, one of the most philosophical and most eminent physicists,

Faraday, thought it his imperative duty to seek to realize in all his researches an element of nature deprived of all material substance, which existed as an entity by itself, and this he found at last in his "*lines of force.*" [v. Notes, app. 80(1)1]. "I think that no particular idea of force has a right to unlimited or unqualified acceptance that does not include assent also to *definite amount* and *definite disposition* of *the force,......*"(*Faraday.*) Now, as "amount" means the aggregate or sum total, we leave it to the reader to decide which is proper, to speak of an aggregate of mode of motion, of affection,—or of an aggregate of something quantitative, an aggregate of a substantive entity, for instance, an aggregate of force-lines. [v. Notes app.]

80. In an article written in 1852, Faraday illustrates how much the idea of lines of force, "the physical condition of which partakes generally of the nature of a current or of a ray," has influenced the course of his investigations and the result obtained at different times, and the extent to which he has been indebted to this idea.—And about the assumption of such lines of force he says: "It is not supposed for a moment that speculations of this kind are useless in natural philosophy. They should ever be held as doubtful, but they are wonderful aids in the hands of the experimentalist and mathematician; for not only are they useful in rendering the vague idea more clear for the time, giving it something like a definite shape, that it may be submitted to experiment and calculation; but they lead on by deduction and correction, to the discovery of new phenomena, and so cause an increase and advance of real physical truth." (v. Notes app.)

81. From what we deduced in preceding paragraphs we may justly and safely assume a real, positive, NECESSARY *existence* of imponderable continuous cosmolineae, an entity by itself, present in every portion of the physical world. As force-lines traversing the universe they are darting across each other with immense speed in every conceivable direction, being as it were, the *web and weft* that fills the immense capacity of the universe.

82. CHARACTERISTICS OF THE COSMOLINEA.

(1.) *Extension* in not more than ONE dimension,—i. e. offering resistance in only **one** dimension, being *penetrated* in all but one single direction in which it is *impenetrable,** and this is the exact direction in which it has its extension.—The cosmolinea must be conceived as having only *one* of the geometrical dimensions, namely length.

2.) *Divisibility.*—The cosmolinea must be conceived as divisible into ultimate fractions or parts called **lineïts** or lineolæ, each consisting of two power-points indissolubly connected in such a manner as to effectually resist any change of distance between them.

3.) *Continuity.*—The cosmolinea must be conceived as being composed of individual lineïts joining each other end to end, so as to form a straight line of indefinite length, either continuous, or merely interrupted by infinitesimal gaps.

---

*If any physical line or cosmolinea A darts upon any other physical line B, A is able (without the least resistance being offered by B) to penetrate B in every possible direction except one, and this is in the exact direction in which B has its extension. This latter is the only direction in which any lineït or any compound physical line is *impenetrable.* Hence it follows that any conceivable number of straight lines, say, for instance, one hundred millions of a pin's length, may be situated around a line C (of the same length) with one of their ends all in one of the end-points of C, and with the other of their ends all within a space as small as a pin's head, surrounding the other end of C, and yet not a single one of these lines might have the exact direction of C, and hence C would be *penetrable* by all of them.

83. CHARACTERISTICS OF THE LINEÏT (the possibly shortest physical line).

1.) *Indivisible.*—No division of the lineït into shorter parts is possible, because being the shortest line capable of existing between two power-points the possibly nearest without both falling into one and the same point, it can have no linear parts, it being composed merely of two *power-points;* and no power in the universe is able to separate this couplet of two power-points, because the power that holds them together is the most elementary power. Even if in imagination the lineït could be divided, it would thereby yield nothing but two unextended separate power-points, but no shorter lineïts; and as a power-point solely and separately existing by itself is a non-reality or a non-entity, only conceivable or to be spoken of in abstracto (46), it follows that dividing the lineït would amount to the same as *annihilating* it, which goes against axiom V.

2). *Eternally existing.* [Unoriginate as well as indestructible].—As according to §46 power-points could never have had an isolated separate existence *singly* by themselves, it is clear that the lineït is as unoriginate as the most primitive power, and as no other power is able to separate the two power-points [83(1)], it follows that the lineït is indestructible, imperishable, and in regard to time eternal, without beginning and without end.

84. 3.) *Convertible* with regard to its functions.—The lineït when in motion is called a *force* or force-lineït. Under differently modified conditions, these lineïts or forces assume different modes of motion and hence different functions or modes of action, and thus result the various forces, such as heat-lineïts or heat-force, gravitation-lineïts [of universal attraction], nerve-lineïts or muscular force, velocity-lineïts or vis viva, polarized-lineïts or magnetic force, etc. These lineïts in their various forms are all convertible, either directly or more or less indirectly, one into another.

4.) *Being present everywhere,* throughout the whole universe from centre to circumference, and being the constituent element of all and everything extended, not only of matter but of force also.*

5.) *Imponderable.*—As the lineïts are the very means by which the manifestations of gravitation and weight are produced [as will appear further on] they can, of course, have no weight themselves.

6.) *Unable to self-change of condition,* i. e. entirely *passive* with regard to change of place or position when by itself, unacted upon by any other but its constituent *power.*†—The lineït, 1st be it at rest or not at rest, can never change either its place nor its position *on its own account,* if not acted upon by *power* able to cause the change—either from without by the power of an adjacent lineït, or in the lineït itself by a power accessory to it—; and 2d when in motion [may the lineït be moving translatory, or may it be whirling rotatory around its end-points] it can of itself neither continue its motion without the motive accessory power it harbors at the time; nor can it decrease or discontinue its motion, i. e. throw off the power that is moving it; nor can it change its course of motion, if not forced to do so by *power.*—Or in other words: the lineït can of itself neither begin to move,

---

*There is something everywhere in interstellar space which to denominate simply "force," as Faraday has done, would be insufficient. Interstellar spaces are full of *substantive* units, namely the LINEÏTS of which the universal lines of force (cosmolineae) are made up. The substance of the lineït is not corporeal in three dimensions, it is substance of *one* dimension, but nevertheless a substance substantial enough to resist in one dimension.

†Though passive in this respect, the lineït cannot be called "inert," because its very essence is made up of active power, namely of two active power-points.

nor when in motion, *neither continue in,* nor change the course and the amount of that motion.*

---

* If the action of a power in moving the lineït be neutralized by another power acting in opposition to it, then the lineït is brought to rest.

SECTION II.

---

85. Two kinds of substantive (i. e. extended) entities.—The existence of the lineït being granted, we are entitled to maintain that in nature there are two kinds of substantive i. e. extended entities; that besides matter i. e. the *ponderable* substantive (substance of *three* dimensions) there exists another kind of substantive entity which, although of only *one* dimension, linear and *imponderable*, admits just as well as the ponderable one, of addition and subtraction with regard to its parts. By *ponderable* or corporeal substance let us always understand MATTER, and by the word "matter" no other but ponderable or corporeal substance. On the other hand, by the *imponderable substantive* let us understand the cosmolineae and the *lineïts*. *Im*ponderable matter there is none. Even the merest atom of the most subtile ether, if you take ether to be matter, must be ponderable.

86. On account of the new and unusual character of the subject we may expect some opposition not only from common prejudice, but also from a too hasty judgment of philosophers with regard to the following view, viz: that matter, or rather its ultimate atoms or monits [6(6)] (offering resistance in *three* dimensions) are the products or compounds consisting of factors of another magnitude of entity, viz: LINEÏTS (offering resistance in only *one* dimension); and again that this latter magnitude, the lineït, consists of the most ultimate and primitive factors, two *power-points*.

87. In these propositions there is, however, nothing extravagant or unheard of, for we find analogous cases in pure mathematics, where an angle, although a magnitude very different from that of a line, is yet the product of two lines joined with one of their ends in such a manner as not to have the two lines parallel; and a mathematical *line* is defined and determined by the position of two points. There is a great difference between the *dividing* of an angle and its *analyzing;* for by dividing an angle we get smaller angles, but by analyzing an angle we get *lines* and not angles.

88. Hitherto in striving to find the most simple things upon which philosophers of nature might build their systems, and chemists build their doctrine of chemical combinations, and in all the divisions and analyses of bodies and phenomena, the inquiries always stopped and rested with the idea of atom as the most simple and ultimate basis that man could find, on which to build the superstructure of physical science. The ingenuity of all ages has been taxed to its utmost in order to find out and discover what this thing, the atom, really is. They have advanced the most varied hypotheses, which to set forth would of itself fill a small volume, but never have they given an explanation or definition to be called satisfactory, as the

numerous disputes about atoms plainly show. The cause of these short-comings must be sought in this: they never conceived that the atom could be a *compound*, something resolvable into simpler constituents or elements which are not matter, but a peculiar kind of entity very different from matter.

89. They never conceived that any remoter more simple factors underlying the production of atom by natural causes and powers, could be traced (119). And they may even yet doubt the possibility of the problem. But that is not to be wondered at, for early and deep-seated prejudice is always apt to operate upon the mind so as to accept the most unfounded assertions if they are only familiar, while new truths, howsoever well founded, if they seem to go against old accepted doctrines, are rejected.

90. " What other simple ideas possibly the intelligent creatures," if there be such, " in other parts of the universe may have"......,says *Locke,* " is not for us to determine. But to say or think there are no such ideas because we conceive nothing of them, is no better an argument, than if a blind man should be positive in it that there was no such thing as sight and colors, because he had no manner of idea of any such thing."

91. Linearium, [or continuum] is the name which we might properly give to the totality of the universal all-traversing cosmolineæ considered collectively as a *medium,*—the space-filling cosmical web or weft within the circumference of the physical universe. (v. Notes app.)

The linearium collectively considered, although extending in three dimensions, is not matter, because its ultimate constitutive parts—the lineïts —are *separable* at any time ; while in matter, on the other hand, the lineïts of which each monit consists, are absolutely inseparable.

For the same reason, what is usually called " universal space" can be no matter, though it extends in three dimensions ; and indeed, if such " space" be considered as something really existing, it will be found to be identical with our *linearium.*

92. TWO DIFFERENT MEDIA IN CELESTIAL SPACE.—Besides the linearium just spoken of, namely : the *imponderable universal* medium which pervades all the universe and every being and thing in it, except the ultimate particles of matter, astronomy has to deal with another more local medium called non-luminous **Ether** consisting of matter, that is: of *ponderable* substance. Between these two different mediums we should always maintain a clear distinction.

93. ETHER (*non-luminous*).—This ponderable medium can be conceived to exist only in certain particular places of the universe, for instance, in the neighborhood of large celestial orbs such as the planets, the sun, and other fixed stars, surrounding them on all sides and extending, may be, a million of miles away from their centres. This is the so-called non-luminous **ether,** the **nebulous** or **cosmical matter,** etc.

94. Being subject to the laws of gravitation, the non-luminous ether must be denser near the celestial bodies, and more attenuated further from them. It is, of course, a resistance offering medium, and may, to some slight degree, also enfeeble the transmission of light. Gravitated upon by the sun it has to follow the sun's rotary motion, at least within a certain distance from the latter, in a similar manner as the terrestrial atmosphere has to follow the earth's rotation. Of this kind of etherial matter the comets and the nebulous or cosmical vapor are supposed to consist.

95. This ponderable medium can never be the one along which are transmitted the light-producing translatory undulations, because it is more local than universal, and because the ultimate particles of ponderable matter can never be continuous to each other, they can never be in actual contact (as will appear hereafter) especially in such a rare attenuated state as the cosmical matter of ether is supposed to be. To this ponderable medium alone should be applied the name of **ether** or **etherial medium**, to indicate its highly subtile though yet *material* nature.

96. The existence of this ether as a permanent independent gas still more rarified and still more elastic than hydrogen is, however, very problematical. If it exists at all as such, it should already have been discovered in the lower regions of our atmosphere, to which by virtue of its elasticity it likewise would be bound to extend. The retardation of Encke's and other comets, which has been said to be caused by this ether, can with more justice be ascribed to the resistance offered by the systems of meteorites pervading, in more or less dense streams, the greater part of the interstellar spaces. To these same meteoric systems may also be due the fact, that the transmission of light from extremely distant celestial bodies is enfeebled to some slight degree, which has hitherto been laid to the ether.

97. The propagation of *light* is effected by means of quite a different kind of medium, namely by that which is mentioned above under the name of **linearium** (or continuum). Its continuous cosmolineæ by the possibly most complete continuity of their *parts*, end to end, and by the ready way in which these parts may be disjoined and rejoined again, and therefore be able to vibrate in all directions at right angles to the axis of the line-bundles, or, as it may be called, in all its azimuths, and thus be made to undulate like the surface of water in progressive true waves, are especially adapted for the transmission of light; where one set of lineïts (i. e. one set of the component parts of the cosmolineæ) when in undulation, determines the motion of the succeeding set of lineïts, producing a kind of swell in the medium, and thus account for the phenomena of *diffraction* more satisfactorily than can be done with the particles of an assumed luminiferous ether, which latter by the way, is said to be of but an *infinitesimal* density. At all events the ether would much more resemble air than water. And yet it is distinctly stated by the believers in a material ether: that the oscillations of its particles are performed in like manner as the oscillations of unelastic water-particles, and by no means like the oscillations of air-particles. That is to say: in sound-waves the particles of air oscillate to and fro in the direction of propagation; in the waves of light, on the other hand, the particles of the ether oscillate to and fro *across* the lines of propagation. While thus the vibrations of the elastic air are longitudinal, the vibrations of the hypothetical elastic air-like ether are transversal. How can physicists reconcile these discrepancies? Not by the adoption of a medium to consist of *material* particles and of a gaseous texture like air, for then the vibrations of that medium could be no otherwise but longitudinal like those of the air. (y. Notes app.)

Of the facts that the vibrations in sound are longitudinal, and the vibrations in light and water are transversal there can be no doubt. But neither, on the other hand, can it be doubted that the vibrations of light would have to take place in a manner exactly like those of sound in the air, and not as in waves of water, if the medium for the propagation of light consisted of *elastic widely separated particles*, as it is said to consist. It will be seen then, that in order to meet the requirements, the luminiferous medium must be so constituted, that if its ultimate parts or portions are forced out in a direction at right angles, and disturbed from their *straight-linear* arrangement into a wavy-shaped one, there should, as in a stretched elastic string, be present another powerful force or principle which always strives to bring the wavy, undulated shape into the straight-linear, even-faced shape called its normal state, and which force or principle works always at right angles to the direction of transversal vibration. Now, all these requirements are fulfilled by our cosmolineal medium, in which the desired force or principle is to be found in the primary power of End-unition.

Properly interpreted, the surface water of a pond may be said to be of similar elasticity with that of a tensely stretched elastic string, because as often as the smooth surface sheet of water is disturbed, and one part elevated above the rest, so often is it forced to come back to its original, smooth and level state. If it be asked: what is it that strives to bring the disturbed surface water back to its level? we answer: the force of gravitation. What strives to bring the disturbed luminiferous medium (the linearium) back to its straight-linear and tense condition? Answer: the primary power of End-unition in trying to bring the lineïts nearer to each other end to end.

97′. Besides this, the cosmolineæ are every where, interstellar as well as inter-atomic, they also penetrate and traverse with enormous speed all material bodies [except the monits (atoms)] organic as well as inorganic, the human body as well as the hardest rock and the densest metal, freely, and are only resisted by the most ultimate particles of matter, the monits (atoms).

98. Having described one of the fundamental most simple compounds, namely: the *cosmolinea* and its **lineïts**, we may now give a description of another most simple compound also composed entirely of lineïts, and which as the ultimate minutest particle of matter we have called *monit,* [6(6) 64 (2).] analogous to, but not the same with atom.

99. The lineïts of the monit are, however, joined to one another in a very different manner from those of the cosmolinea, viz: with one of their ends joined into one common point and the other end free; and besides the power of End-unition these lineïts possess Versatile Activity [6(13)], or an effort and ability to whirl and turn. The lineïts composing the monit are therefore *versatile* lineïts (60), thus distinguished from the *common* lineït of which the cosmolinea is composed.

100. Definition of the monit.—A certain definite number of versatile lineïts permanently joined with one of their ends in one common point, and standing in the shape of fixed rays or radii in every direction all around this point, and thus rotating perpetually around an axis, constitutes a **monit** of matter in its most simple form.*

101. As all lineïts consist of but two power-points, and as all monits are in diameter double the length of the lineït, it follows that all monits are of the same size. A monit of matter thus possessing extension in all *three* geometrical dimensions may be termed a solid or a *corporeal* substantive, to distinguish it from a *linear* substantive possessing extension in only *one* dimension.

102. The sum total of the effort *to turn,* as comprised in all the lineïts of a monit, is called the monit's *Versatile Activity.*

---

*Those who take the atom (monit) to be "something real by itself" are right, as are also those, who should maintain that an atom (monit) is in some respects a minutest pact of a number of force-units, i. e. force-lineïts, all converging into a common centre with one of their ends and with the other turning around an axis. But merely to say [as Faraday did] that matter consists of "centres of force" and is constructed out of the convergence and intersection of infinitely—or indefinitely-long lines of force, would be an incomplete conception. Yet taken in the above sense of an atom consisting of forceline-units i. e. lineïts, it would not be improper to call an atom (monit) a compact of force.

103. This simplicity of form, the monit can have only under certain circumstances, which in reality never occur, namely if the monit has absolutely *no translatory* motion of any kind; by translatory motion we mean motion from one place to another. If the monit has such a motion, then its circumference must be conceived (as will hereafter be explained, §131) to be covered, except in its *equatorial* circle, with additional lineïts attached to the free ends of the monit's radii. These annexed lineïts, however, do not form a permanent part of the monit, and are not essential to its existence, they are liable at any time to be cast off and replaced by others, to be increased and decreased in number according to circumstances (274); they constitute what is called the *velocity*-lineïts of a moving monit, as to be explained further on.

104. As there is good reason for believing that there is in the whole universe no monit absolutely without motion of translocation, either by itself or in connection with other monits, we may describe the MONIT as an immeasurably small globule revolving around an axis, and consisting of lineïts arranged as radii, its extra-equatorial surface covered with velocity-lineïts attached to the free ends of the radii. As the radii of the monit stand out in every conceivable direction from the monit's centre, the monit must be said to have extension and offer unyielding resistance (impenetrability) in all possible directions, and in this sense may be called a *solid.*

105. PROPERTIES OF THE MONIT.

1.) *Extension* in all the three geometrical dimensions.—The monit occupies a certain though inconceivably small space.

2.) *Rotary motion* [an active property].—Rotation around an axis, incessantly kept up by an inherent joint *effort* of the monit's lineïts to *whirl* or turn. The restlessness of the individual lineïts of the monit to whirl or turn we call the Versatile Activity of the lineït. The sum of this effort in the whole monit may be termed Versatile Activity of the monit, or the monit's *power of Versatile Activity.*

106. *Note* 1. While the other two primitive powers, viz: End-unition and Synduction, effect adjacent lineïts, and therefore must extend their influence over infinitesimal distances, Versatile Activity directly influences merely the lineïts it dwells in.

Note 2. Besides End-unition, which belongs to all lineïts without exception, the lineïts of the monit possess Versatile Activity, while the lineïts of the cosmolineæ possess End-unition only.

3.) *Impenetrability.*—By the monit's radii standing out in every conceivable direction and by virtue of the rotatory motion of the monit, the latter offers complete resistance with regard to any infringement on its existence, figure and individuality;—its radii striking aside every lineït that darts upon the equatorial belt, and in case the monit be darted upon and touched in any other place by lineïts, the latter either slide off, or are temporarily attached to the circumference of the monit, but they can never penetrate the monit. With respect to their impenetrability in *all* directions, it would not be amiss to consider the monits as little solids (104), and their whole existence due to *power.*

107. As one of the monit's most essential properties consists in its power of Versatile Activity [105(2)], it would be quite contradictory to assign "**inertia**" to the monit; and we shall speak instead of its inertia only of its:

4.) *Inability of self-change with regard to place or to translatory motion.**

* The monit would be entirely **inert** in regard to change of position if it was not

The monit whether it stay in its place, or whether, in moving translatory it be continually changing its place, can never *begin* to change nor can it *continue* to change its place on its own account, if not acted upon by *power* that causes the change, namely by the motive accessory power it harbors for the time, and which was imparted to it from without; nor can it decrease or discontinue its motion on its own account, i. e. throw off the power that is moving it; nor can it change its course of motion, if not forced to do so by *power*.—Or in other words:

The monit can of itself neither leave the place it occupies, i. e. neither begin to move translatory, *nor continue* in motion, nor change the course and amount of that motion, on its own account.

5.) *Indivisibility into smaller monits.*—Though a certain magnitude can not be denied to monits, their diameter being double the length of the lineït, yet they must also from the peculiar nature of their composition be regarded as absolutely indivisible into smaller monits. For even if in imagination the monit could be divided, it would yield nothing but single end or power-points, because each of the lineïts of which the monit consists, has only one of its two power-points free, the other being merged in the centre-point of the monit; the free-power-point supposed to have been severed by division, however, cannot exist unconnected by itself. [6(1). 46]. As to the centre point of the monit, it has like the geometrical point position only, but no magnitude, and therefore it cannot be bisected or quartered. And even if the dissolution instead of the divisibility of a monit were possible, it would yield lineïts only but no smaller monits.

6.) *Ponderability.*—Monits are ponderable or weighty only in so far as they are acted upon by the cosmolineæ (as explained in 152–155).

By the word "weight" of body in general, or of the monit in particular, is not to be understood an absolute primordial weight persisting and constant in all positions and under all circumstances, not an entity inherent and essential to matter, but a mere relation of pressure upon an obstacle between two bodies mutually attracting each other.*

7.) *Inclination of axis persistent,* and for each chemical elementary body peculiarly inclined.—The monits of all the simple elementary bodies are alike in all other respects except in the inclination of their axes of rotation, which is a different one for each kind of the different chemical elementary bodies. And if in chemical *combination* their axes of rotation are tempo-

---

composed of *versatile* lineïts permanently possessed of the power of Versatile Activity [105(2)]. But though the monit does unremittingly revolve around an axis and, thus continually turning, is never at rest, it does likewise do so only by virtue of the *power* it is possessed of.

The old term *inertia* when applied to the ultimate particle of matter, the monit, is objectionable because the monit, possessing the *active* property of versatile motion, cannot be called "inert."

La Place defines Inertia as "that property of matter by which it (matter) tends to retain its state, whether in motion or at rest." Now, a *tendency* to retain or to effect any thing indicates an active power at the bottom of the tendency. But how can philosophers who thus recognize in "inertia" an *active power,* contend that matter is *inert?* for inertia means inactivity, indolence.

Again in the one case the same "vis inertiæ" is said to retain a body in the place it occupies, in the other case the same "vis inertiæ" is expected to do the very opposite, viz: to make that same body *change* its position continually from one place to another; and whether in a straight line or not in a straight line, it is nevertheless *change of place.* Is not this contradictory?

* For instance, the same body when one hundred miles above the surface of the earth weighs less than when one hundred feet above it; also less on the sea-level near the equator than on that near the poles.

rarily forced into another direction, with the dissolution of that combination they immediately revert to their primordial direction again. Monits (or atoms) may therefore said to be distinguishable only by their differently inclined rotary motions, which is the cause of their difference in chemical affinity (136), and not by size, weight, or figure.

108. DISTINCTION BETWEEN ATOM AND MONIT.—The atom has some of the above named properties (No. 1, 3, 6,) in common with the monit. There are, however, characteristic distinctions between the two. (v. Notes app.)

109. "Atom" is generally regarded as an extended, hard, impenetrable, elastic, inactive, solid particle, and was formerly defined as the smallest ultimate particle of matter that admits of no further division. Recently, however, chemists and physicists had, in view of the combination of gases in simple ratios of volume, to change their views on this subject; for now they speak about atoms of different orders, shape, size and weight. They have even been reduced to the necessity of saying: "we must consider what was formerly assumed as the ultimate atoms of bodies, as groups of atoms" ......This gives us a very confused idea of **atom**, and is in fact a clear contradiction; for in the atom, as its name indicates, there can be no plurality of smaller atoms.

110. How much more definite, after the nature of the *monit* has been explained, is it to say: the chemist's **atom** is *a group of monits.* According to this view we may say: an atom of oxygen consists of a certain number of monits, and not as formerly "an atom of oxygen consists of so many atoms." One of the most eminent chemists maintains that atoms are only in a physical point of view indivisible, and appear to be so only to our perceptive faculties.

111. From the above we see that while the atom of the chemist is still subject to division into smaller atoms, the monit, on the contrary, is *absolutely indivisible* into smaller monits. §107(5).

112. Another distinction between atom and monit is that the latter has a continual *rotary motion* performed by an inherent unremittingly active power, which the atom has not. The atom is said to be hard, inactive and solid, but what the nature of this hardness and solidity is, no one does tell us. The radii of the monit consist of power-points offering resistance.

113. From the most general point of view, matter is at the same time both a compact of pure force, as well as something corporeal and massy capable of being moved. It is force because being a product of power-points* and unremittingly active internally with regard to the rotary motion of its monits; it is on the other hand, something corporeal, because having extension in three dimensions and being the bearer of accessory forces with regard to external translatory motion.

114. With regard to the never ending dispute about the nature of substance in general and of matter in particular, both parties, the idealists or rather the dynamists on one side, and the materialists or rather matter-*per-se* advocates on the other side, could easily adjust their differences to the satisfaction of all concerned. In certain points the one party is right, on other points, the other party. The idealists and the dynamists are right in asserting that in its ultimate composition matter (as well as substance generally) consist altogether of something that is not matter, which the dynamists call energy, force, or effort-exerting power. At the same time it must be remembered that by and through the *most simple* conjunctions of power-points, products altogether new may be possible, for instance, a something extended in three dimensions, maintaining forever its peculiar extension under all circumstances, and as such being a fit object, as a substratum to uphold other power, and in fact to be the bearer of attributes.

---

* "To my mind," says Faraday, speaking about atoms, "the nucleus vanishes, and the substance consists of power."

115. The materialists acknowledge such a bearer and call it matter, but neglect to trouble themselves with the inquiry: what is at the bottom of matter? by what means does it offer resistance? etc., and thus by shutting their eyes and ears against any arguments with regard to the analyzation of matter, they deny and reject the very powers and forces that are the cause of matter, and hence are as one-sided in their view as the idealist who denies and rejects the definite stabile something extended in three dimensions, which for ever maintains its peculiar extension under all circumstances.

116. The idealist and the dynamist are right in saying: matter is no *dead inactive* something existing *per se* that could be capable of existing independent of power; but they are wrong in adding: matter is nothing that in the least could differ from pure power and from spirit.—It most assuredly exists as a stabile indestructible reality of extension, yet as a product the whole inner essence of which is nothing but power.

117. The materialist or matter-*per-se* advocate would be right in saying: matter and pure active power are not the same, but differ very much, matter is a definite *stabile association* that as such may be moved from place to place by force. He is wrong in saying: matter is something inactive, dead, self-subsisting, existing independent of power—an inactive repletion of space—an unknown substratum, with its ultimate minutest particles hard, solid, impenetrable, and yet without active power, possessed only of *vis inertiæ*.

118. How contradictory this! for if anything be impenetrable, it can be so only by *resisting* the attacks of outward power, and resisting denotes the exercise of *active power* seated within the resisting body. The whole trouble seems to be that the idealist and dynamist as well as the materialist are unable to conceive that out of power something stabile (fettered or coupled) may be produced which as such is indissoluble, and retains a permanent existence; but which cannot move from its place unless being impelled by outside forces (v. Notes appended).

119. Being questioned whether we believe in the existence of matter or in that of spirit, we may answer thus: we believe in the existence of matter, real atoms or rather monits of matter which, although indestructible for all time to come, are *not simple* in their essence, they are compacts which are made up of something that is not matter. In a somewhat analogous manner we say: every chemical compound, on being resolved into its elements, yields elements of a very different nature from the nature of the compound. For instance, the molecules of water are made up of elements that are not water, they are oxygen and hydrogen. Speaking still more to the point we may say, an angle in geometry is made by joining one end of a line to one end of another line that has a different direction from the first. Here an angle is made of something altogether different from any angle. The *elements* of an angle are lines, but the *parts* of an angle are angles.

120. The above non-material something of which we suppose the atoms or monits to be made up, are the most simple force-lines i. e. lineïts themselves consisting each one of two active power-points. These lineïts, the factors of the monit (atom) are inoriginate as well as indestructible, and have extension in only *one* dimension. The power-points as the most ultimate, the most primary conception, can never exist singly and isolated by themselves; in their most elementary combinations they always exist as couplets fettered in pairs, thus constituting the *lineït*. These power-points must be conceived as *effort-exerting* power-points operating in accordance with an innate most rudimentary aim, end, or intention, which is unconscious.

121. The power-points having no extension themselves, yet being the factors of the universal *most simple* extension, i. e. a couplet of power-points called lineït, of which latter every existing thing is composed, and which lineïts are (the same as we are wont to think of space) omnipresent in every place of the universe—these power-points must be regarded as the most primitive, most universal principle which is at the bottom of every thing ponderable and imponderable; and thus, although believing as steadfastly in the existence of matter as any materialist, we believe just as firmly in the existence of active power which is *not material*.

SECTION III.

---

122. Without cosmolineæ there can be no translatory motion of monits. The monit being impotent with regard to a self-change of place §107 (4), it cannot acquire motion of translocation in any other way but by impulses *from without.* It is, however, quite impossible for monits to propel in an immediate or direct manner one another translatory through space. To accomplish this, a *medium* is absolutely necessary.

123. The only medium that is at the monit's disposal for this purpose is the cosmolinea (82). We are therefore led to the conclusion that motion of translation of one monit must be performed by another monit, while the latter is making use of the cosmolinea as a mediating agent, which cosmolinea the monit first pulls, and with it and by it pulls along other monits. How this pulling is done will be set forth in the next paragraphs.

124. Monits setting the cosmolinea in straight translatory motion longitudinally. Suppose first, for convenience sake of explanation, the cosmolinea not yet in actual progress of longitudinal motion, but always under the influence of the unremittingly active power of End-unition, which is an innate effort of the lineïts to persist in their arrangement of being temporarily joined endwise to each other to form a *continuous* cosmolinea, and to assume this continuity again as often as it is disarranged or broken.

125. That part of the cosmolinea's extremity which happens to be next to and in contact with the equatorial belt of the rotary monit will be *struck off* by the free end of the whirling monit's radii (with the co-operation of the radii's End-unition), thereby disjoined from the length of the cosmolinea, and in the shape of a **lineït**, that is the smallest linea-fragment, flung aside in a tangential direction.

126. The lineït thus struck off we designate by the name of **detached** or **polarized** lineït, because we suppose it to have polarity, from its anterior end having been touched and operated upon by the monit's radius, while its posterior end was operated upon only by the cosmolinea; the pole touched by the monit's radius we call the *positive* pole.

127. By the striking aside of lineïts in this way, a chance is given to other lineïts succeeding them to follow up the direction of the cosmolinea they are a part of. The lineït following next to the one just struck aside, being urged by its own End-unition and the End-unition of the monit's radii, will move forward to couple its anterior end to the free end of one of the monit's radii, and in rushing up to the rotating monit, this foremost lineït will be struck next, or rather diverted from its former direction and flung aside, and so on with every lineït that comes to be the foremost one.

128. That in this performance the cosmolinea is obliged to move towards the monit, and not the monit towards the cosmolinea is evident, because on the opposite side of the monit is exerted by another cosmolinea a similar and equally strong effort to join, pulling the monit the opposite way, hence it is the cosmolineæ and not the monit which is bound to move.

129. The second lineït (or second portion of the cosmolinea) having touched the monit and having been struck by it, is therefore flung off as readily as the first, and in turn, portion after portion, i. e. lineït after lineït, is treated in the same manner, and thus is established the straight translatory longitudinal motion of the cosmolinea *towards* the monit,—since Endunition of the lineïts always closes up the gaps within the cosmolinea produced by the monit's Versatile Activity in front.

130. As every radius of the monit's equatorial belt is acting in a similar manner, there will be streams of cosmolineæ then converging from all directions towards the monit, which let us call *a* (fig. 2). If now another monit *b* happens to be within range of these streams of cosmolineæ, *b* will be *pressed* upon by the lineïts of these cosmolineæ. The lineïts, of which every *moving* cosmolinea is composed, being always but loosely connected end to end, the anterior end of each lineït as it draws near successively, hits the extra-equatorial portions of monit *b*, and if *b* is not moved by the lineït that strikes and momentarily presses upon it, then does this lineït speedily join its cosmolinea again.

131. If, however, monit *b* yields under the impulse, then the striking lineït *attaches* itself to the extra-equatorial surface of *b* to the free ends of *b's* radii (104). In this manner stored up with lineïts, *b* approaches *a*. The lineïts with which *b* is thus stored we call **velocity-lineïts.**

132. It is only in the equatorial belt *n* (fig. 2.) of the rotary monit that the power of breaking the cosmolinea lies, and as the length of radius in all monits is the same (§101.), and as with good reason we may assume the number of radii to be the same in every monit's equatorial belt, it would follow that only a definite and equal number of cosmolineæ can be operated upon and be disconnected by each monit in the manner just mentioned.

133. From the foregoing assumption of equal rotation and equal number of working radii it follows as a matter of course, that each monit can perform no more than a certain, constant, and unvarying amount of work in striking off lineïts, and thereby induce a certain and constant number of cosmolineæ to move forward; that is to say: no monit is capable of producing more or less than the same certain invariable intensity in the flow of cosmolineæ towards its own body than any other monit is capable of. In this respect then, the monits would individually all be equally efficient as agents causing gravitation.

134. The assertion is true that "No body whose gravity, as compared with its mass," (meaning its total number of monits) "differs in the slightest conceivable degree from that of other bodies, can belong to the system of the universe." This is to say that every monit is of exactly the same energy with all other monits in causing attraction. And it is equally true that "Neither an imponderable body belongs to the universe." But it is nevertheless also true that an *imponderable substantive entity which is not body* does belong to the universe; this entity has extension in no more than *one* dimension, and is in fact the already mentioned *lineït.*

135. From an inspection of fig. 1, it is apparent that outside at each pole of the monit there will be a funnel-shaped space void of inflowing cosmolineæ, although not void of heat. Hence if two or more monits were placed so as to have their respective axis all in the same straight line (fig. 1, *g* and *b*), this line would form an exception to the general rule of attraction. This is the only direction in which the monits thus situated could not act upon each other. But no adjacent monits whose axes are in one and the same straight line can remain near each other; because heat which is found even in these interspaces between the non-attracting part of neighboring monits easily drives the latter apart, so as to allow only monits of different position of axis, that is, monits acting upon each other, to enter between them.

136. CHEMICAL AFFINITY.—The axes of the monits we conceive for each kind of elementary body to be of a permanently fixed type of inclination, peculiar to itself, and different from that of all other elementary bodies. This peculiarity of inclination, which is the cause of the difference in the elementary bodies, gives rise to the many different grades of preference in their mutual attraction which we call CHEMICAL AFFINITY, [107(7)]. When two monits of *dissimilar* inclination of axis have been chemically combined, the product of the combination generally exhibits an affinity differing from that of either of the two monits, because the resultant inclination of the compound's axis must be a different one, just as it is in dynamics with the resultant of a combination of differently directed joint forces.

137. MOLECULES.—As no monits that have their axes in one and the same straight line can stay adjacent to each other, because of their want of attraction when so situated (135) and the thereupon consequent dispersion by heat, and as, moreover, those monits of greatly dissimilar inclination of axis will most readily combine (v. fig. 1, a and d, where *d* most energetically attracts *a*, more so than *d* does attract *g*, on account of the less number of repelling lineïts, which are denoted by dotted parallel lines) it is natural to suppose that no single dissociated monits exist by themselves unconnected with others, at least not under ordinary circumstances;* but that on the contrary, *monits do most generally exist arranged in little groups*, called **molecules.**

138. And because every operative radius of the monit in performing its work of striking and pulling the cosmolineæ, does represent the whole strength of the monit in that very direction; and as, moreover, in any spherical aggregation of monits, i. e. globule of matter, one of the converging cosmolineæ for each monit has to pass through the centre of that globule, *it is clear that this centre will represent the whole number and pulling* strength of all the monits contained in that globule. Hence to the centre of such a little group, or molecule, if it be a spherule, will then flow the cosmolineæ from *all* directions and not, as is the case with a single separate monit, from *nearly all* directions.

139. The explanations in §124-129 were made on the supposition that the pulling monits and bodies did not change their places in the universe. As it is, however, well known that all the planets and their satellites of our solar system together with the sun itself, as well as the double stars, are continually coursing in their orbits, and as it is highly probable that all the celestial bodies descried by means of the telescope follow similar paths through the universal medium, it may be thought at first sight that these facts somewhat modify the whole aspect of the mechanism of our cosmolineal system. Yet this need not disturb us, for in a celestial orb the cosmolineæ worked

---

* In the hottest parts of the sun they may occur in a dissociated state as separate monits.

upon by all its monits can only reach the latter by way of the orb's centre, to which they have to stream first (584-587). Hence the streams of cosmolineæ engendered by the whole orb have only to keep up with the flight of the orb's centre. Moreover, to set the cosmolineal medium newly arrived at by the darting orb, into flowing condition toward the latter, as well as, on the other hand, to check the flow of the part of the medium just passed by, is the work of an instant.

140. Classification of cosmolineæ in direct and in stream-cosmolineæ. With regard to the different manner in which a rotary monit is impinged upon by a cosmolinea, we may classify all cosmolineæ 1st, in such as *m n* fig. 3, which are induced by the free striking radii of monit *m* to flow towards the monit regularly from nearly all directions, and 2d in such as *d m*, which is part of the general *stream* of cosmolineæ *d e f* induced by another monit *e*, or by an assemblage of monits constituting the sphere E H., and which stream in its course happens to impinge upon the extra-equatorial parts of monit *m*. With reference to monit *m* we may call *m n* a *direct*-cosmolinea, and *d m* a *stream*-cosmolinea; while with reference to monit *e*, *d m* is a *direct*-cosmolinea. From this it will be seen that the same cosmolinea may be direct cosmolinea to one monit while at the same time it serves as stream-cosmolinea to another monit; it is also apparent that every monit has constantly to deal with both modes of cosmolineæ.

141. From the peculiar nature of the case it follows that no stream-cosmolinea impinges on the monit in the same manner as the direct-cosmolinea does, which latter on coming in contact with the monit is always shortened.* The stream-cosmolineæ by means of their lineïts exert a pressure upon the monit without being themselves permanently broken or disconnected if the monit is immovable, and in this case the pressing lineïts then proceed unmodified along with the general stream of cosmolineæ toward that particular body, for instance towards E H fig 3, which by the Versatile Activity of all its monits causes this stream *d f e* to flow towards *e*, the centre of E H.

142. If, however, monit *m* is movable, then the very lineït that augments the motion of the monit *m*, attaches itself at the same time to it as *velocity*-lineït (103) of which more will be said hereafter.

143. Cause of outward motion of detached polarized lineïts.—Returning to the flung off lineïts (125, 126), we may here remark, that the cause of the general outward motion of these detached lineïts as they speed *away from* the monit, proceeding towards the periphery of the body of which that monit is a part, is to be found in the action of the rotary monit that hurls aside the detached lineïts and communicates to one of their ends some of its own (the monit's) Versatile Activity. At the same time the detached lineïts are also influenced and moved along by heat (147).

144. Repelling action of monits.—The lineïts thus flung tangentially from the rotary monit will like drops of water from a swiftly turning grindstone diverge in all directions, of course only in plains at right angle to the axis of the monit. They will appear divergent as in fig. 4, *f*, if the monit's axis coincides with the visual ray of the eye; but if the plain of the monits' *equatorial* circle coincides with the visual ray of the eye, then the flung off lineïts will appear not to be diverging, they will present straight parallel lines as in *d* fig. 4.

145. Repelling action of monits takes place in a simple inverse

---

* A stream-cosmolinea, however, on hitting the equatorial radii of the monit, may also be acted upon by the latter and become a direct-cosmolinea.

RATIO AS THE DISTANCES.—From an inspection of fig. 4 it is plain that in adjacent monits the mutual repulsion from the flung off polarized lineïts alone [leaving out the repelling action of heat] *is in* SIMPLE *inverse ratio as their distances;* that is to say: *at double the distance from the monit its repulsive energy will be* ONE-HALF, and not one-fourth as in light and gravitation.

146. No monits of the same type of inclination of axis (136), that is, no monits of the same kind of elementary body, can be held in mutual combination, or stay adjacent to each other, if they are placed with their axes in one and the same straight line (135), as in fig. 1, monit *g* and *h*. If, however, placed with their axes parallel aside of each other, as in *g* and *d*, then they are not necessarily prevented from mutually combining, or from forming what may be called an *elementary* molecule, that is, a molecule consisting of monits of the same kind. Such molecules are, however, with regard to our own planet, by far the least in number. All the other molecules consist of monits of different types of inclination of axis. *These* molecules may be called *compound* molecules. Hence with regard to the latter we conclude that the repelling lineïts of one monit diverge in one plain, those of other adjacent monits diverge in other plains quite different from the first, so that on the whole, the repelling action of a compound molecule takes place in many different directions, though some of these directions may preponderate over the rest. Independent of the repulsion exerted by flung-off lineïts there is another kind of repulsion acting between monits, namely that exerted by *heat*, which will be treated of in another chapter. (v. Notes app.).

147. ELECTRICITY AND MAGNETISM.—As the flung-off or detached polarized lineïts §125, 126, are versatile in only one of their ends, and in other respects passive, they may also by heat, especially by radiated heat, be driven forward until at last they are bound to arrive, in company with heat, at the circumference of the universe. It may well be said that there is no heat quite clear of detached polarized lineïts, and that all the beams of heat, traversing space, are accompanied by an abundance of such lineïts.

148. Following up this subject still further, we feel that in these polarized lineïts we have found the elementary essence or principle of both *electricity* and *magnetism* manifesting itself to our senses in the streams of the so-called electric and magnetic fluids. And it seems very probable that two polarized lineïts tending with their versatile ends in opposite directions ⇄, by uniting the positive pole of each with the negative pole of the other, may be converted into a *neutral* electro-lineït or couplet acting like heat which, however, is liable at any time to be disunited again.

149. MONITS CANNOT TOUCH ONE ANOTHER.—Monits can never come in actual contact with one another, because every monit is kept either by heat, or else by tangentially darting detached polarized lineïts of adjacent monits, at a certain distance from the latter. In the repulsion of molecule against molecule (not monit against monit) heat is the chief agent.

150. Even in those peculiar cases where the axes of neighboring monits are supposed to be in a straight line as in *g* and *h* fig. 1, while there is neither mutual attraction nor repulsion between the respective monits, there is still everywhere and always present a certain degree of repulsion from *heat* which hinders their coming in mutual contact.

151. From the preceding paragraphs, and an inspection of the monits fig. 1, it will be apparent how it is possible that a monit is able to *attract and to repel at the same time.*

152. The pressure exerted by the cosmolineæ of E H (fig. 3), impinging upon body *b* [or rather upon every one of *b's* monits] lying in the path of the stream of cosmolineæ which is flowing towards the centre of body E H, causes the *weight* of *b* towards E H. This pressure is therefore the cause of the *ponderability* of *b* in relation to E H, and is proportional to the number of monits contained in *b*, other things, viz: the distance from *e* and the quantity of matter of E H, being the same.

153. Some hasty objections may here perhaps be raised in saying: a leaden ball *b* is attracted by the earth with much greater energy and exerts more pressure than another ball *c* of the same size made of wood; yet according to your theory both bodies, if placed side by side, are exposed to the same intensity of the stream *d f* (fig. 3), consequently both ought to exhibit an equal degree of pressure in a pair of balances, which they do not.

154. In response I may say, that it is upon the individual monits of these bodies *b* and *c*. and not upon the bodies' surfaces, that the intensity of the stream *d f* is pressing; and that this stream of cosmolineæ is pushing equally *each* monit, whether the latter be by itself or associated with others. And if ball *b* balances twelve balls like *c*, it merely proves that *b* contains twelve times as many monits as *c* does.

155. To make this latter assertion more obvious, let us falsely suppose the monits of the leaden ball to be of the same number with those of the wooden ball. By experiment we find, however, that the leaden ball weighs twelve times as much as the wooden one. In order to sustain our false supposition and at the same time to account for this great difference in the downward pressure of the two balls, we should be forced to assume that gravitation acts twelve times more energetic on the monits of the lead than it does on those of the wood. Now, if this were true, then the leaden ball ought to fall (even in vacuo) twelve times faster than the wooden ball. But we know from experiments that in vacuo the one falls exactly as fast as the other, which proves that gravitation pulls equally energetic in both cases. Hence the greater *weight* or *pressure* of the leaden ball must be attributed to the greater number of its monits, which here must be twelve times as many as in the wooden ball.

Reflecting on §155 the following law becomes manifest:

156. And in all cases *at equal distance from the centre of gravitation will the downward pressure or weight of a body be in simple direct proportion to the number of the monits which the body contains.*

157. Hence also, if the bodies *h* and *g* fig. 3, are of different size but of the same weight, it proves that they are made up of an equal number of monits.

158. PONDERABLE MATTER PROCEEDED FROM SOMETHING NOT PONDERABLE.—All material things in the universe, including their very monits or atoms, proceeded from something imponderable and immaterial, that has always been in existence, even long before matter existed (222).

159. In some of the preceding paragraphs I have endeavored to show how monits are composed of imponderable immaterial lineïts (100), and how the monits came to be *ponderable* (152). As we have no right to regard the imponderable lineït equal to *nothing*, but conceive it as some real substantive something, having an independent existence, we can not properly say that ponderable matter or its monits have proceeded from nothing.

160. TWO OF THE HIGHEST AXIOMS IN PHYSICAL SCIENCE. If we do not want to be set adrift and tossed about in uncertainty, doubt and confusion, without landmark and without compass on the wide ocean of physical inquiries, we must always regard the following two axioms as two of the highest in physical science, not to be abandoned for any consideration.

161. 1st. It is quite impossible that any atom of matter, or any physical thing, force, or power, can be made or proceed out of **absolute nothing,** out of "the perfect negation and absence of all being." (§10, axiom IV).

162. 2d. The ultimate, most simple and primitive substantive entity of extension of which all matter as well as all physical forces consist—whether we call it *lineït* or by any other name, is both in **power** and in **substance** imperishable, indestructible, and in regard to time eternal, without beginning and without end (§10, axiom V).

163. Gravitation.*—The more monits there are in a body S, fig. 5, the more monits' radii will there be at work in striking off lineïts from cosmolineæ, and consequently the greater will be the number of converging cosmolineæ, or in other words, the more dense and efficient will be the stream of cosmolineæ flowing towards the region in which that body S is situated, or more strictly speaking, toward the *centre* of S if S be a sphere.

164. Hence another body E that happens to be in this stream of cosmolineæ will be pushed along by it from without, or pressed upon (not upon the surface of E but upon each individual monit of E) *with a force directly proportionate to the number of monits in S (that is, its mass) and inversely proportionate as the squares of the distances,* because the cosmolineæ *converge* equally from all directions towards the centre of S. And if in fig. 5, plate 2, S m = 2 S l, the energy of attraction, or rather of pushing, in l will be four times greater than that in m, because the cosmolineæ in l are four times more crowded than in m, that is, every monit in l is acted upon by four times more cosmolineæ than a monit in m.—E being thus pushed towards S, is said to *gravitate* toward S, and the effect or phenomenon of this pressure has been called GRAVITATION.

165. That Newton considered gravitation not to be a primary inherent *cause* in bodies, but merely a phenomenon derived from some higher force or property unknown to him, is proved by his own words. He says: "What "I call attraction may be performed* by impulse or by some other means "unknown to me. I use that word here to signify only in general any "force, by which bodies tend towards one another, whatsoever be the cause."

166. Now the ultimate cause of this attraction of gravitation we find in the two contending primitive powers of the universe namely: 1st, **Versatile Activity** of the monits constantly *breaking* and flinging aside in succession lineït after lineït from off the cosmolinea, and thus giving also to

* If you ask an illiterate man why a stone falls, he will be astonished about such a "foolish question" and say, it is self-evident as a simple fact in his daily experience. So also will be the answer with regard to the *continued* motion of a body that received but a momentary impulse, if you ask why does that motion continue if encountering no resistance? That class of scientific men who unalterably stick to their wonted channel of empirical thinking, will perhaps answer: the stone falls by virtue of its force of gravity, and the impelled body continues to move by its "inertia," and they consider such an answer all-sufficient. But with the pronouncing of the two words "gravity" and "inertia" they have in truth said nothing better than this: the stone falls according to certain general laws, and a body continues to move because it is loath to change its habit. To extend the laws of falling to all bodies, celestial as well as terrestrial, is, no doubt, a good step in advance of the illiterate man's position, yet the answer with regard to *how* and *why* stands with that of the latter upon the same grade, it is not in the least any more intelligible. To give an answer res ing upon the most fundamental causes in nature is our endeavor in §163–176. with regard to gravitation.

* Here Newton speaks of attraction as something being *performed.* So does Arnott, who is always very careful not to call attraction "a force" or "a cause," he calls it a **phenomenon.**

the next succeeding lineïts a *chance* to be pulled as close as possible to the monit; 2d, the power of **End-unition** residing in the free end of the monits' radii as well as in the anterior end of the cosmolinea, and in fact in all its lineïts, constantly striving to join endwise lineït to lineït and to keep up the redintegration of the cosmolinea. We may then rightly say: the principal motions of lineït approaching lineït and of their proceeding onward through the spaciousness of the universe, and thereby impelling bodies towards a centre of gravity, are all caused by the two primary powers of *End-unition* and *Versatile Activity*—by End-unition directly, and indirectly by Versatile Activity, which by its action of turning off lineït after lineït gives also to other lineïts, next succeeding them, a chance to be pulled as close as possible to the monit. Without this diverting and turning aside the foremost lineïts, no motion of the cosmolinea, no gravitation, and in fact no motion whatever is possible.

167. The part which Versatile Activity plays in the motion of the cosmolineæ is more by way of inducement in furnishing the requisite indispensable condition for motion toward the monit—namely the *removal* of lineïts by diverting and flinging aside always the foremost ones.

168. In the earth's gravitation we have the same two sets of acting powers. The one, Versatile Activity, *dwelling in* the ultimate *material particles* or monits of which the earth is composed, the other, End-unition, inhering not only in the free ends of these monits' radii, but also more especially in the lineïts of the all-traversing *cosmolineæ*, which are ever present throughout the immensity of the universe, in and around the earth and converging towards its centre.

169. The cause of gravitation, as here set forth in the preceding paragraphs, removes the difficulties hitherto found to exist in the common view which requires the atoms of matter to act where they are not, and which moreover requires them to find out, without an interjacent medium, the exact position of other remote atoms. (v. Notes app.)

The hopes of Faraday that the proper study of forces might "perhaps enable us to know, whether the essential force of gravitation is internal or external, as respects the attracted bodies," are in a good way to be realized, as on examining the subject according to the lineïstic theory, we find that the force causing gravitation is *external* with respect to attracted bodies, but *internal* with respect to the attracting bodies.

170. The question has been raised by Euler and others: can bodies exist without gravity? This question may be answered both by *yes* and by *no*, according as to what is to be understood by the word "gravity." (1.) If gravity of a body is conceived as being nothing more than a primary power or tendency inherent in that body, to *press* and *fall* towards another body, this would be an absurd conception not worthy of being taken notice of, because of its presupposing in them of an occult quality able first to find out without any medium whatever the exact position of other distant, even immensely distant, bodies and their centres, and then to move towards them in a peculiar manner and in a certain precise, steadily increasing, ratio.

171 .(2.) If by "gravity" we understand nothing but the mere phenomenon of the general approaching of all bodies each one to all others, which however should be denominated gravitation [9(10)], then we can in justice say: bodies or matter still exist even if gravity were non-existent, because if the medium, without which the approaching by drawing or pushing cannot be performed is wanting, the bodies although their monits are ever so actively engaged in rotating [and hence exist in all their completeness] cannot in consequence of this absence of the medium, approach or gravitate. And therefore in this case we should be justified in saying: bodies may exist without "gravity." In an absolute vacuum, i. e. a vacuum void of cosmolineæ, it would be impossible for material bodies to gravitate twards each other, no matter how *active* the minutest particles of these bodies may be in trying to produce the phenomena of gravitation. Somewhat analogous to a load being pulled along by means of a rope wound around a fixed windlass, when the latter is turned by a horse. Here the phenomenon of the load *approaching* the windlass will cease the moment the rope breaks, although the *horse continues to turn* the windlass as steadily as ever. The horse is there and still turning the windlass, but no approaching of the load takes place.

172. (3.) If on the other hand, by the name of 'gravity' we solely understand the *versatile* or *rotary activity inherent in monits*, by virtue of which the aforesaid medium of cosmolineæ is set in motion and kept moving, and by means of which medium this activity pulls the distant bodies, then is gravity an inherent and essential property of all bodies. And then we would be obliged to say: bodies cease to be bodies with the cessation of all gravity; because in the very power of Versatile Activity of the monit consists the existence of the monits of which the body is composed. So we see that all the trouble, confusion, and contradictions arise from the indeterminate vacillating meaning of the terms "gravitation" and "gravity." (v. Notes app.)

173. WITHOUT A MEDIUM THERE CAN BE NO ATTRACTION NOR REPULSION PERFORMED AT A DISTANCE [meaning any perceptible distance]. Here we may state the following two propositions which are evident in themselves and hence to be considered as axioms.

174. 1st. Without an intervening medium, a thing can be *struck away* by another thing only either when both are actually in *contact*, or when they are at infinitesimal distances of each other, distances amounting next to nothing. That things with any manifest distance between them, should strike and repel one another without leaving their places or without making use of any intervening medium having extension, is absolutely impossible (§10. Axiom VII*a* and cor. 1.)

175. 2d. All efforts of nearing or attracting two or more things to each other can, without a proper medium having extension, be executed only over infinitesimal distances, distances amounting next to nothing. In order to manifest the dynamic effect of such efforts (of nearing) over greater, i. e. over *measurable* distances, an intervening medium having extension, is absolutely necessary [§10. Axiom VII*a* cor. 2.]

176. *Corollary.* Hence no attraction of gravitation, no attractions nor repulsions of magnetism, of electricity, and molecular forces can at a distance—not even the smallest measurable distance—be performed without a proper intervening medium. And the question: would two bodies gravitate or draw towards each other in "pure and simple space," if the existence of bodies under such conditions were possible, must be answered in the negative.

177. OUTWARD COURSE OF DETACHED POLARIZED LINEÏTS.—But what, we may ask, becomes of the detached lineït (125, 126,) after it has been struck from the cosmolinea and flung away tangentially by the monit.

178. At small distances within molecules, the lineïts flung by the monits, i. e. the detached polarized lineïts, act, as has already been said, as molecular repulsion. The lineït when flung by the rotary monit can by virtue of the Versatile Activity imparted to one of its ends, exert a shock or an impelling act and pressure, yet only *once* as far as regards the very *direction* it was propelled in. Although this lineït after having exerted its pressure once, can have no further impelling or pressing effect *in the direction* received from the monit, yet it still possesses some irregular motion of one of its ends at least, by which it may exert a kind of pressure; and at the same time it may also itself be propelled either by conducted heat from monit to monit, or through celestial space by radiated heat.

179. With the lineïts of a gravitation-cosmolinea their action to exert pressure is kept up in a very different manner from that of a detached polarized lineït; for when a gravitation-cosmolinea encouuters a monit, the individual lineïts of the cosmolinea being worked upon continually by the power of End-unition, it is evident that the same lineït which has already been exerting full pressure in the direction of the cosmolinea upon a monit, is anew set in motion, and thereby enabled to exert full pressure in *the same direction* repeatedly upon other monits in succession, as long as it does not detach itself from the cosmolinea and move along, as velocity-lineït, with one of the monits.

180. In the first mentioned case where the lineït is flung off and detached by the monit, the lineït is the bearer of the momentary striking act of Versatile Activity in the very direction it was sent. This original direction of the impulse is given up by the lineït as momentary *pressure* to the first monit it meets, provided the monit be not moved thereby. The versatile impelling ability of the polarized lineït still remains, but the determination of its direction is then gone, and having Versatile Activity in one end only, it thenceforth falls subject to the sway of moving heat, its positive pole however turning away, i. e. repelling the positive pole of other polarized lineïts.

SECTION IV.

---

181. Before we can proceed any further with the lineïts, we have to figure to our mind's eye an image of the universe, and form a definite idea of this largest of all physical images.

182. Definition of the universe.—The universe is the totality of *all* existing things, including not only ponderable substances, but also all other substantive entities that may not be ponderable. All that exists is contained in *one* immense, and by means of internal powers perfectly connected totality called *universe.* The term 'totality' here signifies the embracing or inclusion of *all* being. Hence the universe is also called "the All."

183. Only a comparatively small portion of the grosser things of this universe have, chiefly by means of *light* and *gravitation*, made their existence manifest to the perceptive faculties of man. Hence we may say, all the visible objects, including all the resolved and unresolved nebulæ, that man is permitted to get a glimpse at, belong to *one* universe connected throughout its whole extent by the common bonds of gravitation, as far as the ever-coursing and traversing cosmolineæ extend—a "distance inexpressible by numbers that have name."

184. Finite extent of the universe.—Although we ought not to depend altogether upon authority, and blindly subscribe to the views of men of fame, yet we certainly ought to be very glad to find that our convictions accord with the views of those giants in the domain of intellect, whose eyes have

> "Caught the mountain tops of distant thought,
> Which man of common stature never saw."—

185. The most prominent philosophers of antiquity, Democrit, Empedocles, Xenophanes, Parmenides, Plato, Aristotle, as well as Bacon, Newton, Locke, Humboldt, and a number of other eminent scientific men of more recent date, speak of the universe as a Whole, complete in its arrangements, and therefore finite.* Newton maintains: "Centrum systematis mundani quiescere." Some philosophers, however, speak of the infinity of the universe, and other inquirers leave this point undecided. Yet it is of the highest importance in our researches that we should have a settled opinion on this question.

186. Let us try then to solve it in the following somewhat syllogistic

---

* We do not here speak of *pure space*, which must always be considered merely as the *possibility for the existence* of physical bodies.

manner: According to §10, axioms I. and II. Cor. 1. Being is Being, and therefore Being has no Non-being in it, i. e. it has no deficiency of Being, or else could not be Being. From this it follows that Being must be wholly complete Being. It is clear 1.) that *besides* (*outside of*) Being there can not possibly be conceived or supposed to *be* any thing else different from Being; but 2.) Being having been admitted as lacking no thing, admitted as wholly and complete, it follows from the two sentences 1) and 2) when taken together, that Being must be *complete in space*, and as completeness in space can be determined only by limits of extent, the universe of Being must be limited or circumscribed on all sides.

187. We never can nor will deny the *possibility* for the existence of matter at any specified distance you may be able to designate beyond the bounds presupposed at first. This, however, is not admitting that the universe *is* infinite, not even that it *may be* infinite, nor that there exist an infinite number of celestial bodies. There is not a single fact to be found in astronomy which justifies the assumption of an *infinite* number of celestial bodies; on the contrary, the harmony of motion amongst them requires a limited number, though that number may be inconceivably great.

188. To the belief that the universe is infinite in extent we can not subscribe. If asked what is beyond the utmost boundary of the universe, we say: the *possibility* for further extension and for the existence of matter. The very name "universum" indicates something finite, it means entireness, something complete in itself, whereas of an infinite thing we can not assert that it is complete, or that it ever can become so. Absolute infinity of substance in extent can not be circumscribed or comprehended by any intellect either human nor divine.

189. In common parlance the word "infinite" is frequently used in its loosest acceptation for the words immense, immeasurable, incomputable; but in science we ought to be as exact as possible and to have only one meaning for it, viz: absolutely without limit, without end. We often have two different names for one and the same idea, but we ought never to have two different ideas under one and the same name.

190. It is utterly impossible, if we admit the idea of *infinity* of extension with regard to the universe, to conceive any satisfactory exposition of its mechanism, or to shape it into any comprehensible system combined and coherent in itself. "The word machine," says a distinguished author, "in its widest sense may be applied to every material system, and the material universe itself." But who can conceive of a machine in successful operation that, however great it may be, could never have any exterior limits? In order to investigate the principal laws of the universe and tread reliable ground, we must have *bounds* set to its magnitude as the chemist and physicist must have limits set to the divisibility of matter, or rather limits to the minuteness of the ultimate particles that matter is composed of. By assigning infinitude to the great cosmological questions, we willfully and effectually stop all further progress of inquiry with regard to them, that otherwise they would admit of.

191. Next it will be asked: what is the universe bounded and circumscribed by? We conceive the universe circumscribed by an uninterrupted layer of horizontal cosmolineæ, the latter parallelly arranged aside of each other, so as to form in its completeness an immense spherical, though imponderable and immaterial envelope [fig. 18. *b. b. b.*] having the centre of the universe coinciding with its own centre. The cosmolineæ of which this envelope is made up are rigid, *immovable*, and *completely at rest;* the lineïts of which they consist being fixed doubly secure, since they possess only the fettering powers of End-unition and Synduction without the least trace of Versatile Activity. Neither have they monits of matter between them.

192. These horizontal layers of immovable cosmolineæ, enclosing the universe on all sides, so as to form a complete spherical but immaterial envelope, I have called **cosmo-velo** (fig. 18. *b. b. b.*). No unconnected extremities project from it into the great concave of the universe. And the latter thus affords to our mind a definite circumscribed though immensely great representation of a reality of which Milton sings: "Thus far thy bounds, this be thy just circumference, O world!"

193. The cosmolineæ of which the immovable **cosmo-velo** is composed can never be started into motion, except by the entering of monits between them to break their continuity. But monits cannot enter, because there are no bodies of matter or even single monits within or beyond the cosmo-velo to draw any thing that way.

194. Relative magnitude of the universe.—The immovable, spherical shaped cosmo-velo embraces within its bounds the immeasurable extent of all Being which is generally denominated the universe. This immense concave is pervaded in all directions by the ever-coursing cosmolineæ, and scattered about throughout its spaciousness are darting myriads of celestial systems. There are the planets and comets, the sun and all the other fixed stars composing the galaxy, besides the stellar clusters and nebulæ, discovered and undiscovered, their numbers and distance baffling all computation.

195. The system of the fixed stars, to which the sun and the whole galaxy belong, is in itself so great that, according to the calculations of an eminent astronomer, it takes nineteen millions of years for one revolution around the system's common centre of gravity. This great system of fixed stars is, however, but one of the thousands of cosmical islands that "float" in the immensity of this concave of the cosmo-velo.

196. "When from our terrestrial dwelling place," says Maedler, "we strive to penetrate deeper and deeper into space, every scale of measurement, however colassal it may at first appear to us, is annihilated, so to speak, before the immensity of the heavens."

197. There are within this universal concave, bodies from which light itself has to travel thousands of years before reaching us—" nay, there is positive inductive reason for believing that from groups of stars and nebulæ the human eye is reached by light which has been 100,000 years in its tireless flight from the distant *verge* of the universe." The preceding considerations have led us to the contemplation of an extent of space which might well tempt us to make use of the term 'infinite,' but never can we justly employ this term in relation to the universe.

198. Nature of the cosmo-velo.—The strata of lineæ of which the cosmo-velo consists, are never penetrated by any of the detached polarized lineïts nor by heat-lineïts, which, commingled with each other, are both streaming at all times towards the circumference of the universe; because these lineïts, on coming up, are promptly made parallel to the above strata by the Synduction of the latter, and having afterwards annexed to the extreme end of the gravitation-cosmolineæ, they then go back on their returning paths as gravitation-lineïts (247, 248). Neither can the cosmo-velo be agitated by any undulations of light, since there is no connection between the linearium and the cosmo-velo. In the cosmo-velo, moreover, all its lineïts are quiescent and rigid, and the union between their ends is most complete and firm, hence incapable of being made to undulate in progressive true waves, and thus unable to produce light, even if the cosmo-velo were connected with the linearium. The cosmo-velo therefore is utter and complete *darkness, coldness, calmness,* and *inflexibility,* or to speak in positive terms: is destitute of light, heat, and motion. What we conceive as cosmo-velo—the world's embracing envelope—must, by no means, be considered as something material.

Having only breadth and length, we find the cosmo-velo to be *an entity of only* TWO *dimensions,* and as it is completely covering a sphere—the universal sphere —it can have neither beginning nor end, in the same sense in which a closed ring is said to have neither. Another, though very different entity of *two* dimensions we find mentioned in §230.

199. While in the cosmo-velo its lineïts are most completely and firmly united end to end, the union of the ends of lineïts in the linearium, i. e. in the *darting* cosmolineæ of the universe, is comparatively very loose and easily yielding, allowing to the ends of those lineïts a certain amount of free play, in consequence of which a kind of swell in progressive true waves—the proper undulatory movement of the cosmolineæ for the production of *light*—is made feasible (97).

200. EXTENT OF THE COSMO-VELO.—How far outward the cosmo-velo extends in depth we cannot define, but it may be surmised that, as it was made up of the parallelly bent extremities of the cosmolineæ (214), it can in depth or thickness be but a mere film, comparatively speaking. Beyond the cosmo-velo's unmoved lineæ there can nothing be conceived except the *possibility* for real extension *to be,* but no real extension existing there—**vacuity** some perhaps would prefer to call it. We, however, ought not to employ this word, because the expression "existence of an absolute vacuum" is in itself a contradiction, for "absolute vacuum" is the same as Non-Being, yet it is only the Being that exists and not the Non-Being. Hence even in a cosmolinea, if it be severed into many parts by infinitesimal distances, there are no vacancies or voids between these parts, for in these minutest of interspaces, which imply merely an interruption of cosmolineal connection, millions of other cosmolineæ, in all different directions but one, may be conceived. [v. Notes app.]

201. PURE AND SIMPLE SPACE.—What some philosophers call "pure and simple space" has no existence, is no real thing, it is nothing more than the possibility for real extension to be—namely: for extension of *one* as well as for extension of *three* dimensions, i. e. lineïts and solids (bodies); just as "pure and simple time" is nothing more than the possibility for repeated execution of vibratory and rotary motion of lineïts, i. e. vibration and rotation of the most ultimate, most simple subtantia* as well as for repeated motion of bodies.

202. This mere possibility, of course, has no bounds, it allows infinity. And only in this sense can *infinite vacuum* be spoken of beyond the utmost bounds of the cosmo-velo.

203. The cosmo-velo must be conceived to have originated at the same

---

*Regarding the question agitated by some inquirers : whether, if the visible creation were annihilated, space could still exist,—we should say, that, as according to our idea *real* space is extension of cosmolineæ in all directions, and these as simple entities not being *visible* and consequently not included in the assumed annihilation, real space could be easily conceived to exist under the above assumption. And if by space is meant : "pure and simple space," which according to our definition (201) means nothing more than the *possibility* for extension *to be,* this kind of space also (although no real entity) may be said to be not wanting outside the universe under the above assumption.—But if the question were asked : whether, if all, both the visible and the invisible real entities were annihilated, space could still exist ? we would be obliged to say : that as regards *real* space it could *not* exist, but as regards "pure and simple space," i. e. the possibility for extension to be, this could never be wanting.

time the monits of matter originated ; the one could not possibly have developed without the contemporary development of the other.

---

204. To readers who are not averse to daring flights of thought and venturous conceptions, the following paragraphs (204–244) are offered as an attempt at delineating the very first stages of cosmical developments and their causal connection, containing some short sketches, as I have studied them out after considerable reflection on the subject. These sketches of the probable development of the present phenomenal universe out of its pre-phenomenal state will also contain suggestions with regard to the origin of the cosmo-velo on the one hand, and that of the monits of matter on the other hand.

205. In trying to recede into the dim mysterious past as far as ever imagination without incongruity can go, to penetrate beyond the first motions of the universe,—beyond the beginning of every created thing,—antecedent to the very existence of matter—we are obliged to listen to the suggestions of intuition, as it were, but at the same time we ought to bridle imagination by keeping steadily in view the teachings of physical science and the laws of mechanical motion.

206. The only material and the only powers allowed us to operate with and deal in, are the already mentioned four inoriginate most primitive entities, namely : three different kinds of primary powers *End-unition, Synduction, and Versatile Activity,* and the most simple *substantive entity of extension* in *one* dimension, the LINEÏT, which also serves as the very substrat requisite for the upholding of any one or more of the primary powers forever unable to exist by themselves. More than these four factors we cannot get, and more we do not need.

207. *Sketch* 1. Let us then, to begin with, first see what would be the result of the state of things assumed to be represented in the following sketch. Conceive instead of what is generally called an indefinite extent of celestial space, nothing but an unbroken sameness of cosmolineæ stretched uniformly along in *all possible* directions, crossing each other for the most part at or near the middle of this space (fig. 18), the ultimate portions of these cosmolineæ, viz : their lineïts, to be possessed of no other of the three primitive powers but that of the lineïts' own constituent power, End-unition.—This would give us a silent, motionless, cold, dark, immaterial tissue, web and weft of cosmolineæ, a primitive principle indeed, a dead substrat for all the phenomena of the world—but which never could develop into a phenomenal world, for want of the vivacious unruly power of Versatile Activity and the steadying re-adjusting power of Synduction, both of which it lacks. Neither outward nor inward manifestation of action could then exist, and permanently all would have remained for ever as it was. Hence we are convinced of the insufficiency of our assumption, if we assume the existence of *only one* of the three primitive powers.

208. *Sketch* 2. MOST PROBABLE STATE OF THE PRE-PHENOMENAL UNIVERSE. To give the possibility of stir and development to the above dead tissue (in sketch 1), let us make use of all the *three* primitive powers, and let it be granted that besides the constituent power of End-unition there existed within the filaments or cosmolineæ of the aforesaid system numberless lineïts *inclined to be versatile,* possessing as such not only the powers of End-unition and Synduction but likewise the power of Versatile Activity, the restlessly stirring, perpetually striving and struggling power which endeavors to keep in whirling motion, round and round, any lineït it inheres in. Let these versatile inclined lineïts be interspersed all along, more or less regularly, between the common or neutral lineïts possessed only of End-unition.

209. Then we have a picture very different from the first one. In this system of cosmolineæ (208) all the lineïts possessed of Versatile Activity and Synduction then exhibit an unremitting tremulous, vacillating motion, though unable to leave their respective places or to move translatory through space; since the two discordant antagonistic parties: Versatile Activity contending for dismemberment and strife on the one hand, and End-unition and Synduction amicably striving for union, connection, agreement, on the other hand, together occupied all the *versatile* inclined lineïts, and thus kept in constant agitation most of the lineïts of the whole system. These antagonistic powers were then, as they are now, never resting or inactive, on the contrary, they were *effort-exerting* unremittingly—Versatile Activity turning the ends of each lineït somewhat out of their normal position which they ought to occupy in the continuous linen, End-unition and Synduction turning as often the same ends back again into line and order, striving to adjust them, and to keep their connection unbroken. Well might it be said with regard to the then prevailing condition of the versatile inclined lineït:

> Two active parties dwell within itself,
> And each repels and each subdues the other.

210. And indeed are we, the more we examine the subject on all sides, induced again and again to the belief that the versatile inclined lineït as it then existed, was a linear being possessing a sort of perceptive faculty analogous to conscious perception [apperception], a kind of *conscious* will and intellect though of the very lowest possible degree, the merest trace of a primary and rudimentary intellect which, however inexpressibly faint it may have been for each lineït, must still be termed *intellect*, resulting from an intimate conjunction and connection of the two will-(or effort-)manifesting (though unconscious) primary powers dwelling in them, viz: the unruly, vivacious power of Versatile Activity and the steadying, re-adjusting power of Synduction. [§64(5)].

211. Excepting this nearly universal, internal, vibratory commotion, the entire domain of the web and weft of the cosmolineæ (linearium) reposed completely adjusted, in equilibrio, with no outward movements of translocation. All the lineïts with their powers, antagonistic though the latter acted in many of them, were yet kept in the bonds of union and fellowship.

212. No material body or ponderable matter of any kind existed at that time—no atom or monit, no gravitation, no light, no heat, no electricity, no translatory motion.—Cold, dark, and silent, yet quivering throughout its whole length, breadth and depth, under the efforts of the two contending power-parties in their struggle for the ascendency, lay the linearium of the world, an immaterial world as yet. No sign of *coursing* life it showed, although possessed of stirring powers within. The quivering emotion alone betrayed its life and busy action. Such we may presume to have been the pre-phenomenal, primitive state of the universe before the latter was developed into a world of phenomena, of matter, and of universal motion.

213. THE PHENOMENAL UNIVERSE BEGINS TO FORM, TO MOULD, AND TO FASHION ITSELF. The beams and rays of cosmolineæ under the influence of the three primary powers, and crossing each other in all different directions, could not have existed without forming a kind of connected system in some shape or other, which most probably would have the outlines of a sphere, for as the *lineïts* composing these cosmolineæ are the *real* extended *Being*, the most simple ultimate extended Being, of which all the other more complex extended Being (matter included) consists, we may well say with Parmenides in regard to the totality of Being:

> "But since the uttermost limit of Being is ended and perfect,
> Then it is like to the bulk of a sphere well-rounded on all sides,
> Everywhere distant alike from the centre; for never there can be
> Anything greater or anything less, on this side or that side;"

At the circumference of this immense totality of immaterial Being or web and weft, the ends of the cosmolineal rays were all unconnected as yet; but in conformity to its nature, the power of End-unition strives even at the circumference of the cosmolineal system to connect the abrupt ends of these rays with each other. (fig. 18.)

214. By virtue of this power the ends of the cosmolineæ at the very verge of the great cosmolineal sphere were forced to bend horizontally at right angles to their former position, in order to meet each other; and wherever at first the greatest number of horizontally bent extremities happens to be in one and the same great circle of the cosmolineal sphere, there will be formed and developed the sphere's equatorial plane, and all the lineïts there will, strenghtened by Synduction as mentioned in §215, be directing all the adjacent ones into parallel lines also. This operation of making parallel would progressively extend further away, more and more, on both sides of this equatorial circle; and indeed, all the other horizontally bent lineïts would therefore, like the parallels of an artificial globe, at last be arranged parallel to their equatorial circle on both sides of it, so that even in this the greatest and most primitive of spheres, i. e. the immaterial sphere consisting altogether of cosmolineæ, two opposite polar places were already indicated on its surface. With regard to this sphere the horizontally bent lineïts would, moreover, on being separated from those that have a radiate position, form a kind of covering or envelope to the whole sphere, and indeed in this its undeveloped state we already recognize the cosmo-velo in its rudimentary condition. All it needs to make this envelope complete and independent is: to get rid of all its Versatile Activity, and in its stead acquire more of the power of Synduction, and then have itself (the envelope) disconnected and severed from the rest of the immense totality of the system of cosmolineæ which is embraced by it.

215. *Sketch* 3. In proportion as the bent extremities spoken of in §213 become more horizontal and parallel, those of their lineïts which possess Synduction and Versatile Activity, having the energy of their Synduction made more efficient by this parallel arrangement, are hereby enabled to expel Versatile Activity, which thereupon diffusing itself along the cosmolineæ, is obliged to proceed more into the interior of the universe,* and is readily taken up by the versatile inclined lineïts there, and thereby the latter lineïts become strengthened in their endeavor to *whirl*, while at the same time they are also enabled to expel from themselves their power of Synduction, which then has to take its way outward along the rays of the cosmolineæ* until it arrives at, and is taken up by the lineïts of the cosmo-velo at the circumference of the universe, and thus gives to the cosmo-velo still more steadiness, compactness and a greater power *to make parallel.*

---

*Because the neutral lineïts are unable to harbor in the least either Synduction or Versatile Activity.

216. The versatile inclined lineïts of the universe, at least a great number of them, are by these events still more freed from the embarrassment of Synduction, and being at the same time constantly strengthened by new access of Versatile Activity, they are at last from versatile *inclined* lineïts confirmed into *thorough* versatile inclined lineïts, enabled to whirl at once from out the ranks of the neutral lineïts with which they have hitherto been so closely associated in cosmolineal union.

217. With the first acts performed by the thorough versatile inclined lineïts of breaking the bonds, and with their whirling from out the cosmolineæ, a more general secession was brought about by the loosening of the whole cosmolineal texture, and as the gaps caused by the departure of the first seceders from the ranks of the cosmolineæ were immediately closed by End-unition, the cosmolineæ along the whole extent were submitted to an unusually severe strain, and when thus their tractility was put to the severest test they had soon to sever their connection in their weakest parts, namely, in the vicinity of their extremities where they were *curved:* that is, near the cosmo-velo. As soon, however, as this severance was accomplished at the circumference of the universe, the Synduction which was still being expelled from the strenghtened versatile inclined lineïts of the interior of the universe was now, instead of escaping outwardly, obliged to go along in an opposite direction, i. e. inwardly, and therefore from all parts of the universe it was driven by the neutral lineïts centreward along the cosmolineæ.

218. In the vicinity of the centre, Synduction thus accumulated rapidly, so that here this power was especially enabled to arrange the cosmolineæ into parallel circles or spiral coils of *convolution* of a spherical outline (fig. 18, *d.*), this being the only shape likely to result under such circumstances and conditions of the streaming of Synduction towards a common central point from all around. In consequence of this *parallel* arrangement, Synduction was enabled to expel from all the versatile inclined lineïts of this central part of the universe all the power of Versatile Activity yet to be found, and thus to change them into *steady* lineïts. The remainder of the versatile inclined lineïts situated between the central part and the circumference of the universe being thus continually more and more strengthened by the gain of Versatile Activity, expelled all the Synduction yet remaining in them, and were then, like their predecessors, also perfected into *thorough* versatile inclined lineïts, and as such easily enabled to break loose from their cosmolineal arrangement.

219. The coherence of the cosmolineæ having thus been weakened, the secession of the thorough versatile inclined lineïts progressed more and more rapidly with each of the latter's departure, until it soon became inconceivably rapid, almost simultaneous. As fast as the thorough versatile inclined lineïts left the ranks of the cosmolineæ, the latter had their own connection restored by closing up again and thus forming continuous lines as before, less however in number of lineïts. By the time the thorough versatile inclined lineits had all seceded, the cosmolineal system was not only freed from all Versatile Activity, but had also severed its connection with the central convolution and left the latter independent. Both the *cosmo-velo* as well as the great *central convolution* were now completely developed and strengthened to greatest perfection.

220. Although the versatile inclined lineïts by secession had gained one of their objects, namely to free themselves from the cosmolineæ, they had not thereby secured their full independence, for there yet remained to the lineït as soon as isolated, the unavoidable danger from the newly re-adjusted cosmolineæ and their [now to better advantage acting] End-unition, of being held fast by at least one of its extremities.

221. To avoid this, the versatile inclined lineïts were immediately on their secession from the cosmolineæ, NECESSITATED *for the sake of their own safety*,* to form pacts of their own, although themselves averse to combination of any kind.

222. The most efficient combination giving protection to these lineïts, and at the same time allowing them to indulge in their propensity of whirling would be: that a sufficient number of thorough versatile inclined lineïts, by virtue of their End-unition, join with one of their ends to a common centre, around which centre they might rotate, but in rotating they necessarily had to rotate around an axis and thus produce the **monit** of matter. Arranged in the shape of a monit, they are no longer called versatile *inclined* lineïts, but are true *versatile lineïts*, and as such they would be secure, because any attack the lineïts of the cosmolineæ may make on them is made ineffectual, by reason of a *united* vigorous rotation and by the End-unition of their free extremities, by which these versatile lineïts (being the radii of the monit) would now be enabled to break and pull the cosmolineæ themselves instead of being held by the latter. How this pulling is effected appears from §124–129.

222'. By virtue of their End-unition which they still possessed, and which no lineït of any kind can ever lose, the versatile lineïts were able to combine. While Versatile Activity urged them to whirl independently, impending danger urged them to unite.

It may here be remarked that the three events: (1) the departure of *conscious* will and perception from the versatile inclined lineïts, (2) their act of secession, and (3) their associating themselves into monits of matter, was all accomplished simultaneously.

223. This well-contrived performance of the versatile inclined lineïts of seceding and of composing themselves into monits, was their *last* action performed with a *conscious* will and effort (intellect), since with their first acts of revolving and forming into a monit, the two powers Versatile Activity and Synduction which together had hitherto animated the versatile *inclined* lineït, had parted for ever, only one of them, Versatile Activity, remaining with these lineïts, which now constituted the monit's radii. Henceforth *no conscious* will and intellect or perceptive faculty belonged to any individual lineït whatever. Yet instead of these numberless mere traces of intellect, there then in consequence of the most intimate commingling and conjunction of all the free and fleeting Versatile Activity upon Synduction [the latter concentrated and within the macrocosmic convolution] arose the ONE great conscious Will and perceptive intellect of the universe, as more fully spoken of in §235.

224. From a retrospection at the preceding paragraphs it would appear that thus, in fact, SYNDUCTION—by silently exerting itself unconsciously in its proper work of directing lineïts parallelly, throughout numberless ages —was *the* power which first of all brought about the BEGINNING towards a gradual construction of the now existing phenomenal universe, because in consequence of this constructing action was induced a general *exchange* of places among two of the primitive powers, and this exchange again gave rise to the production of matter, the cosmo-velo, the central convolution, and so the universal circulation of cosmolineæ.

---

* The versatile inclined lineïts as such possessed, according to §210, *conscious* will and intellect, though of the most rudimentary kind possible.

As the first incipient performance of this general exchange may be called the period of *conception*, so may the accomplished exchange as soon as it was fully completed, be looked upon as the epoch of the *birth* of the phenomenal universe, and at the same time denote the *termination* of the pre-phenomenal *all* immaterial state of being.

225. The aforesaid minutest of pacts (in the shape of monits of matter) at first had no connection with one another, but remained loosely dispersed throughout the universe in the very places where they originated, and thus in a dissipated state they existed as innumerable myriads of *monits*.

226. As soon as the monits had sprung into existence, the cosmolineæ were at once put into motion by them as already explained in §124–129. The general secession of all the thorough versatile inclined lineïts, their immediate formation into monits, and the effectual attack made by these monits upon the continuity of the cosmolineæ, afforded to the End-unition of the latter the first opportunity for a more vigorous action of pulling endwise lineït to lineït, and thereby to produce *longitudinal motion of translocation*; for not only had the gaps in the continuous cosmolineæ, resulting from secession, to be closed up again, but the gaps which resulted from the incessant striking aside so many lineïts at each monit's circumference, had also to be bridged over unceasingly. The cosmolinea, once moving, impels in never ending repetition all the monits it may happen to come upon in its path. Thus for the first time the phenomenon of gravitation appeared, velocity lineïts were attached to monits (131, 142.), and monits themselves, i. e. matter, for the first time exhibited *weight* and *momentum*.

227. Places of greatest energy of action.—Wherever in the wide expanse of the pre-phenomenal universe the most beams of cosmolineæ had intersected each other (v. fig. 18.) there would be the greatest throng of lineïts, consequently there would be the greatest number of monits be formed, ready to operate as a nucleus upon the greatest number of cosmolineæ. Hence there would also be the greatest energy and action of Versatile Activity displayed. And to these points of most vigorous action were then pushed by gravitation immense multitudes of other monits from less central regions. To such places of intersection the newly born matter of the universe was drifting, collecting and condensing into spheres with better success and in greater number than to any other localities possessing fewer intersections of cosmolineal rays.

228. By far the greater number of cosmolineal rays of the pre-phenomenal universe will naturally intersect each other in regions comparatively not very far from the centre of the universe; consequently these will be the regions where afterwards Versatile Activity will be displayed in its greatest energy, and where matter in most enormous quantities was drawn together to form vast numbers of celestial orbs by the side of each other, arranging themselves so as in their aggregate to appear in the shape of an enormous hollow sphere, the **cosmic core**, enclosing the central convolution (218) on all sides.

229. For the same reason that to the centre of every celestial orb there belongs a system of in-streaming gravitation cosmolineæ, a similar system must also belong to the centre of the immense hollow sphere, the *cosmic core*, surpassing in amount of matter the mass of any other collection or aggregate of celestial orbs. And as the centre of the cosmic core coincides with the centre of the universe, it follows that those gravitation cosmolineæ which are operated upon by the monits of the cosmic core, are bound to have the most *direct* circulation, following unswervingly for ever the same straight tracks, because both the centre and circumference of the universe to and from which they are streaming are immovable and eternally at rest. These cosmolineæ are termed **ordinate** cosmolineæ. They pass through every part and place of the universe.

230. NATURE OF THE WORLD'S CENTRE-CONVOLUTION [or of the world's central soul-substance]. The convolution is immaterial, consisting of cosmolineæ parallelly rolled up in spirals. Yet innumerable as these spirals may be [and the whole aggregate of them may even be ball-shaped in outline] (v. fig. 18, d) they are all distinct from each other among themselves. As such each spiral has only breadth and length, and we are here furnished with another case [besides that in §198] of an *entity of* TWO *dimensions*, which in this case gives us the *psyche* or soul. The convolution is made up of no other lineïts but such as the cosmo-velo is composed of, and which contain of the two primitive powers only End-unition and Synduction. As it is with the cosmo-velo, so also with the convolution, both possess neither monits of matter nor the power of Versatile Activity. Within the convolution, by the peculiar duplicating position and convolute windings of its parallel lineæ and the most intimate, though momentarily, yet for ever repeated acts of conjunction by the fleeting, incessantly coming and going, power of Versatile Activity upon that of Synduction, a new faculty is engendered, namely that of **Intellect.*** Intellect is no entity itself, but a faculty belonging to an entity, namely: to the convolution or soul-substance, upon the nature of which the intellect is dependent for its degree or quality. Both the cosmo-velo as well as the convolution are immaterial entities, each of only *two* dimensions containing no monits of matter. While at the cosmo-velo a conversion of heat- and polarized-lineïts into gravitation-lineïts is continually going on, in the central convolution there is continually engendered the faculty of intellect.

231. All three together: the convolution, the cosmo velo, and the *ordidinate* cosmolineæ (229) constitute the immaterial substance of the universal soul in its completeness—the *macrocosmic soul.*

232. FURTHER DEVELOPMENT OF THE UNIVERSE. With the first acts of conflict, which consisted in an attack upon the lineïts of the cosmolineæ by the monits of matter to destroy the connection of the former, dates the most vigorous development of the universe, and the first great phenomena of nature came forth. Motion in all its various modes, and first of all, the universal motion of gravitation—the circulation of the cosmolineæ—was started; scattered monits or atoms thus gravitated upon, were pulled together to form orbs of shining stars.

233. Cotemporary and in connection with the gravitating process were polarized lineïts struck off incessantly within the aggregates of matter (125, 126, 147, 148,) and magnetic streams sent forth from all celestial bodies. Then also, in consequence of the retardation and stopping of the centreward *motion* of monits of matter, heat-lineïts were thrown off, and for the first time streams of heat began to pervade the universe, and floods of light to undulate in all directions.

---

* The immense amount of the vivacious power of Versatile Activity as it is continually chased along the gravitation-cosmolineæ from the circumference of the universe to its very centre, begets—while commingling and conjugating with the aggregate amount of the steadying, re-adjusting power of Synduction—which *within* the central convolution is situate and permanently dwelling—begets the conscious **Will** and **Intellect** of the macrocosmic convolution, or in other words: begets the Intellect of the world's soul. Thus came into fnll vivacity and exercise the most admirable of functions, the **supreme Intellect** of the universe; thus it has been continued till now, and thus also shall it eternally be rejuvanated without cessation.

234. But this was not all. The following occurrences, namely: 1st, the exchange of the steadying re-adjusting power of Synduction for Versatile Activity, and Versatile Activity for Synduction, among all the versatile inclined lineïts, thereby dividing the latter into two opposite classes; 2d, the most complete and lasting separation forever of these hitherto conjunct two primite powers, and 3d, the secession from the ranks of the cosmolineæ performed by the thorough versatile lineïts,—proved to be the grandest events that ever could happen from eternity; for not only did this exchange and segregation give the finishing stroke to the cosmo-velo, but contemporaneous with it was all the matter formed—and around the centre of the universe at the same time was completed the rolling up of the great system of the cosmolineal [immaterial] convolution, that is: the chief and most consummate portion of the macrocosmic soul-substance (230), a fit abode for *conscious will* (or effort) and *highest intellect.*

235. Previous to constituting themselves into monits of matter, all and every one of the versatile inclined lineïts individually was possessed of both Versatile Activity and Synduction, and hence of a kind of *conscious* will and perceptive *intellect* [*which the union of these two powers always begets*] intellect only of the faintest degree though it must have been (209, 210). The merest trace of rudimentary intellect, yet intellect it was nevertheless. But with the forming of the versatile inclined lineïts into monits, all Synduction fled from these lineïts and consequently all conscious will and intellect had likewise to vanish from them for ever. (223).

236. Yet instead of these innumerable faintest of intellects there then [in consequence of the most concentrated commingling and conjunction of the two will and effort manifesting, though *unconscious* primary powers namely, of Versatile Activity upon Synduction and their action and reaction upon each other [v. 64(5). 235] is ONE great conscious will and intellect begotten, —and the **All-Intelligent,** perfect throughout at once, extended and extant in all Its might from centre to circumference, **is** and **exists**;—with Its intellect residing in the world's great central convolution [head-portion of Its soul-system]—Its rays of nerve and strength* all round in physical though immaterial lines, which dart along from furthest points of universe, incessantly converging to the centre, and then as radiant heat and lines of magnetism sent back from whence they came.

237. These *inflowing* continuous lines, which are thus Its soul's converging rays, in fact, Its nerve-like filaments, serve also by their instantaneous speed of undulation as messengers of knowledge, by which the All-Intelligent *perceives* and *knows* all, and at pleasure can influence and stir, and make to vibrate with intelligence such of the genuine souls of mortals, as in their nature prove related to Its own.—This immaterial Being [the cosmic soul possessing intellect] fills with Its rays the concave of the world—the cosmo-velo substantiates Its limits—Its will and faculty of reason dwell in the cosmic centre—Its rays not only visit minds of man, but matter also of celestial orbs, reciprocally acting with material things which are, in fact, that souls co-operating counterpart.

238. From this sketch it follows that the **All-Intelligent** is:

1.) A single Unity.† An Individuality.

2.) Imperishable, i. e. eternal for all time to come.

---

*The system of the *ordinate* gravitation cosmolineæ (229.).

†*A single Unity.* There is only *one central* system of convolutions to the universe, and as no other but the *central* system can be the seat of macrocosmic Intellect, it follows that only one, sole, single **unity** is the All-Intelligent.

3.) Immense in extent and vast as the universe, but not infinite.*

4.) Omnipresent therein, not in thought only but in substance also, though of an immaterial substance.†

5) Omniscient and self-conscious.

6) All exceedingly potent, but not absolutely omnipotent.‡

7) Performing certain functions.||

238′. How long the human mind is to be kept in the trammel of doubt and uncertainty about the most vital question extant, the finding and knowing of the true God, depends to a considerable degree upon its own exertions. Even now, after thousands of years, man's mind with regard to its conceptions of the All-Intelligent, is either swayed by hollow-headed atheism; or cramped by ecclesiastical statutes into absurd caricatures, which aim to pull that Being down to the level of a miserable human likeness, that Being, in comparison with whose universal all-inclosing embrace the whole galaxy of the visible heavens appears as diminutive, as the bright sparks emitted from a burning steel wire appear when compared to the immense domain of that galaxy!—or lastly, the All-Intelligent is by wrangling

---

*The word "infinite" is one of the greatest strongholds of all those who are indifferent to the highest inquiries in cosmical investigation. Because if any one is to accept the predicate "infinite" with regard to the All-Intelligent, then he need not at all try or endeavor to comprehend It, to know It, or to form any conception of It, for this is absolutely impossible with respect to anything infinite. It is impossible for any mind to form a conception of that which is said to be infinite.

†*Omnipresent.* Not only does the greater part of the All-Intelligent's immaterial substance in the shape of *ordinate* cosmolineæ and their lineïts (229), traverse the whole extent of the universe, but they traverse also all matter, however compact and solid the matter may be [the monits themselves alone excepted]—all bodies of inanimate nature as well as those of organized beings. They penetrate the very heart of man and its most hidden recesses. They move within us, across us, on all sides of us; and in truth may we say: within these streams of cosmolineæ—within this soul-substance of the All-Intelligent—we live and move and have our being.

‡*Potent,* but not omnipotent in the strictest meaning of the term. The All-Intelligent can not immediately operate upon monits of matter. It can operate only [by means of the power of Synduction belonging to its macrocosmic soul or convolution] upon free lineïts by changing their direction, and upon the *ordinate* cosmolineæ by setting them into vibration. It is obliged in a great measure to shape its own course of action according to circumstances, which may be brought about by the antagonistic action of Versatile Activity; hence the All-Intelligent cannot be omnipotent in the widest meaning of the word.

The defects and deformities of existing things and beings, or their vicious dispositions and imperfect condition must by no means be considered as the work of the All-Intelligent, must not be attributed to It. Myriads of counter-operations, traceable to the monit's Versatile Activities, indirectly take part in determining and shaping the handiwork of nature.

||Forcibly directing polarized- and heat-lineïts against their own versatile tendencies, and thereby guiding monits and atoms out of their common drift of mere mechanical aggregation, and to group and range them according to peculiar *determined directions* [as is taking place in innumerable forms of organization, and also in the conversion of heat- and polarized-lineïts into gravitation-lineïts at the circumference of the universe]; these are some of the *mechanical functions* of the All-Intelligent performed by virtue of the Synduction of Its own *macro*-cosmic soul, as well as, mediately, by Synduction of the *micro*-cosmic soul of each *vitally active organic cell*, and the soul of each living individual being. The more *mental* functions of the All-Intelligent are: to stir and set into vibration and to influence and animate such of the souls who in their nature are inclined to Its own, and apt to correspond to such vibrations.

The All-Intelligent has never framed or created, nor ever can frame or create *monits of matter.* Framing or making matter has been [as already indicated in §220–222] the work of the versatile inclined lineïts in striving to preserve the independence of their Versatile Activity.

scholastics evaporated into—they know not what—by some into "the Infinite," by others into "the Unconscious," by a third party into "the Absolute," the "Incomprehensible," the "Unapproachable," etc., all of which, scarcely amount to anything better than sheer Nothingness. A sorry aspect, indeed, this universe would present, if all the other habitable worlds of it were peopled with beings of no higher faculties and of no nobler daring of mind than what is possessed by us and the gold-grasping, sensuality-hunting majority of our own race.

238[2]. If not already apparent from the preceding paragraphs, it may be still more distinctly stated that the All-Intelligent is not the indwelling *causa prima* and essence of *all* things, and does not *reveal* Itself in everything; that besides the active faculties of the soul-substance of the All-Intelligent there are other activities at work, viz: the three primary powers operating quite independent of the former; there are, moreover, also monits of matter and physical forces, such as heat-, gravitation-, and polarized-lineïts, existing independent of the All-Intelligent. Consequently not *every* performance and action in the universe is caused and accomplished through It and by It, as pantheists do assert of their Deïty. Our views as set forth in the above paragraphs are very far from being pantheism. And yet, it must be admitted that the ray-substance of the All-Intelligent is everywhere,and in fact does continually penetrate every thing in the universe except the cosmovelo, i. e. the world's envelope, and the monits.

238[3]. According to the pantheistic view, the soul of Nature's God, by Its very action of giving life to nature's schemes and operations, has sacrificed Its individuality and lost Itself in these Its mighty exertions. Such are, by no means, our views with regard to the All-Intelligent. Neither is Itself to be sought in the various physical forces. The One great individuality exists as such for ever, and had not to dissolve Itself, in order that out of It might arise the vast multitude of all the existing separate objects of nature now exhibiting themselves in the universe. To comparatively few of these objects, viz: to the vitally active organic cells, and to any of their inferior combinations, individually belongs perceptive and appreciating power of an inferior degree*—only to the higher organized beings belong conscious Will and intellect of a higher order;—and to the All-Intelligent alone pre eminently belong conscious Will and Intellect of the highest degree possible. All the rest of the universe is animated by the three *primary* powers, who with unconscious but unconquerable earnestness of Will unremittingly pursue their aim regardless of whatever nobleness, beauty, and grandeur may be ruined by them.

238[4]. Our views also deviate from Deism, in as much as that doctrine places God *outside* the world. We place our God *inside.* Around the centre of the universe, unremovable and steadfast, subsists the immaterial cosmic convolution, and within this head-portion of the world's soul substance are constantly engendered the supreme functions of Intellect. Limited to this simple condition the All-Intelligent would, however, be incomplete and

---

* Hence even to living plants, and especially to their *young vitally active* cells, we must allow certain efforts and aims, and an ability, as it were, to judge of what may be subservient to their aims. The fact that tendrils as well as the tender-tips of twining plants reach out and exert themselves towards neighboring poles and other objects to which they may fasten themselves and may cling for support, seems to indicate that the young vitally active cells of these sensitive tips are induced to turn, and stretch, and exert themselves in the proper direction pointed out to them by some kind of emanation which comes upon them, and which is continually issuing from all material objects, most probably as streams of polarized lïneits.

for want of a medium unable to operate upon the outside world around. The COSMIC-CORE like an immense body of mechanism, consisting of innumerable celestial orbs which on all sides encircle the cosmic soul's central portion, i. e. the cosmic convolution, causes and accomplishes* the great circulation of the ordinate cosmolineæ, and by these means makes it possible for the All-Intelligent to operate and act upon the outside world around It, and to be not only a thinking but an acting Being also, and thus all-complete.

238[5]. Hence we see that in this respect it is with the All-Intelligent as it is with man: the head-portion of the soul-substance of both can exist without being connected with matter, but in this state there would be no feeling, no perceiving, and no taking cognizance of what is around and outside.

238[6]. As the brain inclosed within man's head is the central organ of his nervous system, and by its internuntial fibres is connected with every part of his body, and the latter by means of these fibres is in constant communication with the immaterial soul-substance within the brain,—so is the cosmic core with its immense amount of matter, the central organ of the universal system, and is by its ordinate cosmolineæ connected with every part of the body of the universe, and the latter by means of these cosmolineæ can be at any time in constant communication with the immaterial cosmic convolution, i. e. with the soul-substance around the centre. Drawn upon by the immense masses of matter of the cosmic core, the ordinate cosmolineæ are bound to move, and in their routes they *necessarily* have to pass by way of the great universal centre (v. 584, 586,) and thus are issued from the same. As soon as in this outward course they reach the cosmic core, they are by that great body sent divergingly in all directions away to the periphery of the universe, i. e. to the cosmo-velo, from which region by the action of the same mighty cosmic core they then are forced again to return by way of the universal centre, as heretofore.

238[7]. In this manner we conceive that from the centre of the universe, from the head-centre of the All-Intelligent, emanate and spread incessantly in all directions the ordinate cosmolineæ,—that Being's immaterial rays. Darting through everything except the monits, they are turned by the cosmo-velo at the periphery of the universe, whence they are obliged to stream back to the great centre from which they issued. And thus in never-ending circuits, as it were, God's nervous substance circulates in steady imperceptible pulsations throughout the world, so that all nature and, of course, we human beings too, at all times, are penetrated with this divine emanation, which, however, must not be taken for the Deïty Itself.

238[8]. Not by having the Deity's name continually upon our tongue are we made to feel Its grandeur. Rather is it by silent meditation and deep reflection upon Its essence and attributes that we are led to revere and adore God's dignity, and become imbued with sentiments of bliss, sublimest thoughts, and deepest holiest emotions.

238[9]. The universe or, which is the same—the macrocosm—comprises

a) all the most ultimate particles, or units of extension in *three* dimensions, of which all *matter* and material things are composed;

b) all the most ultimate portions, or units of extension in *one* dimension, namely, all the *force*-lineïts, such as gravitation-, heat-, polarized-, and nerve-lineïts; as well as all the macrocosmic soul-substance, i. e. the immaterial most simple compounds composed of lineïts, as there are: the convolutions, the cosmo-velo, and the cosmolineæ.

---

* By the Versatile Activity of the total immense aggregate of its monits.

c) all the power-units or power-points of the three most primitive kinds of power: End-unition, Synduction, and Versatile Activity.

We are therefore entitled to say: The *esse* or being of the macrocosm (the universe) may be divided into three classes, viz: 1) its three primitive powers, 2) its immaterial substances, and 3) its material or corporeal substances. The third of these classes is composed out of the second and first class *excepting* from the latter the *power of Synduction.* And out of the same two classes *excepting Versatile Activity* is composed the macrocosm's soul,* which together with its faculty of INTELLECT constitutes the immaterial All-Intelligent. The All-Intelligent, however, can only exist in mutual retro-action with a corporeal or material counterpart, could not exist if there existed no matter. Matter indeed is coeval with the macrocosmic soul itself—yea, with the All-Intelligent—and as indestructible as the latter.

238[10]. The two ideas of Macrocosm (or the universe) and the All-Intelligent must, however, always be kept distinct. Under the name of the latter is comprised the macrocosmic soul together with the totality of CONSCIOUS Will and Effort—the highest *concentrated* faculty of *intellect and reason*—which in the present *phenomenal* universe is being unceasingly engendered within one single dominion, that is, within the macrocosmic central convolution [§230, 235, 236];† but which in the *pre*-phenomenal universe was being unceasingly engendered as infinitesimal traces of reason in innumerable myriads of versatile inclined lineïts (§210, 235). The macrocosm, on the other hand, being the totality of the material machinery together with the totality of the primitive powers, as well as all the moving motive immaterial forces, and the immaterial most simple compound substances (§238[2]), incloses also the totality of concentrated conscious Will and Effort, the supreme reason of the All-Intelligent. And as the ALL-enveloping cosmo-velo is common to both the All-Intelligent as well as to the macrocosm, so that both are defined in outline by the same circumference, it may in truth be said: *as sure as the All-Intelligent encloses and contains within Itself the macrocosm or universe, so sure does the universe enclose and contain the All-Intelligent.*

238[11]. The particles of matter are constantly shifting, going into combinations, again to be decomposed and alternately to be re-arranged into other shapes and compounds. Our own bodies are thus considered, part of the macrocosmic body. But our souls, although composed of units (or parts) of the macrocosmic immaterial soul-substance, and having sprung forth from the generality of that substance, can not be said to be constituent parts of the macrocosmic soul. They will maintain their individuality after as well as before the dissolution of the material structure by which they were confined.‡ They may even be admitted within the cosmic-core, in nearness to the centre of Intellect itself, provided they be of strength sufficient to take pleasure in all such exercises as through the light of nature lead up to nature's God; to love and to revere this supreme individuality when found; and to practice charity to helpless fellow creatures as readily as to themselves. Such souls, as these, to whom an never-ending intercourse with the All-Intelligent would be a source of highest happiness, can never be dis-

---

*Convolution, cosmo-velo, and cosmolineæ.

†As on a small scale in man, within the convolutions of the soul-substance of the brain.

‡Although, as we have said, no soul could exist if there were no matter, it does by no means follow therefrom that the soul of an organized being must necessarily dissolve with the dissolution of its material frame. For only in case that ALL existing matter were to vanish, could that inference be just and admissible.

solved or have their ultimate parts dispersed again into the generality of the macrocosmic soul-substance, as is the case with souls of all irrational beings. Not only our reasoning faculties and the deep-seated aspirations toward a future more happy and perfect existence, but also the irrepressible desire to be a living witness of the coming fate and change and progress of this earth, to be a spectator of what takes place in other worlds besides—all speak alike against a dissolution of the soul of any human being who seeks to know the All-Intelligent, and does his best to spread such knowledge gained, instead of doing homage to sensual things and mammon.

238^{12}. Freed from every ritualism and ecclesiastical ordinance, the true and holy kernel of all religion is to be found in the earnest desire and longing of the human soul to bring itself into an intimate communion with its exalted psychic prototype, the All-Intelligent,—a communion which may at times, in its sudden promulgation, with awe excite and whirl through all the trembling depths of life and vibrate to the core with overpowering force, at other times in lasting, calm, and uniform exercise stir up the fibres of the soul with gentler tunes of bliss.

---

239. As soon as the central convolution, and the cosmo-velo, the monits of matter, and the darting cosmolineæ, had assumed a definite existence and shape, so soon became the universe to be a universe full of phenomena. After partial condensation of matter, when the heat had subsided sufficiently to allow the free action of chemical affinity, great activity in the development of material compositions took place by combining, separating and recombining the mixed up monits of the different elementary bodies. Then came a busy time, antagonistic jumble, and turbulence supreme, between repelling heat and pulling gravitation ; although allayed at present, incessant strife of antagonistic powers does still excite the pulse of living nature. —Since then abounded mighty work, and stir, and action !

240. If there had been in the primitive nebulous matter of the universe evenly diffused, but one nucleus, then the atoms or monits would all have fallen towards that one nucleus in direct lines to form one immense spherical aggregate, but no vortex motion of the mass could have been produced thereby, because the heat developed by the fall of particles was sufficient to keep them apart and within certain bounds of approach, and where there was no outlet and no giving way on any side, there could be no vortex. If we have only two nuclei a and b (v. annexed fig.) in the whole nebulous mass, it is easy to perceive that those atoms or particles m or n which are not in the straight line $a\ b$ that joines both nuclei, will take a path in accordance with the diagonal of the parallelogram of the differently directed forces, and being more influenced by the nearer or stronger one of the two nuclei, fall in a direction more or less tangential to the same, and if numerous enough cause the nucleus and its system to rotate. These two nuclei, however, will not be sufficient to give a rotary motion to either of the systems if monits of matter are equally distributed on all sides, because the direction of m is then counterbalanced by that of n. But from fig. 18, Tab. 5, it may be seen that under our suppositions a great number of such nuclei necessarily existed, and from their

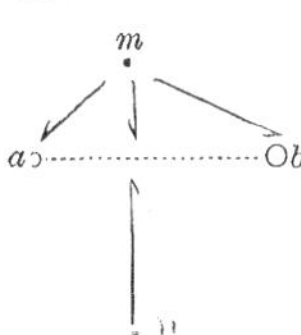

various sizes, peculiar positions, and especially from unequal distribution of monits, under the influence of gravitation, *rotation* of the different nebulous systems is certain to result.

241. By concentration and contraction the rotary motion of each rotating nebulous sphere necessarily increases in rapidity, but most so in its equatorial belt; the rapidly increasing centrifugal velocity of its equatorial belt after having attained a certain strength, hinders this belt very much in its contraction towards the centre of the sphere. Other parts of the nebulous sphere, of less centrifugal force, however, will continue to contract steadily, the more so the nearer they are to the poles, because at the poles the centrifugal force is nothing. And thus the whole sphere will assume an extremely oblate shape. The equatorial belt of a heated oblate sphere cools fastest, hence contracts or subsides fastest, hence increases in centrifugal force fastest, and reaches first of all that certain degree of centrifugal velocity which balances its centripetal force and thus restrains it first of all from any further contraction towards the centre of the sphere. The belt next below the first exterior one has not yet reached its maximum centrifugal velocity, yet still continues to lose heat, hence continues to contract, and is thus obliged to tear itself away from the exterior one, leaving the latter rotating as an independent ring. The inferior belt eventually becomes also detached, in like manner, from the preponderant mass below, and thus begins to form a second separate ring, and so on. Finally these rings break and contract into globes, and in this manner are formed suns, planets, and satellites.

242. Thus 1) by virtue of the powers that are always active in matter [by End-unition and Versatile Activity], and 2) by means of the all-present medium [the cosmolineæ],—it may be said: that by these very agencies which cause gravitation, not only was the primeval ponderable nebulous ether of the universe partitioned into separate immense aggregations, and these aggregations shaped into immense oblate spheroïds, but also were these spheroïds broken up into spherical suns, planets, and satellites, and morover furnished with orbitual as well as with rotary motion. All this may be said was done by *gravitation*, which itself, however, is only a phenomenon due to the aforesaid primary powers and the medium.

243. At a later period when planets, after cooling, became fit for the existence of plants and animals, then it was that by gradual development, from the most simple organized animal beings others of a more complex structure, in gradation up to man, succeeded, all [except the very simplest] propagated in the usual manner by coition. In order to form an immaterial spiral convolution or chief portion of the *soul-substance* (v. 230.) for each of these animal and human germs during conception, lineïts taken from the darting rays of cosmolineæ are rolled up in a similar system of convolutions as that existing at the centre of the universe, though of an immensely more diminutive scale. And if the convolution which is the repository of the supreme will and intellect of the universe, be termed *macro-cosmic* convolution, or chief portion of the *soul-substance of the universe*, then that convolution which is the repository of the will and intellect of man, may be called the human convolution or chief portion of the *soul-substance of man*. This latter convolution encased within the brain, together with the soul-substance within the nervous system of the human body, and made officious by conscious Will, may thus be considered as the *entire human soul*. While, on the other hand, the *macro-cosmic* convolution encased within the cosmic core, and made officious by conscious Will, together with the ordinate cosmolineæ and the cosmo-velo may be considered as the *entire macro-cosmic* *soul*; and in opposition to this immaterial system stands the sum total of all the monits of matter—the macro-cosmic soul's *corporeal* counterpart. (v. Notes app.)

244. All four: 1) the macrocosmic convolution with its faculty of conscious Will and Intellect; 2) the cosmo-velo; 3) the monits of matter; and 4) the system of darting cosmolineæ, together with the isolated lineïts, although they had a beginning, will never end in time. They can never be dissolved into their original constituents, for they are according to §64 the most simple of compounds existing, and therefore the most durable. They, and consequently also the sum of them, the *All-Intelligent* or *macrocosm*, shall remain for ever, and the circulation of the cosmolineæ never cease,* although all other compound things should be dissolved and go to wreck, or be consolidated in one immense immovable conglomerate.

245. Besides the four most elementary of compounds just named we may here mention the fifth, viz: the *soul of human being*, which on account of its superior number of constituent lineïts over those of inferior animals' souls, is indissoluble, and indestructible. Though indissoluble it is liable to become inconscious, whenever its convolution unrolls and spreads out, but is apt to regain consciousness, as soon as rolled up again, by outside power, in its peculiar spiral shape.

---

* With regard to the all-pervading system of cosmolineæ, although lineïts are constantly disjoined from one end of the cosmolinea, and other lineïts just as constantly annexed to the other end, yet the cosmolineal streams shall never cease to circulate.

SECTION V.

---

246. After this short but necessary digression let us now resume our speculations with regard to the detached polarized lineïts (125, 126, 143). The lineïts having been struck and flung aside by some monit—either by the monit of a planet or by that of any other celestial orb—proceed [by virtue of the Versatile Activity communicated to one of their ends] outward betwixt the intervening particles of matter, and at last emerge from the orb's surface. They are also when in company with heat, taken along by the latter.

247. The detached polarized lineïts in their outward flight, either by themselves, or in company with heat, are obliged to reach ultimately the limits of the universe, i. e. the concave inner surface of the cosmo-velo, where, by the powerful synduction of the latter, they all will promptly be made parallel to its immovable strata, at right angles to the radii of the universe.

248. After having been made parallel to the cosmo-velo, the detached polarized lineïts are immediately by virtue of their End-unition joined endwise and *annexed* to the extremity of inward flowing cosmolineæ.

249. Thus moved and redintegrate, the annexed lineïts proceed on their inward journey from the very verge of the universe towards the centre of some celestial orb, once more capable and ready, as constituent parts of the cosmolineæ, to act as gravitation, until in course of time they are from the orb which they go to, again sent forth as detached polarized lineïts or, as the case may be, as heat-lineïts. And in this way again and again they go through similar cycles to other celestial orbs and speed on in circuits for ever, if they meanwhile have not become attached as velocity-lineïts to monits.

250. Hence we find the following procedure to take place continually, on the one hand: the *breaking up* of cosmical threads into linea-fragments (lineïts), which most frequently happens within the dense and crowded masses of gross matter,—on the other hand: the *annexation* and *uniting* of the same linea-fragments to the circulating cosmical threads we call the gravitation cosmolineæ, which happens in places destitute of matter in the free realms of extent, at the very confines of the universe.

251. But for this stopping and making parallel of lineïts by Synduction and for the annexing performed by End-unition, the universe would soon be filled with a chaos of polarized lineïts and whirling heat-lineïts, and eventually all the gravitation cosmolineæ would be entirely broken up and dismembered.

252. MANIFESTATIONS OF OUTWARD STREAMING POLARIZED LINEÏTS. Whether the immense quantities of lineïts that are incessantly detached from gravitation-cosmolineæ by the monits of the earth, and are obliged to leave the earth and dart away from it as polarized lineïts, do make their out-streaming manifest in some way or other, or whether they are playing a part in terrestrial magnetism, we are not quite prepared to maintain with confidence, but it seems highly probable that they make their most frequent exit in the higher latitudes.

253. It will be in the *higher* latitudes not only because the detached polarized lineïts can make their exodus more readily in those regions of the planet which have the least rotary velocity, that is where the least number of monits of matter crosses their paths at right angles, but also because they are for the greater part carried along by streams of heat-lineïts, and these streams, of course, must be incomparably more vigorous in going from the sources of heat of the interior towards the *polar* surface, where the difference of temperature between the heated interior and the cold surface is the greatest, and the distance for escape the shortest of any in the terrestrial sphere. From the arctic as well as the antarctic regions therefore it is that the polarized (magnetic) lineïts, in company with low imperceptible heat issue *en masse.* And this is done in a certain order, that is, with their positive pole directed as much as possible outward.

254. AURORA BOREALIS.—The principal streams of the polarized lineïts will have their origin in that prepondering slice of the earth which directly subtends the wide intertropical belt. These streams will be directed towards north in the northern hemisphere, and towards south in the southern hemisphere. They will be found in greater intensity at some distance below the earth's surface, they will grow stronger and more condensed as they draw nearer to the polar regions, until they issue from the surface of the earth within the arctic and antarctic zones and then, on coming in the higher regions of the atmosphere, where the latter is *rare* enough to be put into a glowing condition [analogous to the glowing of **rarefied air** performed by electricity in *Geissler's* tubes] they proceed along these attenuate strata toward the tropics, causing the almost constant yet feeble auroral issues, still ascending (fig. 19), until at last on leaving the atmosphere altogether, they are unable to set any thing a glowing for want of matter to operate on. This glowing of the higher atmospheric strata will be most intense whenever similar but unusually powerful discharges of electricity [i. e. streams of polarized lineïts] from the faculæ of the sun happen to meet those of the earth; in which case they give rise to those beautiful phenomena, to the fully developed **aurora borealis,** of such extraordinary intensity, as to be visible even in our lower latitudes, (38° N).

255. That from the *sun,* and in company with the sun's heat, similar streams of detached polarized lineïts issue,though on a much larger scale than from the earth can hardly be doubted, and it may yet ere long be demonstrated that the so-called *corona* observed on the occasion of total eclipses of the sun is a real magnetic aurora proceeding from that body. The streams of polarized lineïts from the sun will issue not only from near its polar regions but from other regions also, because the impelling force of heat in the sun is enormous, and the sun's body consisting of rarefied matter in the form of gas, offers much less resistance to the exit of the detached polarized lineïts than the more compact body of the earth does. "The general radiated structure of the corona, and the great comparative outward extent of the luminous radiations in certain directions, have attracted the attention of the observers of all modern eclipses. Some streamers have been seen to extend more than one million miles from the sun, while others did not extend to one quarter of this distance." Prof. Norton says: the corona's "luminous radiations may be conceived either to be permanently connected with the sun, or to be composed of luminous matter actually *streaming away* from the sun, to an indefinite distance into space." If for the word "matter" we substitute: polarized lineïts, we may have it more correctly stated.

256. And as already said in §147, the streams of these detached polarized lineïts may prove to be what is generally conceived under the name of *electric* and *magnetic* fluid; the more so, as the detached lineït must be supposed to have polarity, because its anterior end has been touched and operated upon by the monit's radii, and received a certain portion of Versatile Activity, while its posterior end was operated upon only by the cosmolinea, so that the former, as the more vivacious one, we may call the positive end, or the *positive pole*.

257. That even the heat which finds vent through the craters of volcanoes, and through fissures and hot springs, may also be accompanied by an abundance of detached polarized lineïts is proved by the simultaneous appearance of electrical phenomena on such occasions.

258. There are two kinds of immaterial though extended *emanations* then, continually streaming towards the periphery of the universe. These are 1) heat-lineïts; 2) struck-off or detached (polarized or magnetic) lineïts. Not merely the heat-lineïts alone, but both kinds, as soon as they arrive at the verge of the universe, are by the power of Synduction of the cosmo-velo changed into parallel lineïts, annexed to the gravitation cosmolineæ and become parts thereof (247). Hence we have two *univeral emanations* flowing constantly outward from all celestial orbs, viz: *magnetic*-lineïts and *heat*-lineïts, and only one kind flowing inward toward these orbs' centre, namely *gravitation*-lineïts.

SECTION VI.

---

259. The "first law of motion" as stated in some of the latest and most approved works on Dynamics reads thus: "A body under the action of no force, or of balanced forces, is either at rest, or moves uniformly." The latter part of this assertion is founded upon an error, for according to §10, axiom VIII, a body under the action of *no* force cannot move at all, whether uniformly or not uniformly; neither can it move when under the action of balanced forces.

In the case of a continued uniform motion of a propelled body, the body's monits and the velocity-lineïts attached to the latter, mutually act upon each other, and it is in fact the power of Versatile Activity in the monit which by acting together with the velocity-lineïts, keep up the monit's translatory motion, i. e. change of place.

260. A body at rest, in order to be moved must be moved by power or by action of force—this is not only admitted but insisted upon by Newton—hence motion of body is caused by the action of force, hence where there is motion of body there is action of force (axiom VII), and where there is *continued* motion of body there is *continued* action of force. This law forming, as it were, an axiom, ought to supersede inertia, which to call a force exposes a contradictory assumption.* As long as a body continues moving so long does active force act within or upon it.

261. The motion of a uniformly moving body, which is commonly said to move by *inertia*, can continue only as long as the interaction between the body's monits and their velocity-lineïts does continue; the motion has to cease as soon as the interaction between monits and their velocity-lineïts ceases. This interaction ceases, of course, as soon as the velocity-lineïts are removed from the monits; and the removal of the velocity-lineïts from the monits of a body is effected by contrary forces or obstacles being interposed in the path of the moving body.

262. The above error with regard to inertia seems to have arisen from the doctrine of Telesius adopted by Newton, that the property by which matter sustains itself is altogether *passive;* they did not recognize those two important active powers dwelling in each monit or ultimate smallest particle of matter, by which such particle or monit is kept from being annihilated, by which it can maintain a certain size or volume, preserve resistance in

---

* *Whewell* also observes that "to say motion must continue the same from one instant to another, because there is nothing to stop it, seems to be taking refuge in words."

three dimensions, and be capable of acting upon other particles by means of a medium. These two powers are End-unition and Versatile Activity.

263. By accepting the above doctrine Newton was forced to devise a new quality contradictory in itself, viz: the "**vis inertiæ** or *force* of *inactivity*," an inherent power by which a body resists any disturbance of its uniform rectilinear motion; but if a power or force does act *resistingly*, can it be called a force of *inactivity?* let the unprejudiced inquirer answer. This contradictory character of the "vis inertiæ" is and has been a great stumbling block, and much in the way to achieve progress toward discovering the true nature of the most simple ultimate forces. Hence we have discarded the "vis inertiæ," and trust to explain phenomena which are said to depend on this force, without it. (259, 261, 304).

264. Physicists who still persist in raising the following assertion to a kind of axiom, viz: that when a body is moving it must of necessity continue to move, on account of its *inertia* or inactivity, overlook altogether the active *power* that is the cause of all this *continued* motion and how much light would be thrown upon science if this power was rightly understood. (v. Notes app.)

265. Conversion of gravitation-lineïts into velocity-lineïts.—In order to keep up a close connection among all the parts of the darting gravitation cosmolinea, which is continually shortened by the action of monits (124–129), each of its lineïts is incessantly urged on to press forward by the End-unition of the nearest lineït preceding it, hence any such lineït is, as a part of a gravitation-cosmolinea, able to press repeatedly upon the different monits it may meet in its way.

266. If from some cause or other the monit that is hit upon by a lineït of the streaming cosmolinea, should offer resistance to the aforesaid pressure, then this lineït after impinging ineffectually upon the monit, proceeds in its course without the latter, having exercised only a passing *pressure* upon it.

267. The lineït although exerting a pressure cannot be stopped by the concussion, because it is continually urged on by End-unition to close up again in file with the next preceding lineït in front.

268. Velocity-lineït.—Any lineït of the gravitation-cosmolinea, whenever it can effect an attachment to the monit it hits upon, does at the same time, by virtue of *its own direction* and the interaction between the monit's Versatile Activity and the lineït (261), give motion or speed to that monit in the direction in which the lineït itself moves. The attachment of such a velocity-lineït to the monit constitutes the *dynamic energy* or the *vis viva* of the latter.

269. And the number of lineïts so attached becomes the measure of velocity for the monit. Such an attached lineït we call **velocity-lineït**, (131, 147]. (v. Notes app).

270. Although a monit (atom) may be called **active** with regard to its inherent and innate power, yet with regard to its behaviour when acted upon by extraneous forces which try to change its place it must be called *indifferent*, and the monit being thus unable of itself, without the influence of an outside active power or force, to move from one place to another, it must be assumed that an *accessory* or impressed *active force* is associated with the monit whenever the latter is moving from one place to another.

271. This force which is actually preceding from out a faster moving body into a slower moving body, by which the latter gains just as much as the former loses, and no more, must be a substantive though immaterial entity, and this is the aforesaid velocity-lineït. Bodies having attached this force lineït, provided the latter was taken from the gravitation-cosmolinea, thereby acquire their *speed of fall.*

272. *Force* in a moving body is that which continually urges the body to pass from one place to another. This something which is evidently present in the *moving* body, and absent from the same when the latter is at rest, and which in the calculations of the mathematician goes by the name of *quantity* of *motion*, and which on the sudden arrest of the moving body is converted into a certain quantity of heat, this something, though certainly not matter, is a substantive entity, immaterial, yet very distinct from a mere mode or quality; it is a force, in short, the thing we wish to be understood by the name of velocity-lineït.

273. Not only the lineïts of a gravitation-cosmolinea, but also the *heat*-lineïts, as well as the detached polarized lineïts flung aside by the rotary monit, can impart the momentary impulse in its determined *direction* which they received, to any monit lying in their paths, and when in striking they can effect an attachment to the monit they hit upon, will likewise be converted into *velocity-lineïts*, and thus give speed to the monit. Heat-lineïts in the explosion of gunpowder are to a considerable amount changed into velocity-lineïts. The velocity in this case, however, is also in a great part due to the detached lineïts darting from the repelling monits; but with respect to the air-gun the velocity of the ball is *wholly* due to the detached lineïts darting from the repelling monits.

274. Rules of ratio between speed of motion and the comparative number of velocity-lineïts.—I. In a uniformly accelerated motion of a monit the velocity lineïts increase in number constantly and uniformly; that is: an equal number of velocity-lineïts is added to those already possessed by the monit during each successive second of time;—and the greater or the less speed of a monit indicates the relative greater or less number of velocity-lineïts attached to it.

275. II. Any cause that can and does take away or cast off velocity-lineïts from a moving monit, does thereby diminish or retard that monit's velocity; and *vice versa:* the decreasing motion of a monit or a body tells us that the number of its velocity-lineïts are being diminished or cast off.

276. III. In a motion of *uniform* velocity of a monit, the velocity-lineïts possessed by it remain the same in number, having either their decrease equal to their increase, or having no increase nor decrease at all.

277. The **momentum** of a moving body, that is, the mechanical effect of its motion, is the product of the number of velocity-lineïts of the monit multiplied by the *number* of monits. Or in other words, it is the sum total of all the velocity-lineïts attached to all the monits of the moving body,—the sum of the dynamic energy of all the individual monits of that body.

278. The investigations in the nature of *dynamic energy* are of the highest importance, the more so as in expounding the nature of this force, eminent physicists have made use of terms which are apt to lead to wrong impressions on the student's mind, regarding the convertibility of natural forces. My intention here is not to criticise, but merely to help in clearing up this most important subject.

279. The terms "potential energy" and "possible energy" may be convenient enough to operate with in calculations, but they are rather unfortunate expressions with regard to the true nature of force. (v. Notes app).

280. We read for instance: "By raising it [the weight] I have conferred upon it a motion producing power" [towards the centre of the earth, being, of course, thereby understood]. Suppose the moon could by some force be raised a hundred times its present distance from the earth's centre; instead of having by so doing, conferred upon the moon a motion producing power directed towards the earth and proportionate to the exertion of raising her, she would now exhibit only the 1-10,000 part of her former tendency to move towards the earth, and if her centrifugal force be left unchanged, she will move by means of the latter alone, rise away from the earth, and soon be free of the earth's influence altogether.

281. Another author on the same subject says : "When a weight is raised above the surface of the earth, it acquires potential energy in the shape of an increased amount of the attraction of gravitation." Instead of having by the act of raising increased the attraction of gravitation, the latter has in fact, been decreased between the weight and the earth, for the higher you remove the weight above the earth the more feeble will be the attraction of gravitation between the two, for gravitation varies inversely as the squares of the distances.

282. Again we read : "Before a body falls it must first be raised." Here we may ask, had the meteoric rocks, before they could fall to the earth, first to be raised above it? and if there was a vertical shaft reaching down to the earth's centre, and a weight lying at the upper margin of it, would it be necessary to *raise* that weight first, before it could fall? By no means, for in this case by shoving the weight only a few inches horizontally, it would be made to fall through a distance of 3960 miles to the centre of the earth.

283. There are also many of the modern physicists who will say : so also every body with regard to gravitation "may be compared to a watch wound up, which having the spring of its motion in itself, by the gradual evolution of its own spring produces all the successive motions we observe in it." But then, how will they account for the fact that the same piece of metal if lifted, say one mile vertically above the level of the sea, at some place *near the earth's equator* and then allowed to descend, would fall and strike with less energy of motion, and consequently give out less power in reaching the surface again, than when lifted to the same height of one mile above the sea-level, but this time at a place not far from the earth's pole and there allowed to fall. Yet in spite of all this they assert : "The man who winds the clock communicates to the weight a certain amount of power, and exactly so much as is thus communicated is gradually given out again during the following 24 hours." "And as surely as the force which moves a clock's hands is derived from the arm which winds up the clock."—The force of the arm acts here, no doubt, as a cause, but merely as the cause that removes the obstacle, which makes it possible for the gravitation-stream in the one case, and for the elasticity of the spring in the other case, to exercise their functions, because the obstacles that prevented them from so doing, have been removed by the muscular force of the arm.

284. It is very true that exactly as much energy as our muscles expend in raising the clock weight, is on descending to the spot from which it was raised, gained from it again either as mechanical work, or as heat, or as both, provided the weight is not allowed to fall any lower than the place from which it was lifted, for instance into an adjacent abyss. But in raising the weight, the energy expended by the muscle has gone off in the shape of heat and left the weight.—The wording to state the proposition properly would be : *as much* force as was expended in the exertion of our muscles in lifting the clockweight just as much has in falling been furnished by gravitation, that is from quite a different source than our muscles, and *this* has been used up in driving the wheel-work. But the words: "thus communicated is gradually given out" as above used, naturally leads to the inference that the identical muscular force thus exerted has literally been stored up in the weight, and then converted into the pulling-down force which the weight now exhibits, and which moves the clock's hands. If this is meant in the above cited sentence,* then it must be objected to as an erroneous view. (v. §406).

285. It is true that in raising the weight we momentarily communicate force to the same as long as the act of raising lasts. But it is equally true, that during the weight's *ascent* each successive single effort of the thus communicated force is, after having done its work, instantly cast off again as heat by the action of gravitation exerted in an opposite direction, and as soon as the weight ceases to rise, none of the communicated force remains in store, no more so than that it should remain if the weight had been dragged with great exertion along a rough horizontal surface, where by friction it loses its force of motion as fast as this force is being imparted to it by the muscle.—It is in *falling* that the weight gathers and stores up dynamic energy (*vis viva*), and it is in ascending or in being lifted that the weight loses the dynamic energy which was just being imparted to it in order to make it rise.

286. Yet although by the act of raising and lifting we are unable literally to store up in the weight the requisite force to drive the clockwork, we have nevertheless achieved thereby another object, we have put the weight into a situation or condition, in which it *admits of being pulled along and moved by the gravitation-cosmolineæ streaming towards the earth's centre.*

287. Having endeavored to explain in §163–180 the cause of gravitation, I may here again refer to the subject in a somewhat more general view. From these paragraphs it follows, that we have throughout the whole universe a medium or web and weft of real force-lines,—in their function as gravitation-lines crossing and intersecting interstellar space in every conceivable direction, darting in greater abundance when converging towards any of the centres of the great celestial bodies, and being of more intense array and strength when near them than when further off, according to a ratio inversely as the squares of the distance from the centres of those bodies. Such bodies, on having come nearer to each other, are then attracted with greater force ; but they do not thereby create any new or additional amount of force, they merely have arrived in regions of the universe where the gravitation force-lines exist in much greater throngs, consequently they have come into force-streams of greater intensity and where the pressure, exerted upon the bodies to push the one towards the other, is much more energetic.—Therefore, in order to give velocity to bodies, i. e. to store them with force in the shape of velocity-lineïts [131, 142, 268], all that is requisite is : to remove any obstacles which may be apt to hinder the two bodies from approaching to each other. [v. Notes app.]

287[1]. That this view leads to a satisfactory explanation, and at the same time is in agreement with the great law of conservation of force will readily appear from the following : In throwing a stone upward by means of the muscular force of the arm, the motion thus suddenly imparted, gradually

---

* That this really is the meaning of some authors is evident from the expressions of a Professor, who plainly states that when a stone is thrown upwards, the motion or energy thus imparted as *vis viva* is actually stored up in the stone, and during the latter's ascent is changed into a new form, that is : as the stone ascends the vis viva becomes less and less, being gradually changed into *potential* or *possible* energy ; whenever the stone has arrived at its highest point of ascent and begins to fall, it is a sure indication that all the vis viva or *actual* energy has already been transformed into *possible* energy ; and when the stone is falling back to the earth, all the energy that was stored away is given up again in the form of motion.

disappears. That this force lost to the stone, was on its disappearance not converted *directly* and *immediately* into attraction of gravitation, is evident on considering that instead of augmenting the same in the stone, we know that it has really decreased in proportion to the square of the distance from the earth's centre. Even if we did not know this, our theory shows, that mechanical force of motion or velocity can never change directly into gravitation-force without having first existed as heat [and gone to the cosmo-velo, 385–389]. The force of motion that was lost in the ascent of the stone cannot have been evolved in any other form but that of heat, because the motion in going *against* the gravitation-stream was retarded and arrested, as surely as if it had been done by any other contrarily acting force, for instance that of friction. The heat either radiated away into space or dispersed into the surrounding atmosphere, according to the greater or less tranquility of the air.

The stone after having lost all its mechanical energy by means of which it was carried up, soon *falls*, and on striking the ground evolves a considerable amount of energy or force in the shape of heat, and thus gives us to understand that during its fall it has gathered and stored up mechanical energy of motion. How and from what source this energy has been supplied I have pointed out in other paragraphs in such a way as to have the law of conservation of force fully maintained.

288. A case somewhat analogous to the raising of a weight and then permitting it to get dynamical energy by falling, is presented in the following: If air has been pressed into a vessel by the muscular power of our arm in working a condensing pump, so as to have its quantity doubled, we might in a similar way as in the preceding case be tempted to say: by working the pump we have conferred upon and literally stored up in this air the very identical motion-producing power of our muscle, and as a consequence the air has now, like the suspended weight in the first case, potential energy, by which the one half of the air may drive out the other half.

289. The fact is that by working the pump we simply bring the particles of air nearer together, so that their *repelling force*, which increases in proportion as the distance decreases, can act more powerfully on each other. The monit's stream of repulsion is the real active force, it proceeds uninterruptedly from the monits themselves and from nothing else.

290. We know that a light but large balloon, even if only filled to three-fourths of its capacity with hydrogen gas, rises, and notwithstanding the fact that it is getting all the time into regions of less heat, it becomes more expanded, the gas pressing outwards more effectually against the sides of the balloon the higher it rises. This shows clearly that the force of expansion has its source *in* the particles, and was not transferred to the latter from other outside sources of force; for if no repelling force had uninterruptedly issued from the minutest particles of gas, the balloon, instead of being expanded in rising would have been contracted for want of heat within the colder strata it arrived at. We must confess that all we did do to the balloon was, merely to admit the hydrogen and to put the balloon into a place where it could rise, but we conferred no "potential energy" upon it in the sense of the potential-energy doctrine, in other words we were not obliged to pull the balloon first down from a great height, in order that thereby it may get "potential energy" [as some scientists would insist upon] by virtue of which to make it rise exactly to such a height as corresponds to the muscular force of the arm which had to be spent in pulling it down. The whole work, not only that of *lifting* to a great height, but also that of *expanding* the balloon and pushing its sides further apart, even to such a degree as to burst and tear it to pieces, is the work of the force of repulsion issuing 1) from the particles of the *atmosphere* in lifting the balloon, and 2) from the particles of *hydrogen* in expanding the balloon.

291. Another analogous case may be found in a revolvable wheel stuck upon a stationary axle, over which wheel runs loosely a leather band driven by the expansive force of heated steam by means of an engine. Suppose the wheel stuck loosely upon the stationary axle in such a manner that in shoving it sideways, it may in one place of the axle turn freely upon the latter, but when shoved to another place of the axle it may be held unmovable there by a projection or catch existing upon the axle. Now when held by the catch the wheel is stationary, and the leather band glides swiftly over its periphery, and we could say with the same propriety as regarding the suspended weight in the first case: this wheel now has *potential* energy, because as soon as we slip it free of the catch,* it at once exhibits *actual* or *dynamic* energy in turning swiftly around its axle, and thereby setting other machinery, with which it is connected, in motion.

292. But can we assert that by the mere act of taking the wheel to the axle, shoving it upon the catch and applying to it the band, we have conferred upon and imparted to this wheel a motion-producing power [may be, equal to several horse-power] derived solely from our muscles? By no means; for if we have no heat in the steam-boiler, the wheel, no matter by how great an expense of muscular power it was stuck upon the axle, can have neither actual nor potential energy to revolve. The expanding force of heat is working in this case as continually, yet ineffectually, over the fixed wheel as the force of gravitation in the other case is working upon the weight suspended and hindered from falling.

293. Let us, in order to compare the preceding three cases, put them in juxtaposition in the following manner:

I.	II.	III.
By muscular force of the arm	By muscular force of the arm	By muscular force of the arm
I pump and compress air	I lift a weight and suspend it	I shove a wheel [connected by a band with an engine] upon a stationary axle and
Into a strong vessel.	By a string.	Upon a catch of the axle.
The vessel holds the air.	The string holds the weight.	The catch holds the wheel.
I open the valve,	I cut the string,	I push the wheel from the catch,
The surplus air is expelled,	The weight falls,	The wheel revolves,
It is driven out by the *repelling force of the monits* (atoms).	It is pulled down by the *force of gravitation.*	It is turned round by the *expansive force of heat.*
This force is not derived from the muscular force of the arm.	This force is not derived from the muscular force of the arm.	This force is not derived from the muscular force of the arm.

The muscular force of the arm in the above three cases merely has put the air, the weight, and the wheel in such a place and position, as to give

* Analogous to cutting the string in the case of a suspended weight.

the respective three forces just named the proper chance to operate upon them.

294. To illustrate the nature of dynamic energy (*vis viva*) more fully let us offer another case. The lineïts of the cosmolineæ in their course towards the centre of the earth continually impinge and press as gravitation upon the monits of all terrestrial bodies. If for instance a four pound iron weight rests upon a man's hand extended horizontally, the man in his effort to keep the same extended, will soon be made aware of the efforts of some downward tending force [which here is the pressing action of the lineïts] by the pressure exerted upon his hand by means of the iron. Yet he may be able to counteract this pressure and keep the iron at rest for a considerable length of time. But if more iron be added, there will be more monits to be pressed upon by the lineïts pushing downward; and in thus adding successively monits to monits [of iron], the power of pushing down the hand may be increased to such a degree that the muscular power of the hand is overcome and then the weight begins to fall.

295. From that moment, as long as there is no resistance to the fall, the lineïts that now strike the monits of the iron give increased motion to the latter in being allowed to *attach* themselves in the shape of velocity-lineïts to these monits, instead of glancing off from them and thereby being turned aside as heretofore (294) ; and if another hand 50 feet lower was extended in the path of the descending weight, the effect would be very destructive, and very different from what the weight performed on the hand when the latter was merely exposed to the weight's pressure.

296. But why does the weight when allowed to fall exercise a more crushing effect upon the hand held at a distance below, then when it is permitted simply to press with its resting mass on the same hand ? Because if the weight is at rest, i. e. effectually supported by something underneath, the lineïts of the centreward rushing cosmolineæ that strike the monits of the iron are not allowed to attach themselves to the monits, since each lineït after exerting a certain momentary pressure* upon the monit it strikes, is obliged to leave at once by way of glancing off, hence no *storing up*, and hence no combination of the vivacious Versatile Activity of the monit with the direction-determining lineït can take place, which combination is most efficient and fully entitled to the name of vis viva (the same with velocity-lineït).

297. The longer the unobstructed descent of a falling body continues, the more velocity-lineïts (vis viva) will its monits gather. And the greater the velocity of the falling monit is, the greater will be the number of the velocity-lineïts supposed to be possessed by it.

298. As there is no particle of matter in the universe of which we can assert that it is not under way in a translatory motion of some kind or other, it may well be assumed that *every monit* in existence is covered more or less with a certain number of stored-up velocity-lineïts. Hence we may assume that every monit in existence possesses a certain amount of dynamic energy or *vis viva*.

299. TWO MODES IN WHICH ORIGINALLY ALL THE VELOCITY MUST HAVE BEEN IMPARTED TO MONITS. Every monit has originally received the vis viva or velocity-lineïts it possesses, in one of the following two ways : either 1st by FALLING, in being pushed along by the stream of gravitation-cosmolineæ flowing either towards another single monit, or towards the centre of a more or less concentrated aggregate of matter (assemblage of monits) ;—or

---

*Caused by the End-unition of the lineïts of the gravitation-cosmolineæ.

2*d*: by FLINGING the detached polarized lineïts being hurled by monits against other adjacent monits. (125, 126, 143–145.)

300. But it is especially due to the 1st mode, namely to *falling*, that not only all the planets of our planetary system, but also all other celestial bodies must necessarily have received, at one time or other, all their velocity-lineïts, and hence their momentum or vis viva, which they possess in their orbitual as well as in their rotary motions.

301. LAW ABOUT THE DIFFUSION OF VELOCITY-LINEÏTS. Velocity-lineïts whenever added to a closely connected assemblage of monits [to any material body or connected system of bodies] always diffuse or spread *towards* those parts of the body in which the monits have *less* velocity-lineïts of the same direction, until all the monits possess alike an equal number of velocity-lineïts of the same direction.

302. Hence if a non-elastic ball of nine pounds weight and being at rest, but easily movable, be struck by a similar ball of one pound weight, yet having a velocity of ten inches per second, the two balls will proceed together with a velocity of one inch per second. Suppose for instance, each velocity-lineït of a monit to represent that monit as moving with a velocity of one inch per second, then if a monit has ten velocity-lineïts it will move 10 inches per second; and if the one-pound ball has one million of monits and moves, previous to having struck the nine-pound weight, at the rate of 10 inches per second, it is clear 1) that this ball will possess ten million velocity-lineïts, and 2) that the nine-pound ball consists of nine millions of monits with *no* velocity-lineïts. But immediately after the concussion of the one-pound ball against the nine-pound ball, both balls having together ten millions of monits will be moved by ten millions of velocity-lineits, so that each and every monit of the ten pounds possesses one velocity-lineït, thus moving one inch per second.

303. If into one side of a cannon-ball a hole is bored and this hole filled with a wooden plug, we can make to deviate the course of the ball either to the right or to the left of the object aimed at, according as the wood-plugged side is placed to the right or left, when loading the gun. Because the wood-plugged half of the ball, not having as many monits of matter as the opposite side, cannot get the same number of velocity-lineïts, and hence in overcoming the resistance from friction of the gun-barrel has to lag behind the other half, by which a partial turning of the ball on leaving the mouth of the gun takes place, bringing the unplugged half more in front, and hereby the ball is made to deviate from its original course. In like manner the direction of the shot can be made to deviate upward or downward by placing the plugged side up or down when loading the gun. If the plug is loosely put in, it will during the ball's flight be pushed in somewhat tighter, by resistance from the atmosphere if the plugged side is placed in front when loading the gun.

304. TIME REQUIRED FOR THE SPREAD OF VELOCITY LINEÏTS.—The reason why a large and heavy body when *at rest*, cannot be overcome and moved instantaneously by any applied force, even if the latter be superabundant, is to be found in the inability of velocity-lineïts to distribute themselves *instantaneously* over all the monits of the resting body, and is not to be sought in an impossible and itself contradicting power, the so-called "*vis inertiæ.*" The lineïts need a certain length of time in spreading themselves over a certain amount of surface.

305. A man endeavoring to give a very swift rotary motion all at once and instantaneously to a heavy grindstone, will find that it is impossible for him to do so, and that only by steadily exerting his strength for a certain time [short though this may be] he is enabled to give to the turning of the grindstone the desired velocity. The cause of this phenomenon has been attributed to the *inertia* of the particles of matter tending to retain their state of rest. But the true reason why the motion of the grindstone is sluggish at first, is because it takes *time* for the lineïts, when being disengaged from the hand, to spread from the centre over all the monits of the grindstone, the circumference of which needs by far the most lineïts.

306. The reason why so-called "inertia" in a fast moving body of great weight, for instance a heavy railroad train, cannot without destruction to the cars be overcome instantaneously by resistance offering impediments, lies in the inability of the velocity-lineïts to depart from the material particles of the moving body *instantaneously*. For departing, the velocity-lineïts need time as well as for spreading, and the quicker or more suddenly a train is stopped the more will all the different parts of the cars suffer, and the sooner will the cars become dilapidated.

307. If the wheels of an exceedingly fast running railroad train could be fastened and fixed to the rails *instantaneously*, the cars of the train would thereby be broken up into a promiscuous heap of pieces, the metallic and heavier material tearing away from the lighter material and going in advance of the latter. If the stopping could be done in a vacuum, the heavier material would not separate from the lighter, all the parts of the cars above the wheels would be carried forward in one *connected* body and dashed to pieces against the first obstacle they came to.

308. If the number of velocity-lineïts be exceedingly great *for each* monit, as for instance in a fast moving musket ball, the velocity-lineïts of the ball coming upon a plank freely suspended in the air, take along only those particles of the plank which they hit, and thus make a hole without moving the plank. This is done before the densely contracted stream of veocity-lineïts of the ball and their immense number had time to diverge and to spread over the whole plank in which case the ball would have pushed the plank ahead instead of cutting a hole through it. Hence the particles of the plank are shoved out and the ball still keeps velocity-lineïts enough to move farther on.

309. If, on the other hand, the ball is hitting a somewhat *yielding* non-elastic body, *time* is afforded to the velocity-lineïts to spread gradually over a greater surface and mass, and therefore the ball cannot proceed very far, and soon stops.

310. Again if the spreading out of the velocity-lineïts could be instantaneous, no bullet hole in the plank could be made however fast the motion of the ball might be ; but in this case the suspended plank would either be moved as by a gale of wind, or be rent to pieces.

311. Recapitulating some of the propositions concerning velocity-lineïts and adding others, we say :

1) The motion of a body is due to the motive action of the velocity-lineïts that are attached to that body.

2) The continued motion of a body is due to the continued presence of its velocity-lineïts and their incessant action while in that body.

3) If one body impels or sets in motion another body, velocity-lineïts pass out of the impelling body into the body impelled.

4) Velocity-lineïts attached to a body make that body move, but as soon as opposed in its path by an unremovable obstacle, the velocity-lineïts will flow out of the moving body, yet they cannot enter and pass as velocity-lineïts through the obstacle, because there is nothing at hand to continue them in their mode as velocity-lineïts. Hence these velocity-lineits, being left

to themselves have to appear in an independent mode of active motion, namely in the *whirling* motion which is peculiar to *heat-lineïts* (315). With regard to the lineïts of gravitation it is very different; here if a lineït, in striking a monit, glances off, it is readily connected and ranged into the cosmolineæ again.

5) When a sufficient number of velocity-lineïts—so great as to overcome the other forces, such as cohesion, gravitation, &c., that are tending to hold the obstacle in its place—is thus communicated to the obstacle, the latter will be moved, and only in proportion to the resistence overcome will *heat-*lineïts be developed.

6) But so long as the velocity-lineïts are flowing out of the active body against the obstacle without moving it, so long do they (after having first exerted a certain pressure) disperse as heat-lineïts. For instance in the case of muscular exertion against a too heavy log. These velocity-lineïts are, however, evolved as heat not from the obstacle but from the active body itself; as for instance, from the muscle by its contraction and exertion to push aside a log without being able to move the latter.

7) In an obstacle acted and *pressed* upon but not moved by gravitation-lineïts, the latter after exerting the pressure, pass into and *through* the obstacle and do not turn into heat-lineïts, because beyond the obstacle they are connected again to, and unchanged conveyed away by, the gravitation-cosmolineæ.

8) As during the mere pressure from gravitation-lineïts no heat-lineïts are set free, so also are no heat-lineïts set free during the mere pressure from an elastic spring; hence there must also exist with regard to the elastic spring some connection and conveyance of lineïts in some analogous *closed system of circulation* issuing *from* the elastic spring.

SECTION VII.

---

312. In the preceding chapters we endeavored to show how lineïts,being detached from the gravitation-cosmolinea, and joined or attached to monits of matter, have thereby experienced an important modification, having been converted into *velocity*-lineïts. These velocity-lineïts, at any time thereafter, may by the counteraction of other forces which thus act as obstacles, be obliged to leave the moving monit to which they are attached, without having an opportunity of entering and giving motion to another body; having therefore no chance to continue in their peculiar mode as velocity-lineïts, and neither being able directly to renew their former connection [with the continuous cosmolineæ, to act in the capacity of gravitation] these velocity-lineïts will be left to themselves, but their acquired Versatile Activity remaining with them, they are bound to appear in an independent form of active motion, viz: the whirling or versatile motion of themselves, and thus as whirling *heat-lineïts* they give rise to the sensation of heat.

313. The fact that there are insurmountable difficulties in attempting to reduce the conception of heat to that of an undulation of a so-called ether, analogous to that which produces the phenomena of light, is yet abundantly recognized by many physicists, because 1) there appears nothing in light analogous to the slow *conduction* of heat; 2) the light-producing undulations of the ether have no tendency to produce expansion in illuminated bodies; 3) heat can be confided and fixed to a substratum, and can be confined between non-conductors of heat for a great length of time, even when the surrounding atmosphere is of less temperature, as may be strikingly illustrated in the Norwegian boxes of felt to preserve a temperature for cooking without any additional fire. 4) The specific heat of different bodies, and the capacity of solids and liquids for "storing up" heat, as well as the *binding* of heat in evaporation, and the liberation of the very same quantity again on condensing. All these are stubborn facts pointing out, that while light is but a phenomenon extending by undulation of a continuous medium, heat *proceeds* as a separate entity *per se*, from place to place.

314. A moving monit *a* may hit upon a movable monit *b* that is at rest, and then both will go on together. In this case half the number of the attached lineïts of *a* will spread over the movable monit *b*, and both monits will proceed with *half* the former speed of monit *a* (301). Here then, even those of the attached lineïts that have been disengaged from *a* and gone over to *b* continue to act as velocity-lineïts.

315. There is, however, another case possible. The moving monit *a* may instead of striking the movable monit *b*, hit upon another monit *c*, which being fixed by other forces, completely resists and thereby stops b in its progress. This, however, cannot stop the motion of the attached *velocity-lineïts* of a; having had imparted to them Versatile Activity by the monit a, they are bound to *move* in some way or other, because Versatile Activity can never be driven out by anything except by Syduction of the cosmo-velo. In the case of the *resisting* monit the velocity-lineïts leave monit a, and as they can find nothing to attach to immediately, they become free of *all* connection, and depart with a new mode of motion as independent **whirling** lineïts, manifesting themselves to our sense of feeling as **heat.**

316. A certain amount of the power of Versatile Activity, which is the cause of the velocity-lineït's motion of translocation, was imparted by the monit's Versatile Activity to this lineït as soon as the latter left the cosmo-linea and attached itself to the the monit as velocity-lineït—and this is always a most important epoch in the lineït's mode of existence.

317. The lineït when in the form of velocity-lineït, has translatory motion in a certain direction, and affects monits accordingly by pushing them along with it. But on having been detached from the monit and liberated to shift for itself, the lineït keeps its appropriated part of the monit's Versatile Activity, assumes a whirling motion, and is thus enabled to agitate monits, striking and pressing them and even making them move translatory.

318. Heat is not "matter," neither is heat "a motion of the ultimate particles of matter," nor a motion of a material "ether." That not all the eminent physicists have subscribed to the doctrine that "heat is a peculiar shivering motion of the ultimate particles of *bodies*" is evident from the following admission of one of the highest and latest authorities. "In the dynamical theory of heat, which is based upon the experimental fact that *heat is motion*, many formulæ are at present obscure and uninterpretable, because we do not know **what** is moving, or **how** it moves."—(Thomson).

319. We may define heat as follows: Although heat is nothing material, it is in itself something substantive,* it is in fact the imponderable lineït appearing in the character of *heat-lineït* whenever possessed of a peculiar, brisk, *whirling* motion which was imparted to it by the Versatile Activity of the monit.—It strikes adjacent heat-lineïts as well as monits of matter. The quantity of heat is determined by, and proportional to, the *number* of heat-lineïts,—the temperature is proportional to the *quickness of whirling* of the heat-lineït.

320. *The heat-lineït's whirling motion, i. e. its temperature, is capable of being made still more violent and brisk on being struck back by adjacent heat-lineïts as well as by the ultimate particles of matter*, that is *by monits*, which are always rotating. Although by this striking back of monits of matter upon heat-lineïts, the motion of the latter may be made more brisk, no more heat-lineïts or *new* heat can ever be produced thereby.

321. Each heat-lineït is continually repulsed by other heat-lineïts as

* In his natural history, Bacon maintains that "there is in every tangible body, a spirit or body pneumatical, which fills the pores of all gross bodies:—that it is not some virtue, or action, or trifle, but a *real* and *quantitive substance*, though rare, invisible, and without weight." That this spirit or body pneumatical was ment to represent what at a later period was called *heat*, and not "ether," is apparent from the fact that Bacon alludes to it also as the cause of evaporation and other phenomena, which have always been considered as the peculiar effects of heat. And it is equally plain that by choosing the terms "spirit" and "body pneumatical without weight" he meant to represent something substantive that was not matter [because there is no imponderable matter] and yet not entirely without extension. These requirements are completely fulfilled by the heat-lineït exposed in the present pages.

well as by monits of matter striking against it, and all the heat-lineïts being thus, to use Lord Bacon's expression, "restrained, repulsed, and reflected, become alternately perpetually hurrying, striving, struggling, and irritated by the re-percussion."

322. This augmentation of the whirling motion in heat lineïts mutually striking each other, may be expressed in a general law as follows: *If in a given compass of space the number of heat-lineïts be doubled, then their whirling energy and pressure outward will be four-fold, that is as the* **squares** *of the number of heat-lineïts.*

323. If a monit has on its surface double the velocity-lineïts it had before, then the whirling energy of the heat-lineïts at the moment of being liberated and disengaged from the monit will be four-fold, that is, they will at that moment be able to execute four times the mechanical work of what they could do when they had only half the number of velocity-lineïts. For instance, if a heavy, perfectly elastic ball falls through a vacuum and strikes the ground with a velocity of 8, (vide annexed fig.), it will rebound, and if there be no resistance will rise to the height it fell from, that is, it will ascend through 16 spaces; but if it strikes the ground with double the velocity, viz: with 16, it will rise through 64 spaces, or four times the space it rose in the first case. Now as in the same weight, the work performed is in proportion to the height it is lifted, it is clear that here the work done with double the velocity was four-fold. This shows that not only by *newly acquired* velocity-lineïts is the falling body propelled, but that the velocity-lineïts previously attached, still continue to exercise their action.

Seconds.	Spaces fallen each second.	Velocity.	Total number of spaces at the end of each second.
		0	
1	1 .	1	
		— 2	1
2	3 .		
		— 4	4
3	5 .		9
		— 6	
4	7 .		16
		— 8	
5	9 .		25
		— 10	
6	11 .		36
		— 12	
7	13 .		49
		— 14	
8	15 .		64
		— 16	

324. Hence if we impart twice the number of velocity-lineïts to a body, the temperature, i. e. the whirling motion of the lineïts, manifesting itself when the motion of that body is arrested immediately after will be fourfold, although the number of heat-lineïts will be no more than double; because, as we have seen already (§323), if to the doubly increased velocity an upward direction be given, then the body will rise to four times the height it would have risen if possessed only of half the velocity.

325. From this exposition it follows that we must be very careful in keeping up a clear distinction between the meaning of the two words "temperature" and "heat-lineïts;" for while the latter in itself is a certain indestructible subjective quantity, the former is the varying quickness in whirling of the heat-lineït, a more or less briskly whirling, specially adapted to execute molecular work, such as expanding, etc.

326. Heat is a whirling motion, but the peculiar view I wish to establish and to impress upon the reader is: that the thing substantive which is whirling—the thing to which this whirling motion belongs—is an *imponderable lineït* (the heat-lineït). Heat is not the shivering condition of the ultimate minute particles of ponderable matter, as has been assumed of late.

327. Repelling action of the heat-lineït.—Even among themselves the heat-lineïts will constantly in meeting each other, strike and repel one another. Thus repelled, the tendency of heat-lineïts is always to go to places of *less* heat, that is where repulsion is less energetic. In this way the heat-lineït acquires besides the whirling motion a *translatory* motion, but the acquisition of the latter [the translatory] is always at the expense of the *whirling* motion.

328. The whirling and at the same time translatory moving heat-lineït coming upon a monit strikes the latter, and, if unable to move it, receives a stroke in return, and bounds over to another adjacent monit which it strikes likewise. And so the heat-lineït continues to give and to receive blows, to fly hither and thither [to and fro] as long as it is kept between monits.

329. Thus can one and the same heat-lineït continually act as a repelling agent for an indefinite length of time between monits of matter, until it escapes from matter into free space, or else until in going to places of less heat, it actually *moves* the monit which it has been pressing upon, and in this case it attaches itself to the monit and becomes a *velocity*-lineït.

330. Conducted heat.—Between the monits of a solid, a fluid, or even an æriform body, the heat-lineïts that are whirling amongst them must necessarily, in going to places of less heat, be rebuffed more or less in their progress, according to the peculiar position of the monit's axis of each substance; and thus hampered and impeded in their escape. These heat-lineïts go under the name of *conducted* heat, because in this their entanglement they will make comparatively slow headway from particle to particle, as if led or *conducted* towards the surface of the body or towards any other part of the same where there is *less* heat.

331. Radiant heat.—Whenever the heat-lineïts, instead of having to travel through dense masses of badly conducting bodies, come upon heat-transmitting bodies, or else enter more rarified matter where monits are in a less crowded and in a *diathermanous* state, and consequently where they find but little impediment, then their *whirling* motion changes more into a rectilinear *translatory* motion, a rapid motion of transit from place to place. They thus dart onward in rays as **radiant heat**, unhindered in their course towards regions of *less* heat. But as soon as impeded or arrested in their rectilinear course, their translatory motion changes again into a whirling motion, which makes itself felt as thermometric or repelling heat.

332. Latent heat.—Heat-lineïts when shut up between monits and molecules in such a manner that they cannot go outward even if their immediate neighborhood be of *less* heat, are said to be **latent.** When in this state, they may whirl as lively as ever in full repelling activity, but they are not permitted to come out, and hence cannot become manifest to our sense of feeling, nor can they affect the thermometer or act as outside motory force. They are neither paralyzed nor dormant, they are locked up, actually shut up, yet vigorously active within their constraining tiny enclosure.

333. If we are allowed to use a comparison, tolerably well though not exactly representing the case, we should say that the heat-lineïts pent up in the organic molecules are like so many myriads of particles of highly *compressed* air held imprisoned within minutest films; the more sudden and simultaneous the destruction of the latter is, the more energetic and powerful can the force of the liberated air make itself felt.

334. When water is converted into steam, i. e. when it is changed from the liquid into a gaseous state, a certain amount of heat-lineïts is employed and made latent in whirling between the monits of oxygen and hydrogen of each molecule [not between the molecules themselves] in order to bring and keep the water in gas form. Any more heat-lineïts that may be added after this merely push the molecules further apart, that is, they expand the gas more or less, according to the greater or less number of heat-lineïts added.

335. By the above process of imprisonment during the molecular change, the heat-lineïts become *latent*, seeking, however, continually to break from confinement, and they are sure to escape whenever by a change in the degree of extraneous heat, or by chemical affinity, their prison films are broken. With regard to the breaking by means of extraneous heat, this may be done either by a *reduction*, but more generally by an *elevation* of temperature, as in the burning of fuel.

336. In the condensation of steam, for instance, the confining films are broken by a *reduction* or abstraction of exterior heat, by which means the interior heat, that is, the latent heat acting betwixt the monits, is enabled to break the prison films by superior pressure from *within;* while on the other hand, in igniting and burning of vegetable matter this breaking is accomplished by attacks from *without* by the exterior heat that has been added; as in kindling and burning a pile of wood, a candle, etc.

337. In combustion, however, it is not the attacks from outside heat alone that breaks the heat-confining cells, consisting of monits of carbon, of hydrogen, or of any other combustible elementary matter, but it requires the affinity of oxygen, sulphur, or any other negative electric element, at the same time. For without the presence of these negative electric elements we cannot combine or burn the more positive electric ones, no matter how hot they are made. Carbon consists of molecules each composed of a number of *monits* of carbon; hydrogen consists of molecules each made up of a number of monits of hydrogen, and so on with all other elementary substances. These molecular enclosures confine the latent heat-lineits.

338. Reflections on latent heat in wood.—What a marvellous object the little pile of dry wood is, as it lies in the stove or fire-place ready for kindling on a bitter cold morning. Here in this woody tissue are heat-lineïts, pent up, perhaps, a hundred years ago. They were engendered in the sun, at a distance of 93 million miles from the place where they are now held prisoners.

339. The wood itself feels cool. Shivering with cold we hold a lighted match to the shavings, and in a moment the liberated heat-lineïts rush forward, dance briskly against our hands and face, and send warmth and comfort through our frame.

340. But if instead of dry sticks we have wood soaked in water put on the top of the kindling, the heat-lineïts just liberated from the latter will be pent up again by the monits of watery vapor (steam), which is just forming from the water contained in the wet wood. The vapor or steam thus carries off in a latent state, through the flue of the chimney, the heat-lineïts that ought to have ignited the sticks, consequently the kindling is robbed of its heat, and extinguishes before it can set the other wood on fire. And even if the top wood instead of being quite wet, be merely green, it may still be made to burn, yet yield but little heat, for most of the heat-lineïts which are set free by combustion are immediately made latent during the formation of steam, and carried away, and although the little pile of wood may have been thus consumed by burning, our room is left nearly as cold as it was before.

341. Rules with regard to the evolution of heat-lineïts.—It may be necessary here to remark that in the following rules the amount or *number* of heat-lineïts, and not their more or less energetic whirling is being considered.

(1.) In the same ratio as the motion of a body is retarded by friction, by concussion, or by any contrary acting forces whatsoever [without, however, transferring any of its *motion* to other bodies] will velocity-lineïts be set free, that is: be evolved with another mode of motion, as heat-lineïts.*

342. If, for instance, the retardation be gradual, the evolution of heat-lineïts will also be gradual; if retardation be very sudden, the heat-lineïts will be evolved at once or *en masse.* But in either case will the total amount of evolved heat-lineïts be the same after the body has come to a complete stand still.

343. (2.) The whole amount of evolved heat-lineïts of bodies of the same velocity but of different weight, on being arrested in their motion, no matter whether this be done gradually or at once, will always be in proportion to the respective weight of each body. And in bodies of the same weight but of different velocities, the number of heat-lineïts [not their energy of whirling] will be in proportion to their respective velocities.

344. (3.) Just as many heat-lineïts are evolved from a body when arrested on striking the ground in falling through a vacuum, as that body had velocity-lineïts acquired during the fall by which it gained its speed, provided there was no *motion* transferred to the ground by the concussion from the falling body.

345. (4.) If the falling body has not the accelerated motion of a free falling body, but if it be retarded by friction or otherwise, so as to keep the same speed all the time, then the moving body receives constantly as many additional velocity-lineïts from the gravitation-cosmolineæ as it loses in the shape of heat-lineïts by friction, so that a constant number of velocity-lineïts is always kept up.

346. (5.) A body driven upward by the force of an explosion or by other means, will evolve during its *ascent* just as many heat-lineïts as it received velocity-lineïts from the forces driving it upward. Here the heat-lineïts engendered in the combustion of the explosive materials have first been converted into velocity-lineïts, and the latter, by the gradual checking and final stoppage of the body's motion during its ascent against the stream of gravitation, again reconverted into heat-lineïts. (352, 416, 421.)

347. THREE CASES WHERE HEAT IS EVOLVED BY BODIES IMPINGING UPON OTHER BODIES.—If $b\,a$ and $c\,a$ in the annexed fig. represent the relative strength of force, that is, the number of velocity-lineïts with which the two bodies b and c [having an equal number of monits, that is, equal weight] impinge upon each other, the following three cases of heat-evolution may be presented.

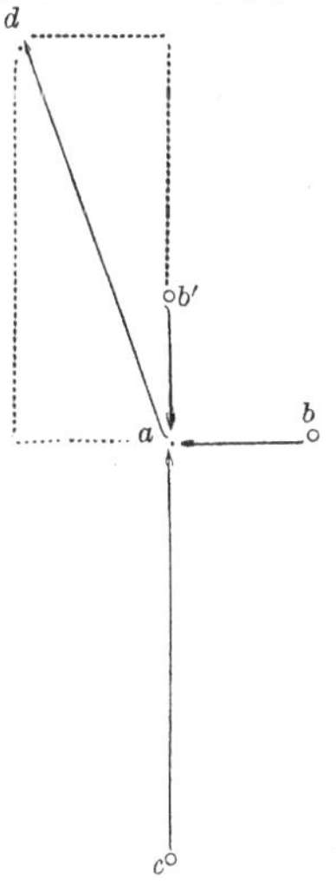

1ST. If the course of b and c happens to be in the same direction, and c overtakes b, both these bodies will continue to move in this direction, each one with half the sum of all their velocity-lineïts $= \frac{ab + ac}{2}$ (301) without evolving any heat.

2*d*. If b and c strike each other simultaneously at an angle, they both will go together and take the direction of the diagonal $d\ a$, each one with a velocity $= \frac{ad}{2}$ and evolve heat-lineïts equal to $ab + ac - ad$.

3*d*. If b and c strike each other diametrically opposite, they will both go on in the direction of the body that has the most velocity-lineïts, each one with a velocity $= \frac{ac - ab'}{2}$ and at the same time evolve heat equal to $2\,a.b'$.

---

* We speak here of bodies in general, in some peculiar cases electricity is also made to appear in company with heat.

348. *Coroll.* If in case No. 3 $ab' = ac$, then both b' and c are stopped and the *whole* number of their velocity-lineïts evolved as heat-lineïts.

349. If the two bodies b and c are of different weight, that is, of different numbers of monits, then the weight of each has to be multiplied by its velocity, and the product proceeded with as in the above cases.

350. Elasticity. A moving body impinging upon an immovable object disengages velocity-lineïts in the mode of heat-lineïts only in case of its motion being stopped or retarded. But if the moving body, instead of stopping, rebounds with undiminished speed into another direction, it shows that the velocity-lineïts, instead of departing, continue to adhere to the monits, they only change their direction, and we say the body is perfectly *elastic*, and in this case it can disengage *no* heat in striking the immovable object, because it retained the whole number of its velocity-lineïts on rebounding from the obstacle.

351. This kind of elastic body may be defined as a body to which the velocity-lineïts adhere with such extraordinary tenacity that, whenever *suddenly* prevented from proceeding any further in their wonted direction, they are changed in their course, instead of being disengaged or detached as heat-lineïts [as is the case with non elastic bodies]. If, however, the retardation of an elastic body be gradual, this change or reversion of the velocity-lineïts does not take place, because now the lineïts have *time* to depart from the body, and are then as heat-lineïts, necessarily scattered over a long distance, and therefore cannot be concentrated. This happens when the elastic ball, impelled along a horizontal plane, is gradually stopped by the resistance of air, or if ascending vertically, it is stopped by the counteraction of gravitation. The reason why an elastic ball when suddenly hitting an immovable obstacle is reflected, is the same as in a very swift cannon ball when, suddenly striking an immovable obstacle, it retains its velocity-lineïts and is obliged to cut a smooth hole through the obstacle, if at all possible, before its velocity-lineïts have time to disengage and spread themselves over a large surface, or else to detach themselves and appear as heat-lineïts.

352. The fact that a perfectly elastic body on striking an immovable obstacle and being deflected thereby, yields no heat, while an inelastic body, being *stopped* thereby evolves heat, proves conclusively enough, that it is not the *concussion*, but that it is the *checking and arresting* of the energy of mass-motion which produces heat, no matter by what means or in what manner this arresting may be accomplished. And in this we have the concurrence of Tyndall on our side in the following words: " generates the motion of the mass, and the *stoppage of that motion* produces heat." Just the same amount of heat will be produced whether the falling body be arrested by striking the solid floor, or whether in its fall it be arrested by a string fastened to the ceiling, to the end of which string the body was tied, so that the latter when falling cannot come in contact either with the floor or any other obstacle, provided, however, the height of the fall in both cases to be the same. It would even make no difference in the result if the arresting of a moving body was done by some invisible means working against the motion of the body, as, for instance, in projecting a ball against the stream of gravitation (346); or in moving a conducting wire across the lines of force in an excited magnetic field. In all these cases heat would be evolved, its amount being exactly equivalent to the resistance overcome.

353. In striking and repelling each other, the heat-lineïts will always more or less assist in the molecular repulsion of monits of matter, according as the number of heat-lineïts (as well as the number of monits) is greater or less within a given space. For the monits strike the heat-lineïts, and the heat lineïts strike the monits. Hence by introducing heat-lineïts into the air of a partially expanded bladder, the bladder gains in expansion; it likewise gains in expansion by forcing more monits of air into the bladder instead of introducing heat-lineïts.

354. These views will do much towards explaining the following cases of pressure from air:

Case 1. Suppose a closed vessel A made of heat-conducting metal, and filled with densely compressed air, the temperature of this air having in due time cooled down to exactly the same degree as that of the outside air. According to a well known law, heat cannot move translatory unless there is an adjacent place of *less* heat [temperature] to which it always will go. And yet, if by opening a valve or cock of the above vessel, we allow the inside air to follow its own tendency, a portion of the enclosed air will rush out on account of being driven out not only by the action of the remaining portion of air but also by its own reaction against the latter; at the same time all the inside air becomes chilled. Now we may ask two questions, 1st. What is it that drives the air out? For the heat, before opening the valve, being of the same degree inside as outside of the vessel, can in its state of equilibrio not do the driving, much less can, on opening the valve, the instantaneously reduced heat of the chilled inside air move the particles of the latter towards a place of *more* heat outside.

355. According to our lineïstic theory of heat we should answer thus: All monits are constantly flinging (144, 145,) detached polarized lineïts against each other, and thus repel one another in an inverse ratio as the distances. The 2d question, What chills the air remaining in vessel A? may be answered thus: Immediately after opening the valve, the *number* of heat-lineïts in the vessel is the same as before the valve was opened, because the opening did not in any way facilitate or induce the *escape of heat-lineïts* in the least, as any surplus heat can at any time easily escape through the heat-conducting sides of the vessel; but on account of the *less number of monits* in the vessel after opening the valve, the heat-lineïts are now struck upon less frequently because there are fewer molecules, and hence fewer monits to strike; hence the whirling of the lineïts is less brisk, and operates less upon molecules generally, as well as upon our nerves, less upon the mercury of the thermometer, and less also upon the face of the thermo-electric pile. Thus the air within the vessel is said *to have become cooler* or to have been chilled, and to this place will also tend heat-lineïts from without, and penetrate through the heat-conducting walls of the vessel A, until the contents of the vessel have acquired the same temperature with the outside, that is, until the heat-lineïts within and without have an equal energy in whirling. And then both the heat and the molecules inside are in equilibrio with those outside.

356. *Case* 2. Next if we take the aforesaid vessel A, as we now find it,* close it and connect it with another vessel B, containing highly compressed air of the same temperature with A, and then open the valve that is between them, what will happen? The denser air of B (fig. 2′), having its molecules nearer to one another, their monits repel each other with greater energy than those of the less dense air of vessel A. Hence on opening the valve the air of B, although of no higher temperature, will stream into vessel A, and will there generate heat, not

Fig. 2′.

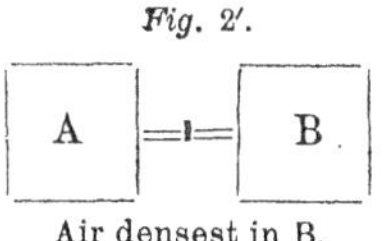

Air densest in B.

*Viz: the outside monits and heat-lineïts in equilibrio with those inside the vessel.

only on account of being arrested in its course, but *cheifly* because the adding of more molecules and their monits gives new energy of whirling to the heat-lineïts in A; thus the temperature inside of A is raised. In vessel B, on the contrary, the temperature is lowered on account of a reduction in the number of molecules and their monits, as already explained in case No. 1 (354).

357. Relying upon §356, we may predict that the burning of the same quantity of combustible matter mixed with the requisite quantity of highly condensed atmospheric air, ought to yield a much higher temperature than when burning in the same quantity of atmospheric air very much rarified. The most refractory metals might be melted with ease if only the gases in a furnace could be kept enormously condensed under a sufficiently high pressure.

358. Let a small but strong vessel be half filled with gunpowder loosely poured in, then let atmospheric air cautiously be pumped in and gradually raised to a pressure of three or more atmospheres. On igniting this gunpowder, the temperature as well as the explosion ought to be much more energetic than if, in the same quantity of atmospheric air, though intensely rarified within a larger vessel, the same quantity of powder had been ignited.

359. If within a closed vessel the air be enormously compressed, for instance by a column of water 260 feet in height, as was done in Schemnitz in Hungary, comparatively but *very few* heat-lineïts are required to keep the compressed air at the same temperature with the outside air, because these heat-lineïts, although comparatively few in number, are here agitated and kept briskly whirling by an immense number of monits of air. Hence as soon as a stop-cock was opened so as to allow the air to escape, the hitherto brisk agitation of the few heat-lineïts inside the vessel abated at once to a vanishing degree; and the enormous low temperature resulting therefrom became at once apparent in the icicles that formed around the pipe from which the air issued.

360. *Corollary.* If the two connected vessels A and B in case No. 2, fig. 2′, are exactly of the same size and temperature, and if they had, previous to the opening of the valve, been immersed into a tub of water, it would have been found that the water in the tub at the close of the experiment [no matter how great the difference of density of the enclosed air had been in the two vessels] had experienced neither gain nor *loss* of temperature, proving thereby that as much heat as A gained after opening the valve, just so much heat B lost by the same operation. Ample experiments have established this fact beyond doubt.

361. The same results of compensation of temperature will be obtained if A, in the preceding case, instead of containing air of inferior density, had been entirely exhausted of air previous to opening the valve, provided however, the inside of both vessels were of the same temperature.

362. *Case* 3. A cylinder A C (fig. 3.′) open at the top, and half way between *a* and *b* an airtight fitting piston *p* [which for the sake of simplifying our explanations we shall suppose to be without weight and without friction] the air beneath it to be of common atmospheric pressure as that above, and call the quantity of air in A, 2 volumes. Let another closed vessel B of the same capacity as A, be connected with A by a pipe furnished with a stop-cock, and let B contain double the quantity of air that A contains [i. e. 4 volumes] both of the same temperature. If we fasten *p* and open the stop-cock, one-fourth of the air of B will rush into A, and the air in A will be

Fig. 3′.

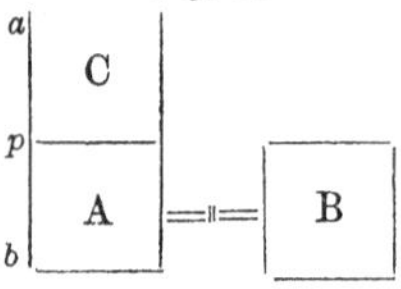

a C p A B b

warmed by just as much as the air in B will be chilled (359). Each of the vessels A and B now contains 3 volumes of air.—But if the piston *p* is not fastened, it will be carried outward to *a*, and both A and B will become chilled; and if C, A, and B were immersed in water, a reduction of temperature ought to manifest itself.

363. To explain this we need to remember that piston *p* in going to *a*, shoves before it only the molecules of air, but leaves the heat-lineïts of C where they are, and thus gives to the air in A the whole room of C to expand in, and each of the vessels C, A, B, will contain 2 volumes of air. And as 2 volumes, i. e. the same number of monits that used to be in C, are now there again, the temperature of C has to remain unchanged; but in B instead of 4 volumes there are only 2 volumes of air now, hence the molecules of this air will now be further apart and therefore unable to agitate the heat-lineïts as much as they had done before. B will consequently be chilled, and a reduction of temperature ought to manifest itself in the water in which the vessels are immersed.

364. It has been said in such a case as this that the temperature thus vanished, has done work in lifting the piston. But really all the work done here was the shoving of the molecules of air contained in C *from out their places*, because we assumed neither friction nor weight of the piston.

365. *Case* 4. Suppose we have a cylinder A C, two cubic feet in capacity, (fig 4′) open at the top, and an air-tight fitting piston *p* resting upon the air, half way between *a* and *b*. If air is heated it expands by $\frac{1}{273}$ of its volume [which it has at 0° Cent.] for every additional degree centigrade; and if we wish to double the elastic force or *pressure* of the air in A, keeping its *volume* constant, we need only to heat that air from 0° to 273° Cent.

Fig. 4′.

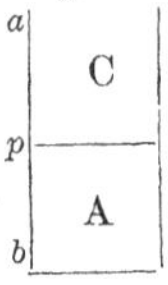

366. But if on the other hand, we wish to allow *two* cubic feet of space instead of one to the air of A keeping its *pressure* constant, whereby piston *p* is moved up to the top of the cylinder A C, then we shall be obliged not only to heat the air in A that is, one cubic foot, from 0° to 273° Cent., but we shall have also to give to the thus *expanded* air as existing in the *whole* cylinder A C, or in two cubic feet of space, a temperature of 273° Cent. That for this purpose more heat, i. e. heat-lineïts, are needed than in the case of constant volume (§365) is evident, for if in cylinder *A C* after heating *A* to 273°, piston *p* was moved up to *a*, the air of *A* streaming into *C* would be chilled not only by rarefaction of the air, but also by rarefaction of the heat connected with the warm air. By this streaming of the air into *C* there was not heat enough generated to compensate for the chilling effect in *A* as in §360, because the temperature of *C* at the time of opening *p* was yet at 0°, while that of *A*, was at 273° Cent., whereas in §360 the two connected vessels were supposed to be of the same degree of temperature.

367. Now the requirement, viz: that in our experiments in heating *A* from 0° to 273° Cent., the temperature of *C is to be left as it was, that is, at 0° Cent.*, seems to have been overlooked by philosophers; consequently they have drawn conclusions which will be found not to hold out against the test of experiment.

368. They say for instance, let in fig. 4′, the top be closed, *C* be a vacuum, and the air in *A* be heated from 0° to 273° Cent. If piston *p* were then removed, the air would expand in *A*, it would be chilled, but in *C* it would be heated, and mixing both portions together, we should have the whole column at a temperature of 273° Cent.

369. It is true that *A* would be chilled while *C* would be heated, and there would be no loss nor gain in temperature, provided the vacuum *C* also had previously been heated from 0° to 273° Cent. Yet this is not to be presumed; on the contrary, it must be presumed that the temperature of *C* was left at 0.°—Thus *the heat itself being transferred from A to C*, the air in the whole cylinder will be of a temperature much lower than 273° Cent., and it would require an additional quantity of combustible matter to bring the whole column of air up to 273° Cent.

370. THE FORCE OF VELOCITY OF ALL MOVING BODIES, that of celestial orbs as well as that of the driving snowflake; the velocity of the ball as it leaves the cannon's mouth, as well as that of a car [whether pulled by steam or by the muscular force of horses] may all be traced successively from link to link through a series of inferences, until at last we are always led to the following most simple mode of motion:

The FALLING—of monits towards each other and towards assemblages of monits, as well as the falling of larger and smaller bodies and particles of matter towards the centre of large celestial orbs, caused by the pushing streams of gravitation cosmolineæ (299), these latter being set in motion by the monits of matter; as will be made more apparent in succeeding paragraphs.

371. Although it may be said that the velocity of a steamer is due to heat, and that heat gives velocity to innumerable things, yet this very heat which we get from the combustion of fuel is after all nothing but the velocity-lineïts in their converted mode of whirling motion, and its origin can be successively traced to flow from the gradually retarded and arrested motion of *falling* particles of matter darting diagonally through the sun, as explained in §465.

372. All the immense amount of heat-lineïts that were first evolved in the universe during its formation and development, owed their emission as such to the retarding and stopping of centrewards *falling monits*, when in the remotest periods of time the general centreward motion and condensation of matter first took place to form celestial orbs, immediately after the formation of monits of matter.

373. VERSATILE ACTIVITY INDESTRUCTIBLE.—The primary power of Versatile Activity inherent in the lineïts of which the monit is made up (102) and in other versatile lineïts [for instance, in heat and in polarized-lineïts], existed before monits ever were formed, for it, as well as the other two primary powers [End-unition and Synduction], and also the lineït, is eternal and indestructible (§8); its total amount in the universe remains constant, never growing more, nor less, nor inactive.

374. The power of Versatile Activity can never exist by itself, *outside* of a substantive entity having extension [the most simple of which are the lineïts]; and as the immediate presence of this power must be sought in the most simple extension, Versatile Activity can therefore have nothing else but the lineït for its substrat, and it may either have a protracted stay in the latter or *move along* continuous lines consisting of lineïts. As Versatile Activity can never be at rest, it must, when dwelling protractedly in the lineït, either 1) be moving *rotatory* as in the monit's radii and in confined heat-lineïts, or 2) it must be moving *translatory* as in the velocity-lineït and the radiate heat-lineït, and 3) when not dwelling protractedly in one and the same lineït, it must be moving *along* the lineïts constituting the continuous cosmolineæ, i. e. gravitation-cosmolineæ.

375. VERSATILE ACTIVITY TRANSFERABLE.—Although Versatile Activity cannot exist outside of the substantive that bears it, i. e. outside of the lineït, yet it is capable of being shifted or transferred along lineïts from one to another, provided the ends of the successive lineïts are in actual contact; over vacui—even the smallest void imaginable—Versatile Activity cannot pass.

376. Versatile Activity when existing in lineïts that are ranged as in the continuous cosmolinea, i. e. in actual contact with each other's ends, can never exist there in a *stationary* condition, but is bound to move along swiftly, beyond all expression of language, from lineït to lineït, and while thus moving cannot manifest itself in its usual *rotatory* function, as it does when in the free unconnected lineït, as in confined heat.

377. As long as the heat-lineït enjoys this free unconnected condition, and is not by attaching itself converted into a velocity-lineït, so long is the *whirling* or rotary motion of the heat-lineït persevering, lasting, and can neither be stopped by other lineïts nor by monits in striking or pressing against them. It can be stopped only by Synduction in being made parallel, and then having its Versatile Activity transferred to a continuous gravitation-cosmolinea (198, 386, 387,). After exercising a shock upon an immovable body, the heat-lineït rebounds, but does not lose its power of exercising new shocks and pressure, repeatedly again and again.

378. Comparison between heat-lineït and gravitation-lineït.—The lineït of the gravitation-cosmolinea in striking an object, when unable to move it exerts only a pressure on the same, and proceeds on its way as before, connected with its fellow-lineïts; the heat-lineït when unable to move an object, rebounds in another direction after having exerted its pressure. And as the lineït of the gravitation-cosmolinea constantly acted upon by End-unition can exert renewed pressure afterwards, so the heat-lineït constantly acted upon by Versatile Activity, can exert renewed pressure over and over again. But whenever able to move the object they strike, then both kinds of lineïts go on as *velocity-lineïts* attached to that object.

379. Such a velocity-lineït when stopped in its translatory motion becomes a heat-lineït again, and thus the lineït remains efficient, whether it moves in the mode of a confined heat-lineït or in that of a velocity-lineït; in the former it has *whirling* motion, in the latter it has *translatory* motion.

380. Knowing the weight or mass of each planet and their satellites as well as that of the sun, besides knowing their diameters and periods of rotation, as well as their velocities through their respective orbits, and shape and size of the latter, it is not impossible to calculate the amount of velocity-lineïts (vis viva)*—mechanical force or dynamic energy, if you please—still possessed by all the known members of our planetary system.

381. To calculate the amount of dynamic energy (mechanical force) which in bygone times they have already lost in the shape of heat, since the planetary system began to condense from cosmical or nebulous matter, is impossible, because we can never know the height or distance through which the different particles or monits had to fall before they were arrested, while assembling to array themselves into orbs.

382. It may easily be conceived, however, that the dynamic energy resulting from the action of aggregating into condensed assemblages of matter to form our planetary system, must have been at least one hundred times greater than what at present remains in it.

383. What then has become of this immense amount of at least $\frac{99}{100}$

---

* Namely those dependent on this planetary motion, for besides this they may possibly have a still higher motion around some more distant and more powerful orb.

parts of wasted energy? It was emitted as heat, of course. But what has become of all these heat-lineïts? This is the question to be pondered on, and we shall try to make it appear that they have been *converted back into gravitation-cosmolineæ*, from which they first were detached and converted into velocity-lineïts.

384. Moreover, within the bodies of myriads of suns [as will hereafter be explained] lineïts of the gravitation-cosmolineæ are even at the present time, constantly changed first into velocity-lineïts and afterwards into heat-lineïts. As these heat-lineïts are incessantly sent abroad by those myriads of suns, the monits of the diagonally up-and-down-moving masses within the suns (§456) would soon become deficient in Versatile power, consequently the lineïts attaching themselves to falling monits as velocity-lineïts be more and more scantily supplied with Versatile Activity, and the rise and fall of matter within the suns would gradually cease, and the suns themselves would fast grow cold and be gradually extinguished, while at the same time heat-lineïts would have accumulated to an enormous amount within the bounds of the universe. This would certainly take place if the powers of Synduction and End-unition did not constantly do their share to re-modify the heat-lineïts into their former condition, that is, *into gravitation lineïts*, and send their Versatile Activity back to the partially depleted monits of the suns, as set forth in the next following paragraphs.

385. Transfer of Versatile Activity and conversion of heat-lineïts into gravitation-lineïts.—Whenever from out the gravitation-cosmolinea, a lineït is being attached to a monit as velocity-lineït, the Versatile Activity of the monit in distributing itself gives a proper share of its power to the newly added lineït. When after this the monit happens to be arrested and the lineït is then obliged to leave the monit, this lineït *takes its share of Versatile Activity along*, and having at the same time become isolated, manifests itself now as a more or less intensely whirling or rotating **heat-lineït.** But this share of Versatile Activity which has been taken trom the monit, has to be restored again to the same in some other way, or the monit will become deficient in Versatile power. This restoration is effected in the following manner.

386. All heat-lineïts go to where there is *less* heat, that is to regions where they meet with less counter pressure. Hence all free heat-lineïts find their way ultimately to the cosmo-velo, that is, to the verge or boundary of the universe, and there by most powerful Synduction, the versatile *rotary* motion of the heat-lineït is subdued and changed into *vibratory* motion, because the Synduction of the cosmo-velo by making the lineïts **parallel** to its own immovable cosmolineæ, makes it impossible for Versatile Activity any longer to act upon its lineït *rotatory.*

387. The heat-lineït, under the influence of the cosmo-velo's Synduction, now merely vibrates, and as soon as one of the ends of this lineït *touches* the free extremity of a continuous cosmolinea, which are never wanting, it is joined or annexed to this extremity by End-unition, and from the vibrating lineït the Versatile Activity is instantly sent swiftly along the gravitation-cosmolineæ, towards the centre of some celestial orb.

388. And as every gravitation-lineït is incapable of entertaining even for a moment the Versatile Activity, the latter is bound to move from lineït to lineït, along the gravitation-cosmolinea in unspeakable haste. In this way, after passing through the centre of the celestial orb, at last it reaches the monits, which are thus constantly replenished with Versatile Activity. Versatile Activity cannot fail to reach these deficient monits, as it most readily goes to such cosmolineæ as are most bare of this power, namely to those which directly stream to the sun and to similar other heat-emitting celestial orbs. In this manner Versatile Activity starts *from* places where it is being unfettered incessantly, and where it would otherwise accumulate in undue quantities, and it goes *to* places where it is always needed, always most lavishly spent for the use of the ever rotating monits of matter.

389. Here then at the cosmo-velo—in celestial regions farthest removed from any gross matter, at the verge of the universe—it is where Synduction performs its grand task of driving Versatile Activity from out the heat-lineïts as well as from the polarized-lineïts; and here it is also where the great work of annexing of lineæ, and with it the conversion of heat- and polarized-lineïts into gravitation-lineïts goes on uninterruptedly in all its energy. In these seemingly destitute and forsaken realms of the universe it is, where the most stupendous work is done, for here are unceasingly busy:—Synduction aided by End-unition—two of the three mighty primitive powers.

390. The *circumference* of the universe is, however, not the only region of the universe entirely destitute of matter, where Synduction performs its work. In and around the *centre* of the universe, within the great central convolutions (196) it is, where Synduction [not as in the above case aided by End-unition, but] acted upon by the vivacious power of Versatile Activity, in never ending yet fleeting conjugation performs another kind of stupendous operation—constantly engendering and keeping incessantly exercised the faculty of the world's great Intellect (230).

391. Light.—If heat-lineïts by any process whatever are fast multiplied aside of each other, faster than they can disperse; and if at the same time they have a sufficiency of monits intermingled with them, these lineïts by being thereby circumscribed within more narrow bounds, are obliged to rebound much more frequently from monit to monit, and being besides this also struck back by a greater number of monits, they have their whirling motion incited and exercised to such a degree as to set the monits themselves into a peculiar vibratory motion, which these monits communicate to the linearium [the so-called luminiferous ether] in that particular manner detailed in §97, so as to cause the latter to undulate in progressive true waves, and thereby produce the phenomenon which to the optic nerve of the eye is **light**. (v. Notes app.)

392. From the preceding paragraph it follows that the greater the number of monits is within an inclosed space in which heat is evolved, that is to say: the greater the pressure to which the monits of gas, surrounding a flame or any other source of heat, are exposed—the more brilliant with light will this pressure make the flame or other source of heat. Even the flame of the common spirit lamp might by these means be made to burn with a bright light.

393. Light then is an undulation in progressive true waves of the linearium [the so-called ether]. This undulation being produced by the peculiar vibratory motion of monits [the ultimate particles of matter] induced by the intense whirling of heat-lineïts, re-acting upon and striking the monits of matter.

394. While *light* is an undulation of a medium set in motion by the vibration of monits, that is by the ultimate minutest particles of ponderable matter,—*heat* is the whirling motion of the imponderable immaterial lineït itself, capable of setting the monit into vibration.

If it be asked, what is it in *heat* that vibrates, we may say: it is the immaterial heat-lineït. In *light*, on the other hand, it is the ultimate minutest particle of matter which by its own vibration sets the linearium (luminiferous ether) into undulations.

395. Heat-lineïts cannot act upon the linearium in an immediate manner, although traversing it continually in the shape of most energetic sunbeams. Even if ever so much crowded, heat-lineïts are not capable directly to make the cosmolineæ quiver or undulate. But they can do it *indirectly* by first setting monits of matter into a quivering motion, and thus by means of a comparatively small number of monits of matter they can accomplish, what all the strength of the enormously crowded heat-lineïts of the sun could not do alone without matter, namely to produce the phenomenon of *light*.

396. In the flame of a burning candle the heat-lineïts shake the monits of carbon that linger in the centre of the flame, and these monits of carbon shake the linearium and make it to undulate as light.

397. Having now had under consideration the three primary powers and the principal kinds of force-lineïts of nature coming within the scope of these pages, as well as the monit (or atom) of matter, it will not be amiss to add the following remarks.

398. Force or Force–unit.—A lineït associated with and acted upon by a primary power so as to be kept in *motion* constitutes a force-lineït, or force in its possible least quantity, termed **force-unit.** [§6(5)].

399. Now there is a peculiar kind of motion of some of the lineïts, viz: where one end of the latter is held in the same place or point, and only the other end of the lineït revolves, as is done in all the lineïts constituting the monit (atom); from being the constituents of the monit they are termed *constituent* force-lineïts. This is the only kind of force-lineït, or lineït in motion, that can never be set free, can never be converted, and can never be transferred from one body to another, as all the other forces can, and on which account these other forces are comprehended under the generic name of *accessory* forces. These accessory forces also can be converted into one another, but the constituent force-lineïts of the monit can never be converted. Hence all the forces may be distinguished into two genera, namely: the *constituent* force and the *accessory* forces.

400. But although the atoms (monits) of matter may be said to consist of lineïts of force, and these latter again to consist of power [units of power or power-points] it would be wrong to say that matter, force, and power are but one thing. We are amply justified to believe, and it is no fallacy of the atomist (as some authorities say it is) to imagine "that conceptual constituents of matter can be grasped as separate and real entities." Power as well as Force and *Matter* are real facts. The analysis and classification of all physical reality into Matter, Force, and Power is a correct one, but none of these three must be omitted, though it must be remembered that Power cannot be found to exist except in force and in matter.

401. The whole universe consists of the following primary powers and fundamental entities, a schedule of which is hereby subjoined.

IN PHYICS.*

<table>
<tr><th colspan="3">POWER.
POWER-POINTS.</th><th colspan="6">FORCES.
LINEÏTS.</th><th>MATTER
MONIT.</th></tr>
<tr><td>Constituent.</td><td colspan="2">Accessory.</td><td>Constituent.</td><td colspan="5">Accessory.</td><td></td></tr>
<tr><td rowspan="2">End-Unition.</td><td rowspan="2">Synduction.</td><td rowspan="2">Versatile Activity.</td><td rowspan="2">Constituent lineit of the monit.</td><td rowspan="2">Heat lineit.</td><td rowspan="2">Gravitation lineit</td><td colspan="2">Velocity-lineit.</td><td rowspan="2">Detached Polarised lineit.</td><td rowspan="2">Monit or Atom.</td></tr>
<tr><td>Vis-viva</td><td>nerve-lineit.</td></tr>
</table>

* In Mathematics the *abstract* items representing these three physical realities are: the mathematical *Point*, the math. *Line*, and the math. *Solid*.

SECTION VIII.

Conservation of Force.

402. "The highest law in physical science which our faculties permit us to conceive, namely, the *conservation of force*." These are the words of that eminent physicist, **Faraday**. We trust that by this time the great truth of the conservation of force has been adopted pretty generally by physicists, although we may find but few who have a clear perception of its true bearings. If this principle be involved in any of our inquiries and researches, it is our duty not to lose sight of it, and place unrestricted confidence in the consequences it may lead us to, no matter how discordant they may be with our former conceptions, if only these consequences are not contradictory to facts.

403. With regard to the production of heat in a mechanical way, it is generally said that either compression, percussion, collision, or friction, of one body against another, is absolutely necessary. But on going deeper into the study of physical forces we find that percussion, collision, friction, are mere secondary conditions, they are some of the means by which the chief object, namely: the RETARDING and ARRESTING *of the movement* of a body is accomplished. With the rebound of a perfectly elastic ball no heat is produced although concussion took place.

404. The mere fact that a body has movement or is in motion, already indicates that there is an *active force* in that body; and the possibility that by applying force a moving body can be stopped as well as that an arrested body can be set in motion, points to some force staying with the body as long as the latter is moving, and being absent from the body whenever the latter is at rest. That this force is *indestructible* has by the greatest lights of modern science been recognized as the highest law in physical science. Accordingly, if a translatory moving body be stopped, the force itself that moved the body is thereby not destroyed, but is still existing, though in some other mode than that of translatory motion.

405. If by a string we pull, say a four pound weight to the height of 70 feet, we have *not* thereby [as some authors seem to think] stored up in the raised weight, or *imparted* to it, the identical muscular force thus exerted, and which will again show itself after the weight has been cut loose and fallen 70 feet. All we can claim of having done in this case is: we have put the weight in a proper condition or position, so that it can, on being cut loose, be moved by the gravitation of the earth and *therefrom* can *gather force* (285–287′). This is a cardinal point differing widely from what has been the generally adopted view.

406. That the weight, as long as it hangs in its elevated position, possesses no more force than when it was lying on the ground can easily be proved, for if we place our hand half an inch below the pending weight, and then permit the latter to fall, the hand will experience hardly more than a mere pressure from the weight; but what a crushing effect the latter will exhibit on another hand held 70 feet vertically beneath the falling weight, may easily be conceived.

407. It is evident that the efficient force was added to the weight not before but after it had struck and slipped from the hand placed in the higher position; for at the time it did the first striking, it had not yet force enough to crush the hand. Where then did this force come from that crushed the hand when placed in the lower position? It could not have come from nothing, it must have existed already in some other form or mode of motion. The mode of motion we are looking for, we find in the darting lineïts of the ever-present gravitation-cosmolineæ (225, 226,) attaching themselves to the monits of the falling body.

408. The falling weight gathers its *force*-lineïts from the earth's gravitation-lines. The accumulated force with which the falling weight thus moves cannot be annihilated or destroyed, and if the weight be arrested in its course, the force of its motion must manifest itself either 1st, in a change of direction of the same body, or 2d, in a *translatory* motion of some other adjacent object or body, or 3d, in a *vibratory* motion of some adjacent matter, or 4th, in a peculiar *whirling* motion of its own self, viz: the force-lineït, then called **heat**, which some authors define as a shivering motion of molecules. And as sooner or later each one of all these newly induced translatory as well as vibratory motions of the adjacent bodies are by the influence of counteracting forces made to subside, all the motion of this falling weight will eventually have been transformed into heat.

409. In the above case, if for instance the falling weight be arrested by a floor, it is not in the weight alone that we have to seek for the evolved heat, but also in the floor struck by the weight; and in proportion as the floor is more yielding, the more of motion will be imparted to the same, and the less of heat will be found in the weight. Some of the heat will also, no doubt, escape by radiation and some by conduction over the surrounding air.

410. The motion of a body may be retarded and arrested by other means than those of percussion, collision, and friction. Any force, be it cohesion, be it gravitation, or some other kind which, by acting in a direction contrary to the motion of the body, accomplishes the latter's retardation, will also develop heat. Some of the principal cases of this retardation we will now take under consideration.

411. (1.) If a 77 pound weight be tied to the end of a chain ten feet long, the other end of the chain fastened to the ceiling, and then the weight allowed to drop from the ceiling, there ought to be developed by the arresting of the weight's motion at the end of the fall just as much heat as if the weight, after falling ten feet, had struck the floor instead of being held back by the chain. In fact, it ought to be even a little more in the latter case, on account of the falling chain's motion also being arrested. The heat developed in both cases, if it could be kept from dispersing, would be sufficient to raise the temperature of one pound of water one degree Fahr. Here too, the developed heat is not to be sought in the weight alone, but also in the more or less vibrating ceiling, chain, and air.

412. (2.) Suppose, by the aid of gun-powder, a one-pound ball could be sent through a space void of a resisting medium to the height of 770 feet vertically, it is clear that according to the law of the mechanical equivalent of heat, the ball on leaving the gun must possess dynamic force equivalent to an amount of heat sufficient to raise the temperature of one pound of water one degree Fahr. And it is certain that this much of heat, by the time the upward force is spent, must have been evolved again, either gradually or all at once, from the ball, according as the motion of the ball is to be arrested gradually or all on a sudden.

413. Now if this ball, in being shot vertically upward, meets an unyielding rock a few inches above the gun's mouth, it could easily be made evident to our senses that the ball had developed heat in being stopped. But if that same ball had met nothing to obstruct its path, what then? As soon as this ball has ascended through 770 feet, its energy of upward motion is exhausted, gone,—gone as surely as if it had been stopped by friction; and in one sense this going against the stream of gravitation is the same as being exposed to friction. And yet it may be impracticable to ascertain by experiment any gain of heat in the ball. Are we in consequence allowed to assert, as many a one would be ready to do, that this upward force of motion has been annihilated during the ball's ascent? By no means, for the law of conservation of force is contrary to this assertion, and "no assertion of fact should be credited that denies this law." Joule established the fact that for every foot-pound of force which is lost, a definite quantity of heat is always generated.

414. Hence we are justly and fully entitled to infer, that an amount of heat sufficient to raise the temperature of one pound of water one degree F., was actually evolved during the ascent of the ball, and that this heat, if not found in the ball itself, must have escaped into the air.

415. Let us try to illustrate this principle by another example. Experiments made at Basel with conical shaped leaden bullets weighing 40 grammes, and fired at a distance of 100 paces against an iron plate showed that by the impact a considerable part of the lead projectile was *melted* off, the molten lead found in little globules close by, only 13 grammes remaining unmelted. Calculation shows that in this case which we may designate with *a*), almost all the impetus of the motion of the body is transformed into heat,—a result which was indeed expected, seeing that the iron plate was but very slightly affected, and the projectile rebounded but little.—By far the greater part of this heat was used in melting the lead, but little was lost by conduction and radiation.

416. *Case b.*) Instead of having the gun-barrel placed horizontally, let us place it in a vertical position and shoot from it, upward with the same charge of powder, a bullet of the same figure and weight as used in case *a*. In case *b* the bullet's motion, although encountering no iron plate, will be stopped also as was that in case *a*; all the difference is that in case *a* the bullet was brought to a halt very abruptly, that is, its bodily motion was converted into heat-motion all on a sudden, therefore fully concentrated in one and the same place; while in case *b* the bullet was brought to a halt gradually as in friction, being checked by innumerable successive little impacts exerted in a direction contrary to its flight, that is, the bullet's bodily motion (velocity-lineïts) was converted into heat-motion (heat-lineïts) gradually and successively little by little over innumerable different little spaces, and consequently by far the greater part, if not all, of the evolved heat was dispersed by conduction and radiation by the time the bullet had reached its greatest height, especially towards the termination of its upward course when the bullet moves slowest. If the heat evolved in the ascending bullet should prove incapable of measurement in the bullet itself, are we therefore justified to conclude and to maintain that no conversion of velocity-motion into heat-motion has taken place in the above case *b*? No impartial man who understands the principle of conservation of force aright, will deny it in the one case and assert it in the other.

417. In firing the gun and propelling the ball, a great amount of heat evolved by the combustion of gunpowder lost its whirling motion, and with it, its heating character, because by their action of driving asunder the gaseous particles of matter, the heat-lineïts changed into another form of force, viz: into velocity-lineïts, which performed the transit of the ball from one place to another, in other words: the *whirling* motion of heat-lineïts changed into the *translatory* motion of velocity-lineïts taking along the ball. But in moving upward, the ball is seen to lose more and more in energy of this translatory motion until if stops, and if something be then put underneath to support it, it remains at rest.

418. The force of translatory motion which thus carried the ball up being gone, must, according to the law of conservation, either have been transferred to other bodies, or changed into an equivalent of some other form of force. Now, as there was in the vacuum no other body to which this force of translatory motion could have been transferred, and as this motion had been evolved from heat, and actually would have appeared as heat on being stopped by an immovable obstacle, we are justified to conclude, that on being *retarded*, no matter whether by opposition of a rock, or by friction, or by gravitation, it reverted back again into heat, either on a sudden or gradually, according as retardation was performed all at once or gradually. Into attraction of gravitation the translatory motion could not have been converted, for we know that a body in going further from the surface of the earth *loses* in energy of attraction, because the latter is in an inverse ratio as the squares of distances from the centre of the earth. There is no doubt that in the case before us, the motion of the ascending ball was changed into a motion of heat in all the molecules of the ball, and that at the end of the ascent all the upward motion was gone only, because it had by the counteraction of gravitation-force been gradually converted into a whirling motion of heat. The aggregate amount of this heat must exactly be the same with what it would have been, had the ball immediately on leaving the gun, been arrested all at once by concussion against a solid wall or iron plate; only in the latter case the heat would be more concentrated, having had no time to disperse.

419. If in a gun we store up force in the shape of gun-powder, and by means of it drive forward a piece of metal sliding along a rough plain, then 1st, by friction the metal is exhausted of its store of energy; it it also evident that, according to dynamists, the metal 2dly, in overcoming resistance viz: friction, has performed work; but at the same time it has 3dly, generated heat. Exactly the same things happen in the ascending of a heavy ball: 1) by the counteraction of gravitation it spends its store of energy, 2) in overcoming the resistance of gravitation performs work, and 3) its expended energy of upward motion has to appear in that particular mode of motion called heat.

420. (3) ELASTIC BALL. If it were possible to have a *perfectly* elastic heavy ball, and to let it drop from a height upon a solid floor, within a perfect vacuum, we might be able by these means to produce a never-failing supply of heat-lineïts by permitting the ball alternately to rise and fall continually.

421. With every *downward* movement or fall, the ball will be stored with a certain amount of translatory force which *taken from the all-pervading* *gravitation-cosmolineæ* is being attached to the molecules, or rather to the monits, of the ball; and with every *upward* movement the during the descent acquired force- or velocity-lineïts are turned off again from the monits, by streams of gravitation-cosmolineæ going and pressing against them in a contrary direction, and hence obstructing the ball's path as if by some dense viscid medium. The turned off velocity-lineïts being thus detached, take a whirling motion and now appear as *heat* as fast as the upward motion is lost, which heat, however, disperses or radiates away as soon as evolved. When the elastic ball in falling reached the floor, its motion instead of being arrested [as is the case with a non-elastic ball] was only turned back by the floor—the force or velocity-lineïts in the ball merely reverse their direction, yet remain in the ball and drive the latter upward. As the perfectly elastic ball at the moment of rebounding loses none of its velocity, no heat can be evolved by the concussion.

422. Whilst *ascending*, then, the ball [no matter whether the latter be elastic or non-elastic] throws off heat-lineïts after heat-lineïts successively. In a vacuum, with every rise of a *perfectly elastic* ball of 77 pounds, previously having fallen ten feet, there would be evolved heat enough to raise the temperature of one pound of water one degree Fahr.; and a kind of perpetual motion, yielding heat at the same time, would it be indeed. But as a perfectly elastic ball as well as a perfect vacuum are not within our reach, we need not try to carry the design into practice.

423. According to Rankine's Mechanics: "A body alternately accelerated and retarded, so as to be brought back to its original speed, performs work by means of its retardation exactly equal in amount to the potential energy," or rather as we would say, equal in amount to the attached velocity-lineïts, "exerted in producing its acceleration; and that amount of energy may be considered as *stored* during the acceleration; and *restored* (expended) during the retardation."

424. Thus we see from the preceding that by means of retardation, work is performed, according to Rankine, in the *ascending* of a heavy ball, and as by the same author, forces that "do work" are considered as those which "accelerate *molecular motion*" that is to say, disengage heat, he will admit that the ascending ball during its ascent, ought to disengage heat—most during the first instant of time, least during the last instant.

425. (4) PENDULUM. If it were possible to keep a pendulum of 77 pounds' weight continually oscillating so as with every rise to make it ascend ten feet above the level of its lowest point of descent, we should be able to evolve the same amount of heat-lineïts as in the case of the elastic ball.

426. Here it seems would be a chance for the construction of an apparatus to procure, in an easy manner heat without fuel, if it was not for the *circular curve* the pendulum has to describe in rising to any considerable height, and it is only from such heights that we can expect any considerable quantities of heat. In a clock the rise of the pendulum is quite inconsiderable; its path of oscillation don't deviate much from the straight line, and hence it is easy by means of a sinking weight to keep the clock pendulum constantly oscillating. The problem to keep a heavy pendulum oscillating through the whole sweep of a semicircle of 10 or 20 feet radius is, however, a very different affair from that of keeping oscillating a clock pendulum. To compensate the great loss of velocity caused by the short curve of a high ascending pendulum would probably require so great an amount of outside mechanical force as to make the whole operation unprofitable.

427. (5) Suppose there was an open tunnel running in a straight line directly through the centre of a solid celestial sphere, the latter, however, having no rotary motion, nor being gravitated upon by any other sphere, and the tunnel to be void of any resistance offering medium. A heavy body, say a piece of metal, dropped into one of the mouths of the tunnel would fall and gather velocity-lineïts, i. e. force of motion, all the way until it reached the centre of the sphere.

428. If we divide the time of falling into three equal parts, and the length of the radius into eight equal parts or space-divisions, by far the most force of motion will be gathered during the second, that is, the middle part of *time* of the whole fall; and with regard to space-divisions the most force of motion will be gathered in the 2d and 3d and part of the 4th space-division, that is, in the strata situated about one-fourth of the length of the radius below the sphere's circumference; because within a sphere, gravitation pulls with only one-half of its energy at one-half of the distance from the centre that it does at the circumference. The least force of motion will always be gathered in the vicinity of the sphere's centre.

429. Arrived at the centre the falling metal can not stop there, but rushing through with amazing speed, it will ascend towards the opposite mouth of the tunnel until that is reached, and then it will begin to fall back again and thus continue to oscillate up and down. In its outward or ascending course it encounters the resistance of the downward, that is, centreward going streams of gravitation-cosmolineæ, and is affected by them obstructively as by friction (v. 421). It will therefore in ascending be obliged to part with its force of motion, i. e. with its velocity-lineïts, and hence evolve an immense amount of *heat* in the same ratio as it previously, during its fall, had received force of motion, that is: it will evolve the least heat near the centre of the sphere and the most in the upper strata of the same, some distance below its circumference; because within a sphere filled with matter, the pulling power of gravitation affects a body less, the nearer that body is to the centre. In such a sphere the attraction is, in fact, proportional to the distance from the centre.

430. If the metal were dropped outside of the tunnel, ⅛ of the length of the radius *above* one of its mouths, then the metal as soon as it reaches the centre will ascend to the other side of the sphere, ⅛ the length of the radius above and beyond the opposite mouth of the tunnel, that is, it will go so much higher outside or above the circumference of the sphere than in the first case. In this case of §430 the greatest amount of force of motion [velocity-lineïts] will be gathered in the 1st and 2d space-divisions, that is, in the two uppermost spaces or strata of the sphere. In the same strata, though on the opposite side of the sphere, will also take place with greatest energy the evolution of heat. Hence the height from which the metal *begins* to fall is a most important circumstance always to be taken into account, if we wish to calculate at what depth of the sphere the greatest amount of heat is likely to be evolved.

431. (6.) Now suppose, instead of the solid sphere in the preceding case No. 5, another celestial orb consisting throughout of gaseous matter extremely attenuated by heat, and having no rotary motion around an axis.

432. If anywhere from the circumference of this orb the metal be dropped, it will fall to the centre, then rise on the opposite side, and evolve heat as in case No. 5, with this difference, however, that from the gaseous matter it will experience a certain degree of resistance, and consequently cannot rise through the same distance it fell. The paths of the metal's motion would gradually become shorter and shorter, and at last it would find a resting place in the centre of the orb.

433. But if an extraneous force is exerted, sufficient to give to the metal a new downward impulse, every time it begins to sink again after having come near to the surface on the opposite side of the sphere, the loss of the speed, which the metal had suffered from resistance, might thus be fully restored or compensated.

434. A comparatively small supply of extraneous force, properly applied, might thus be able to keep the metal passing diametrically through the whole sphere, alternately one way and back again, thus fluctuating to and fro for an indefinite length of time. And in this way the fluctuating, to-and-fro-coursing, metal within the sphere may be made to become a constant source of heat to the sphere, especially if instead of one small piece of metal, thousands are made to fall and rise, each one of immense volume.

435. (7) REVOLVING GASEOUS SPHERE. Let us now substitute, instead of the solid celestial sphere of case No. 5, a gaseous one like that in case No. 6, but revolving with considerable velocity around its axis. If from the equatorial circumference of this sphere the metal be dropped, it will be obliged to take quite a different track from that in No. 6, although in all other respects it will behave very similar. Here the centrifugal force, which we find, as we go downward, to decrease in a direct ratio as the distances from the centre, is the disturbing cause. The falling metal can never pass exactly through the centre of the sphere, but will describe courses as shown in fig. 9, which represents the sphere, bisected along the equatorial plane.

436. Having reflected on the preceding seven cases of motion, we are now prepared for a train of ideas having in view the solution of one of the most interesting themes which natural philosophy and physical astronomy have to offer, namely : THE SOURCE OF HEAT IN THE SUN.

437. The principal theories hitherto brought forward to assign a source from which solar heat proceeds are the following :

I. That the heat sent forth by the sun is simply the remainder of its primitive heat left, after cooling down from a more intense degree of its heated matter—gradually losing its primitive heat by radiation, without receiving any supply.

438. This is considered by many authorities as quite untenable, because if the sun had no other source but the remainder of its primitive heat to draw from, he would at the present rate of emission cool down and become dark in a comparatively short time. On the other hand, to obviate this objection, it has been claimed by the defenders of the theory that by the *condensation* of the sun's body which follows its cooling, new heat is developed, and thus the time of cooling, itself protracted.—It may, however, be replied that here the condensation does not result from an extraneously applied pressure, but is merely the consequence of an insufficiency of interior heat inducing *contraction*, hence in this case to speak of generation of heat by condensation, like that of atmospheric air in a match-syringe, is altogether out of the question.

439. The only heat that could be gained from such a contraction of the sun's mass would be from the arresting of the centreward directed intermittent motion of solar matter, while contracting at short intervals. Yet aside from this consideration there is the *repelling force of atoms (monits) of matter* to be taken into account, which works most powerfully in opposition to and against the contraction of the mass, thereby hindering the centreward motion or falling of the particles to take place in proportion to the loss of heat ; for, the nearer the gaseous particles approach each other the more energetically are they mutually repelled.

440. Even if this contraction were able to disengage the enormous amount of heat necessary to equalize the sun's expenditures, which is evidently impossible, it is very clear that the tranquil, *gradually* subsiding, and settling down of particles by cooling, can never produce those immense commotions—violent beyond the boldest conceptions of man—of which the surface of the sun gives innumerable tokens by its ejaculations and eruptions in the shape of protuberances, faculæ, etc.

441. II. That the heat emitted from the sun is due to chemical action among its constituent materials, or in other words: that the heat is produced by combustion, by a conflagration of the sun's body.

To prove the untenable nature of this hypothesis, it has been demonstrated, that if the sun contains within itself all the necessary elements of combustion, it could scarcely have lasted 8000 years without its whole mass being consumed, if by its own burning it generates the heat which is actually emitted.

442. III. A third hypothesis is that of aerolites falling into the sun. Aerolites from remote regions of stellar space, whenever they happen to come within the domain of the sun's pulling action, are attracted by the sun and, falling into the latter, develop heat by being stopped in their motion.

443. It has been calculated that the quantity of falling aerolites necessary to develop and keep up the heat of the sun, as emitted at the present rate, would have to be so great as to cover the whole surface of the sun to a depth of thirty feet in one year. The quantity of extraneous matter thus falling into the sun during a century would be equal to the whole mass of our planet, the earth. Hence for 10,000 years it would require masses of matter equal to one hundred planets like that of the earth.

444. That this hypothesis, on account of the enormous quantity of meteoric matter which it requires, meets with many objections, and does not give the true solution of the question with regard to the source of heat in the sun, is obvious, and seems to have been fully exposed. One of the most eminent physicists of the present day, **Tyndall,** says: " I do not pledge myself to this theory"......" it is a noble speculation; and depend upon it, the true theory [if this, or some form of it, be not the true one] will not appear less wild or less astounding."

445. In the theory which is to be propounded in the following pages, but a very limited quantity of falling aerolites is required. They will be required merely to compensate for any loss of motion by friction, that the trains of heavy chromospheric matter, coursing to and fro diametrically through the sun's body, may experience from the latter's gaseous texture. [v. §432–434, and 456]. The quantity of aerolites necessary to compensate for the friction will be found, no doubt, so small that a sufficiency of it may at all times be furnished by the Zodiacal light without being missed from the latter, which Zodiacal light, moreover, is being constantly replenished by meteors and aerolites coming from remote stellar regions. This new theory, it is hoped, will thus offer less difficulties and have a better claim of satisfying the student's mind than either one of the three theories above mentioned.

SECTION IX.

---

446. Gravitating energy of the sun. The diameter of the sun is 882,000 miles, its density 0,254 or about one-fourth of the earth's density, so that the molecules of the sun's matter, notwithstanding the prodigious gravitating energy of that body, must be at a much greater distance from each other than those of which the mass of the earth is made up. The sun's weight or mass of matter is 354,936 times that of the earth, that is, the sun attracts equal to an aggregate of 354,936 such planets as the earth. But the sun's surface being 111½ times more distant from his centre than the earth's surface is from the earth's centre, this energy of 354,936 has to be divided by the square of 111½, which gives us 28½ for the gravitating power of the sun upon a body placed on his surface, so that a one-pound weight, if taken to the surface of the sun, would bend or pull an elastic spring there to an equal degree as 28½ pounds do to the same spring when tried at the surface of the earth.

447. Each overlaying stratum of the sun's matter presses with its weight upon the lower ones; it must therefore be deemed most remarkable that matter exposed to such enormous pressure, as that to which the great bulk of the sun is subjected, can occupy so much space without being condensed into much smaller dimensions or to collapse at once; especially when it is remembered that the identity of a great many of the materials which compose the sun, with those composing the earth, has been demonstrated. The fact that the matter of the sun does keep up its loose texture under the above almost inconceivably great pressure, proves clearly enough that an intense heat prevails *throughout* its whole mass, by which the elasticity of the solar matter is reinforced and rendered capable of resisting the pressure.

448. Constitution of the sun. The central part of the sun can be neither an opaque *solid* nucleus, nor can the whole visible body of the sun be an incandescent *liquid* globe. For if according to the doctrine of the first supposition, we conceive the opaque nucleus surrounded by a photosphere which is said to be the seat of solar heat and light, it can not well be comprehended how the nucleus, surrounded by such an intensely heated envelope, should not share in the same temperature, and why therefore, it should remain opaque and solid. For a well-known law in physics teaches that heat always tends toward places of *less* heat, and accordingly the nucleus, if colder than its surrounding photosphere, would thus be attacked from all sides, and however feeble a conductor of heat that nucleus may be, after the lapse of a sufficient number of ages, and certainly by this our present time, it would have been raised to the same temperature with that of the furnace embracing it.

449. Or if on the other hand, according to the second of the above suppositions, the sun throughout the whole diameter of its visible disk be an incandescent *liquid* globe in fusion, and of a much *higher* temperature (in the proportion as 2 to 1) than its surrounding chromosphere, of which latter the heat is known already to be so great as to volatilize the most refractory metals contained in that chromosphere, it is again difficult to conceive how the sun's body should endure in its *liquid* state, without being evaporized to an equal degree with the materials that are contained in its chromosphere, and which have only one-half as high a temperature. It has been proved by physicists that the most intense light of the sun must necessarily be between the volatilized metals of the chromosphere and the sun's centre; and, moreover, Arago has proved that this most intense light of the sun proceeds from *matter in gasform.*

450. From many different aspects which the case presents I have come to the conclusion that with regard to the sun's constitution:

1st.) The whole body of the sun, as far as its visible disk extends, consists of matter in a gaseous state. This gaseous sphere, that is, the luminous body of the sun, is in some parts especially rich in volatilized *metals*, besides containing many other materials in vapor-form [which with less heat could only exist as solids and liquids], and is throughout of an intense, but not uniform heat and light.

451. 2.) Some distance below the sun's equatorial surface, arranged all round in a kind of concentric zone,* we find what may be called the breeding places of heat and light, for in this zone it is where the disengagement of heat-lineïts most energetically takes place, and while thus evolved, they set the molecules of matter, and through them, the luminiferous ether (linearium) in most intense wave-like undulations. This zone may therefore justly be called the *zone of intensest light.* The zone of intensest light extends downward from near the surface to a considerable depth. Upward or exterior to this zone, the temperature of the main body of the sun decreases rapidly on account of radiation, and through these cooler strata the heat-evolving trains of metallic chromospheric matter (458–468,) shoot up with the most astonishing rapidity, lifted not only by their vis viva or velocity-lineïts, but also most powerfully by their steadily growing temperature, until they break forth from the periphery of the sun with explosive violence, carrying everything before them [even the hydrogen of the upper strata]. Crossed in different directions by such extraordinary heated trains of matter, the body of the sun cannot be of a uniform temperature.

452. 3.) This intensely brilliant gaseous sphere (the sun) is encompassed or covered (as if by an ocean) by a less brilliant, reddish looking envelope of specifically *heavier* gases (metallic as well as non-metallic). This red gaseous sheet or envelope is continually being pierced, cleft, and fissured by innumerable specks, mounds and ridges of a more brilliant matter, boiling up from below and consisting of various metals, such as sodium, magnesium, barium, iron, chromium, nickel, etc., all in vapor-form, and giving rise to the phenomena of *faculæ* and the mottled appearance of the sun's surface. The different parts of this envelope are always in great commotion, caused not only by the gushing and shooting upwards of great masses vertically, but also by immense horizontal currents streaming and whirling rapidly in different directions; and this great commotion, like that of an

---

*If the sun be bisected along the plane running through both poles, this zone in its section will appear in patches horizontally elongated, on both sides of the equator.

immense chaldron in full boiling, is the cause why specific *heavier* matter can also move and for some time keep itself afloat upon the surface.

453. This matter, especially rich in metals, boiling up in the shape of faculæ, if pouring itself over and spreading along the sun's surface, forms what is called the *chromosphere*, and assuming a colored hue after having by radiation lost one half of its temperature. The chromosphere, though still enormously heated, is of a less brilliant light than the main body of the sun, of a more or less red hue, its heat being to that of the main body somewhat less than 1 is to 2, yet is still hot enough to keep volatilized and in gasform all the various metallic substances which it contains in great abundance.

4) Resting upon this chromosphere are the *strata of hydrogen* together of a depth of from 5000 to 7000 miles.

454. 5) The strata of hydrogen and the chromosphere are encompassed by a non-luminous atmosphere of extremely elastic and attenuated matter, unable to keep any of the chromospheric matter suspended; this atmosphere is of but moderate height, its upper limit is where the effects of gravitation counterbalance the atmosphere's elasticity; and its bottom, which is the sun's visible circumference or disk, is the line where the metallic gaseous particles of the sun are balanced between the two opposite efforts of gravitation and upward shooting matter. This outline of the sun is constantly fluctuating up and down, according as the heat from below becomes alternately sometimes feebler sometimes stronger in its energy, thereby disturbing greatly the equilibrium of the sun's level, while gravitation, on the other hand, is working to re-establish that equilibrium.

455. 6) When the faculæ, instead of merely pouring over, ascend with a rush in immense jets for thousands of miles above the disk of the sun, they give rise to what is called the rose-colored *protuberances*. Both the faculæ and the protuberances consist of the same material, only the protuberances being propelled upward with far greater force—and protruding high into an attenuated atmosphere—lose heat and light very fast and assume a colored tint. Every protuberance emerges first as a facula or group of faculæ before it rises higher; by radiation it loses heat and assumes the rose-colored hue. And as the chromosphere is nothing more than the accumulated matter ejected by the faculæ, it follows that the chromosphere, the protuberances, and the faculæ contain similar if not the same metallic materials, which ultimately are carried down by way of the solar spots, to rise again as faculæ and protuberances from the opposite side of the sun's surface.

456. *Within the sun, diagonally through its body, heavy matter in long trains descends and ascends alternately.* Let us suppose a large quantity of the molecules of the metals and of other *heavy* substances of the sun, in gasform hove up from below and spread out as *chromosphere* upon the sun's surface. Having radiated much of their heat into free space, the heavy metallic particles of the chromosphere thus cooled will soon begin to fall through the aeriform body of the sun, which is by most enormous heat perfectly elastic and so bare of every thing like cohesion, as to allow a nearly free and unobstructed passage through its mass. Their courses will be directed *obliquely* towards the sun's central part, 441,000 miles deep. Sometimes these cooled metallic masses are collected in exceedingly great quantities, and in a vortex sink down like an immense cataract, as it were, steadily renewing its length in the rear, and fed by the chromosphere like a river fed by a lake.

457. As *solar spots* we may recognize all those places of the sun's surface where the heat-losing metallic matter of the chromosphere sinks down and is engulphed. An uninterrupted stream of these falling heavy substances may thus continue for weeks, so that during all this time the resistance from the gaseous matter would in a great measure be obviated. In some few cases solar spots have been observed of a diameter twice as great as the circumference of the earth is long; frequently spots last for six or seven weeks, the greatest duration being about six months.

458. Though the fore-part of the fiery cataract when it is beginning to descend, encounters resistance from the gaseous body of the sun, yet all the long trail that is following uninterruptedly for weeks and even months will find its way comparatively clear, and and fall with an accelerated velocity.

459. When the cooled descending metallic matter falls in such immense continuous cataracts from a height of 441,000 miles, and is urged on in its fall with such astonishing energy of gravitation [28 times that of the earth] —its store of acquired force of motion (velocity-lineïts) must be immeasurably great by the time it comes within the neighborhood of the sun's centre; and it is easy to imagine how all along the sides of such a channel, any lateral intrusion from the sun's permanently gaseous matter is shut out, so that in the interior of this immense tube or channel of the sun, the comparatively cooled specifically heavier metallic mass moves with great freedom.

460. Arrived within the region of the sun's centre, at the lowest point of descent, the falling heavy matter does not stop there, but sweeps through that region with all its increased speed and accumulated force of motion, for here it has attained its greatest velocity.

461. If the sun is supposed to be bisected so as to let the plane of section pass through both its poles (vide fig. 8.), all the falling masses of metallic matter leaving the circumference, will seem to proceed in straight lines towards the central regions of the sun. Very few of the many continuous trains of falling matter can, however, come in line with the centre, because they all crowd towards the same region. Their course will be deflected more or less in the neighborhood of the centre, as shown in fig. 8., and from thence their paths will present the appearance of straight tracks running toward the circumference of the sun.

462. And thus in two great belts parallel to the sun's equator, one on each side of it, as in fig. 8—the very belts in which we see the great majority of spots—the great trains of metallic matter of the chromosphere continue alternately to *emerge* and to *sink down.* Trains may occasionally sink down in other regions, but that none can successfully sink and rise at right angles to the resultant plane of the majority of the trains, is apparent on a further examination of the subject. The reason why the sinking and rising of the trains takes place in belts near and to both sides of the sun's equator will be explained in a subsequent paragraph (470^1).

463. Fig. 8 is to represent the course of the downward and upward trains of metallic or chromospheric matter in the sun, if the latter is bisected so as to let the plane of section pass through both of his poles.

464. If, however, the sun be bisected so as to let the plane of section coincide with that of the equator, then the downward and upward trains of chromospheric matter will be as represented in fig. 9, for we must not forget that that the sun has a rotary motion around his axis, and that therefore his centrifugal force at the circumference is twice as great as that which he has at half the radius, and amounts to nothing at the centre.

465. Most probable source of heat in the sun. If, as assumed in the preceding pages, great continuous masses or trains of heavy metallic matter pass to and fro, alternately descend and ascend diametrically through the entire body of the sun, from circumference centreward, and still onward from the centre to circumference, then the molecules of these masses when *ascending*, that is: when going from centre to circumference, are necessarily bound (as has been set forth in §429) to convert their force of motion—which they had acquired previously [during their fall centreward]—into another motion, namely that of heat, and in this way evolve heat until they (the metallic masses) have reached the highest point they are able to attain, which generally is the circumference of the sun, or frequently even a considerable distance above it.

466. Having carefully read the paragraphs on heat-yielding motions, especially §427–430, and assuming many such alternate up-and down-motions simultaneously to operate, the reader may now be prepared to comprehend how a never failing supply of heat may be furnished to the sun, especially in those portions not very far below its circumference.

467. So astonishingly rapid is the fall of the masses of the chromospheric matter and so great the width of the channels through which they fall, that the excessive heat of the intensely heated sun's body will not have time to reach the cooled and *falling* particles before they begin to ascend. Only with the moment that they pass by the centre and ascend on the other side of it, as has already been intimated, will begin the conversion of the force of translatory motion into heat; sparingly at first, but in greater and still greater abundance as the moving chromospheric matter proceeds, so that on drawing near to within one-fourth the radius' length from the surface of the sun, heat in immense quantities will be evolved, and the metallic particles throughout the entire width of the chromospheric channel be rapidly volatilized to an excessive degree.

468. Arrived at the sun's circumference, the ascending, now extremely volatilized particles of metallic matter, having by counteracting gravitation been obliged to give up all their force of motion, stop. They next spend by radiation into interstellar space a great deal of the accumulated heat, and consequently get to be comparatively cool, and thus they constitute a part of the chromospheric layer enveloping the sun. Liquid *may* in some cases be the metallic particles of the chromosphere on their way down from the circumference of the sun towards its centre, but vaporized they certainly *must* be when in ascending they approach the sun's circumference.

469. The sun is surrounded by an immense lenticular-shaped aggregation of matter, known by the name of *Zodiacal-light.* This matter does not, like an atmosphere, rest and press upon the sun; on the contrary, its several parts move by independent velocity in more and more narrowing orbits around the sun, without being connected with that body. Its greatest plane of section coincides with the sun's equator, and extends on each side of the latter from 40 to 90 degrees, that is: to beyond the orbits of Mercury and Venus. It is more than probable that this great lenticular body consists entirely of gross matter, and contains myriads of smaller and larger ponderous bodies, such as asteroids, aerolites, and other stony and metallic meteoric masses which are continually falling into the sun.

470. On reaching the sun's body, these falling meteoric bodies are not at once arrested, and therefore their motion is not directly evolved into heat, but on the contrary, their motion is most generally *transferred* to the downward passing trains of chromospheric matter which is already sinking continually into the abyss of solar spots, and thus are added velocity-lineïts to velocity-lineïts, increasing the downward speed of those trains. Hence by bodies falling into the sun, are the great descending currents or trains so much reinforced in their motion that they are enabled, in spite of friction, or other retarding causes, to ascend through the opposite half of the sun's body, and to as great a distance as they just had been descending from,—and indeed, to be driven as high in their one millionth excursion as they had been in their first. They will rise to, or sometimes even far above, the surface of the sun's luminous body, not merely *piercing* the chromosphere, but rising for thousands of miles above it, where, by continually losing heat, they then appear of a still deeper hue, viz: that of a rose-color.

470[1]. Our knowledge that the longest diameter of the zodiacal light coincides with the equator of the sun, goes far to account for the fact that the rising and sinking of the chromospheric trains take place almost exclusively in *belts near and parallel to the sun's equator*, on either side; because the longest diameter in the zodiacal light indicates that in this direction exists by far the greatest amount of meteoric matter, and thence only can be expected the greatest shower of aerolites upon the sun.

471. After emersion, the volatilized metal masses may be looked upon as part of the chromosphere. They will soon spread horizontally, lose much of the remaining heat by radiation, become more dense and less luminous, and flow over to a neighboring vortex, where they sink and partly are sucked down into a whirlpool-like mouth, which is the *solar spot*.

472. ROSE COLORED PROTUBERANCES. Occasionally the chromospheric trains in the act of sinking down, may by means of unusually great supplies of meteors and other cosmical bodies falling into the sun, have received so much additional headway as to speed with uncommonly great velocity through the sun's body, and emerging on the opposite side shoot for thousands of miles beyond, i. e. *above* the sun's disk, where in a nearly isolated condition, by greatly facilitated radiation, they lose heat to an excessive degree, though still existing in a state of red hot vapor, and then they appear in the shape of *bright* rectilinear *jets* inside of the *rose-colored protuberances* noticed at the sun's circumference. In cases like these, the cooled matter when arrived at its utmost height has no substratum to *spread* out as in the more normal cases, and as its path is an inclined one, it is apt to topple over.

473. It may here be objected that the spectroscope showes the protuberances to consist of hydrogen. We ought to consider, however, the presence of hydrogen merely as a phenomenon accompanying the ejection. The strata of hydrogen encircling the sun are said to be of a depth from 5000 to 7000 miles; hence there is nothing strange in the fact, that the jets of denser matter in passing through these strata with astounding velocities, should take along and be enveloped in hydrogen. And when we recollect that according to recent researches the layers of the chromosphere and the jet itself contain not only hydrogen but also barium, cobalt, chromium, iron, magnesium, manganese, sodium, nickel, titanium, in considerable proportions, we then begin to realize that the jets are made up of heavier substances.

474. That none of the traversing chromospheric trains can pass through the very centre of the sun, and only a few may pass in close vicinity of the centre, is evident; by far the great majority are obliged to pass at a considerable distance from it, and do not interfere in their paths one with the other.

475. REGIONS IN THE SUN CONTAINING THE MAIN SPRINGS OF SOLAR HEAT.—As all the heat that originates in the sun is evolved only from the *ascending* chromospheric trains, especially in that portion of them which begins some distance [one-fourth to one-eighth of the radius' length] *below* the sun's circumference and reaches up to the surface, we must consider as main fountains of heat all parts of the ascending chromospheric trains of matter, whenever they have come up to within a certain distance below the sun's surface, say one-fourth or one-eighth of the radius' length; mostly in those regions of the sun which comprise the two great belts parallel to the equator, where the most faculæ are to be seen.

476. REGIONS OF MOST INTENSE LIGHT IN THE SUN. In a burning candle the greatest heat is in the outside parts of the flame, in particles chemically combining, i. e. in particles being consumed, and thereby yielding heat; the most intense light, however, proceeds from the *interior* of the flame, from particles being heated to an enormous degree without being consumed. In a candle-flame the place of intensest heat, therefore, does not coincide with the place of intensest light.

477. In the sun the case is very different. Here the region of intensest light exactly coincides with the region of intensest heat. The particles of carbon on the outside of a candle-flame in being chemically consumed, yield up the requisite heat necessary to set other particles [those of the interior of the flame and not in reach of the oxygen] into vibration. The *vibration* of these more interior particles, which while they are heated are not thereby consumed, sets the so-called luminiferous ether into undulations of light. Here then, the special exclusive function of the one set of particles is to furnish the heat, the special function of the other set is to *vibrate, and thereby to set the luminiferous ether (the linearium) into undulations*, i. e. to give *light.*

478. In the sun, heat is produced without combustion, that is, without any particles of matter being chemically consumed. Thus all the particles of the ascending chromospheric trains do not only furnish heat, but at the same time are ready to serve as vibratory particles also. Each particle therefore performs both of these functions simultaneously. Each particle furnishes the heat necessary to set its adjacent particles in vibration, and is at the same time set itself in vibration by the latter.

479. And as this vigor of action of the particles, mutually setting each other into vibration, will be as the *squares* of the number of heat-lineïts within the same compass of space (322), it is clear that the particles will most energetically vibrate where the most vigorous disengagement of heat takes place; consequently wherever the most energetic vibration of the particles of matter is going on, there also will be produced the most energetic undulations in the luminiferous ether, and thence will issue the most intense light. From this it follows that in whatever region of the sun's body the greatest heat is to be found, there will also be the greatest source of light.

480. From §430 it appears that if the heavy material of the chromosphere begins to fall from a great distance, say 50,000 miles *above* the sun's visible circumference, the greatest amount and intensity of heat and light will be produced in that region of the sun which extends from immediately below the circumference to a depth of about 100,000 miles, but on that side of the sun opposite to where the fall began. If, however, the fall of the heavy material begins *at* or *near* the circumference of the sun, then will the region of most intense heat and light be about 50,000 miles *below* the surface, and extend to a depth of 100,000 additional miles further down. But these distances will, of course, be somewhat modified by the resistance of the medium that has to be overcome.

481. Hence if the height to which the jet of a protuberance ascends, is very great, the temperature with which that jet emerged from the sun must also be proportionally great. Zollner finds the absolute minimum temperature of the place from which an eruption of a protuberance of 1.5 minute's height issues, to be 40,690° Cent., and that of a place from which a protuberance of 3 minute's height issues, to be 74,910° Cent.

482. Faculæ and penumbra. The conclusion readily suggests itself that the mighty commotion observed on the surface of the sun, and the rushing up of immense masses of matter, is produced by the above mentioned ascending chromospheric trains of intensely heated metallic and non-metallic matter in gas form; and it is very natural that the breaking out or boiling up of *faculæ* in the shape of flat mounds or in ridges is accompanied by the most intense light and heat. On the other hand, the darkest places on the sun's surface will indicate the central portion of *spots* where the already cooled and less luminous matter sinks down, while the less cooled and somewhat more luminous masses are still lingering around as *penumbra* before merging into the downward speeding stream.

483. Both the faculæ and the protuberances, consist of the same material and are produced by the same causes, namely: the rushing up of the chromospheric trains as explained above. And observations are not wanting, going far to prove their identity, because of their similarity in shape and position. The only difference between them is that the light of the faculæ is generally more intense than that of the other part's of the sun's surface; while on the contrary, the protuberances are only of a moderate red light. That the faculæ should appear brilliantly white, while the protuberances are red, is not to be wondered at, if we reflect that the faculæ just emerging from the disk of the sun must be yet full of intensest heat, while the matter of the protuberances during its ascent and isolation at great height, must have lost an immense amount of heat, though the lowermost parts, i. e. the base of the protuberance, is most probably as white and hot as the faculæ themselves are.

484. And thus we have arrived at the remarkable inference that faculæ, protuberances, and the *chromosphere* are of the same nature and composed of the same material; all three constitute a wondrous system intimately connected, and performing most important functions in the economy of the sun's existence.

485. After our endeavors to dive deep into the mysteries of the sun's heat-, light-, and magnetism-producing mechanism, let us now for a few moments reflect on its stability. It is very natural for all of us to ask the question: is the mechanism of the sun a kind of "perpetual motion," or is it bound sooner or later to run down and stop? To this a positive answer can be given with confidence. No matter which of the different theories of the sun's source of heat we go by, we meet the verdict: It has to stop at last.—

486. In adopting the theory developed in the preceding pages we will find it comformable that the ponderous chromospheric trains in their alternately ascending and descending course, may be said to represent the pendulum of the great heat- and light-giving clock of our planetary system—"the orb of day"—while the cosmical bodies that fall, in the shape of asteroids and meteors, from planetary space into the sun by way of the system of the zodiacal light, represent the raised clock weight; because they furnish the requisite motive force to make up for any loss in velocity of the up- and down- speeding trains, which the latter may have suffered from resistance and friction by the sun's gaseous body.

487. It is believed that at present there is a sufficiency of outside cosmical matter in the shape of meteoric streams, to operate upon the sun in the manner just described, and to be to the sun for a long succession of centuries what the raised clock weight is to the clock. But conformable to inflexible physical laws, the time will surely come when the supply of sunward-bound meteorites shall be exhausted.—What then will be the consequence?

Then the alternately falling and rising chromospheric trains, diagonally through the sun, have to become shorter and shorter in their paths, unable any longer to reach the surface of the sun or to emerge from it as faculæ and protuberances.

488. Constantly acted upon by resistance and friction, these trains will grow more and more feeble in their movements, and shorten their paths with every succeeding journey they make, until the whole chromospheric matter, as the specifically heavier, gradually has settled down around the centre of the sun.* The latter then turns slowly to an incandescent liquid globe surrounded by a cold and rigid crust of solid matter.—

Dreary indeed will our planetary system be, when the swing of these solar pendulums shall shorten in—the clock run down—the sun grow cold—his body shrink—his light expire—silence and quietude settle around in darkness and death.

489. Impending consolidation of all matter. Having spoken of meteorites (487), we may ask: what are meteorites, and where does all this immense amount of cosmical matter that seems to flow in never ending streams come from? Meteorites are the debris and fragments of exploded celestial spheres.† In the whole range of the sun's domain, that is as far as his activity with regard to attraction extends, we may confidently expect to find converging from all sides, more or less interrupted streams of meteorites and aerolites of all sizes, obeying his mighty pull, and speeding to his great rendezvous of matter (487). All interstellar space seems to be well stocked with fragments of millions of broken-up celestial spheres. These fragments leave [mostly in parabolas] the dominions of other fixed stars and, getting into the sun's domain, they either *follow* suit, or else are gathered up by him as he himself proceeds along his sweeping path through space.

490. Not only do these streams of cosmical matter constantly increase the mass of the sun, and thereby give him additional strength to pull more forcibly upon all planets and satellites, but these meteors on being struck by a planet in its path, are the means of gradually lessening somewhat the planet's centrifugal force. Thus in two different ways do interstellar meteorites give to the sun a steadily increasing advantage of power over the planets, so that each one of them has to succumb at last; either being in one inviolate mass drawn into the sun, if the planet's exterior crust has always granted readily the escape of heat and heated gases from below, or else the planet will have to burst into fragments, whenever its thick and solid crust should at any time prevent the opening of natural safety valves [in the shape of fissures and volcanic vents (512-524)]. In the latter case many fragments will be quickly drawn into the sun, while others, driven in an opposite direction, will stray off as meteorites in space. Many fragments, however, may be hurled in directions so as still to be obliged to continue in more or less eccentric paths around the sun.

491. Yet, besides the causes assigned in §490, there is another one to induce all secondary celestial orbs to be at last engulphed into their heat-spending primaries. The streams of heat issuing incessantly from the sun, no doubt, contribute their share of action, comparatively small though it may be, to retard the planets in their approach to the sun (505). This *repelling* efficiency of the sun's heat has been observed with regard to com-

---

* But very little heat, comparatively speaking, will be supplied by the contraction consequent upon the cooling of the sun. (v. 439).

† For the cause of this explosion see §520-522.

ets and their tails, when drawing near him. By the above action of meteorites (490), the planets may continue gradually to decrease their solar distances; and even do so still later, when the fall of meteorites has discontinued to the sun, for then his heat producing action fails—no sun-beams will be there to act repellingly—and thus the planets are enabled to continue approaching to the sun, and never can their final doom to mingle with his body be averted. In a similar manner all planets and satellites, one after another, are swallowed up in one vast tomb. The concussion from each, it is true, will evolve immense amounts of heat within the sun, yet never can they (except for a short time) re-animate his body, after the exhaustion of the life-sustaining flow of meteorites has once set in.

492. What happened to our sun would likewise, in the course of time, happen to other heat- and light-emitting spheres, to the fixed stars, and even to those higher dignitaries among celestial spheres, round which the distant suns and stars may circle; until after ages "inexpressible by numbers that have name," the fatal catastrophe of failing heat and light overtakes the last grand cluster of brilliant orbs that circulate around the cosmic-core. And even the COSMIC-CORE itself—the halo that enshrines the sanctuary of the *centre*—shall at last, when no longer receiving its wonted supply of falling matter, grow dim and cold, and form a rigid shell, and all the matter of the universe be thus consolidated into one total aggregate, dark—heat-less—mute—and motionless.

493. But notwithstanding all this, the cosmolineæ continue for ever [and now as *ordinate* cosmolineæ] their circulating course, steadily streaming from the circumference of the universe inward to its very centre, whence in the shape of detached polarized-lineïts they are obliged, as heretofore, to stream back to the circumference again, the only region where, by being constantly used up, there always is a scarcity of them; and where by their annexation the cosmolineæ are always restored to their full length.

494. The world would then present the following picture: all the matter, i. e. all the monits of the whole universe, collected and consolidated into one immense concentric shell, with Versatile Activity in all its monits still at work, as usual, breaking the continuity of the cosmolineæ and scattering the fragments in the shape of detached polarized-lineïts, thereby continually giving rise, around the cosmic-core, to the most astounding outbursts of *auroral* phenomena, never to die out or to grow faint.

495. All *translatory* motion of matter is now suspended for ever. And when this state of quiescence is fully established, then, of course, no matter does fall and no more heat is being evolved. And as the most of the then remaining free heat-lineïts shall have been converted into gravitation-lineïts, the temperature of the universe will be diminished to an inconceivably low degree. All matter has been driven towards the central regions, and its monits there held captive. No haughty flight through the sublimer regions, no roaming and no circling in grand orbits will be for them henceforth. Monits are then bereft of all their motion except the monotonous spinning around an axis, which never can be stopped.

496. Thus, when in the beginning of the phenomenal universe the versatile inclined lineïts [of conscious will possessed] by their struggle for unrestrained liberty, broke loose from the companionship and gentle restraint of the then stabile cosmolineæ, and formed into monits of matter, they shall find themselves at this distant future date whereof we speak, shut down to perpetual servitude, to give translatory motion to the cosmolineæ, all of which shall then as ordinates, in never ending paths sublime, dart from the very centre of the cosmic soul to distant verges of the universe and back again,—the monits, on the other hand, of which the seceded versatile inclined lineïts now are parts, will be fixed steadily to their places of captivity, doing the *requisite draft-power service* by reeling in the same monotonous manner continually and for ever around their own axis.

497. The All-Intelligent at that future distant day shall have no more the guidance of organic structure, no new designs to make; yet the two great powers, Synduction and End-unition, of which Its soul partakes, will still have to be unremittingly busy in restoring and maintaining, at the very verge of the universe, the continuity of the cosmolineæ, and by means of the latter which are always acting as gravitation, to hold in subjection the monits of matter. Thus the All-Intelligent shall imperishably exist and act for ever and ever, though at that late date performing functions far less diversified than in the phenomenal world at present. Its chief delight will always be to influence and animate such of the souls who are inclined to and corresponding to Its own.

498. No further changes can then take place; and in this condition the world will continue to exist through all of eternity's long waves, as they roll on one after the other in endless succession.

499. Thus have we been led to a landmark of time in the distant future, when the whole machinery of the *phenomenal* universe at last shall have run down;—when, so to speak, the universe has sunk to rest—into persistent death.—When all the darkened suns and stars are cast* in one great cosmic shell—long after this gay earth and all its sister planets, plunging beneath into the sun, have been consumed with incandescent heat.—

500. Contemplating upon the coming of such events, the reflecting mind may ask: to what purpose has been all this onward striving and struggling, this agony and suffering of hosts of good men to promote progress, if all these acquisitions and grand results by the coming waves of time are to be swept away? The answer to this interrogatory may be given in a future essay.

---

* As in founding or casting.

SECTION X.

---

501. SUNBEAMS. The heat-lineïts of the surface region of the sun radiate, enormously crowded, from thence rapidly into universal space as solar rays or *sun-beams.* And as our hand is turned to the rays of the sun, it is touched by the whirling heat-lineïts which, not long since, were yet attached to some gaseous particle of our great luminary.

502. The sun-beam, like other radiant heat, when freely traversing interstellar space, does not raise the temperature of the latter, except when met by sun beams streaming from other fixed stars or suns in an exact opposite direction. If even so near as, say, ten million miles from the sun a hollow pyramidal non conducting screen could be fixed so as to have its apex directed against the sun, in order to throw his rays aside, and a thermometer be placed behind, inside the screen, and its temperature examined, it would, no doubt, be found of a very inferior degree of heat, less perhaps than 200° F. below freezing point (331).

503. But the temperature will be a very different and much higher one in the inside space of the pyramidal screen, if the latter be turned so as to have its open base directed toward the sun. In this case the heat-lineïts will be arrested in their translatory motion and assume the whirling motion, and thereby make the mercury of the thermometer rise considerably.

503[1]. Much has been said about the waste of the sun's heat, only one part in 230,000,000 is being received by the planets. Yet this supposed immense loss of heat will after all be found to be no utter waste, because on further reflection it may easily be conceived, how the total amount of radiant heat from all the suns of the universe must necessarily give to interstellar space, i. e. to the linearium, a certain temper ; in this way : that every planet and other celestial orb, by continually meeting and stopping heat-rays which dart in an opposite direction to the course of such an orb, receives a certain amount of heat from this universal web and weft of heat-rays, no matter whatever direction that orb or body may move in.

504. Heat-lineïts in being intercepted, and having reached at last a certain degree, become very much crowded, and their effort to go to places of *less* heat is increased to such an extent, that they escape as fast as they are received.

505. REPELLING ACTION OF SUN-BEAMS. As heat-lineïts exert motive power in going from a place of more crowded heat to a place of less heat, and as they are always more or less accompanied by detached polarized lineïts, it follows that in the neighborhood of the sun where the lineïts of the sun beams are enormously crowded, the sun's repelling force must also be very considerable; and this seems to be strongly corroborated by the fact, that the tails of comets actually experience the effect of such a thrusting force in being repelled, as was observed in Halley's comet in 1835, and others.

506. HEAT DISENGAGED BY PLANETS IN MOVING ALONG THEIR ORBITS. Let yFxH, fig. 6, be the planetary orbit. Suppose the planet within a fortnight's time to move by tangential force alone, from *B* to *c*, if there was no centripetal force at S to act upon it; and from *B* to *m* by centripetal force alone in the same length of time if it was not affected by tangential force. If both the tangential and the centripetal forces were impelling the planet simultaneously, it would at the end of the fortnight be in *C* instead of *c*. Now if it be found that the resultant *BC* is less than *Bc*, it shows that a part of the tangential force has been lost, and this loss will be in proportion as *BC* is shorter than *Bc*; if it be found that the resultant is greater than the tangent, as for instance *gi* greater than *gh*, then it shows that the tangential force has been increased. Taking *x* to be aphelion, *y* perihelion, and applying the parallelogram of forces all round the planet's orbit, we find that from *x* by *H* to *y* the tangential force increases, from *y* by *F* to *x* the tangential force decreases.

507. From fig. 6 it is seen at once, that when the planet describes an elliptic orbit, the motion will not be uniform, but will be, as indicated in fig. 6, for each succeeding $\frac{1}{26}$ of its annual time [i. e. for each fortnight], going the course as indicated by the arrows. 1) With regard to the different degrees of efficiency of the centripetal force (gravitation) to accelerate or to retard the planet, we find the points of perihelion and aphelion *y* and *x* to be the only two places which in regard to situation correspond to the curve of a circle, consequently there is only in these two places of the orbit a uniform motion, no increase nor decrease of orbitual velocity. 2) If we take notice of the arches passed by the planet in equal times, we find from *x* by G to *y* the velocity of the planet all the time to increase, from *y* by *F* to *x* all the time to decrease, greatest in *y*, least in *x*. 3) Taking notice of the angles of projection *SB*1, *SC*2, *SD*3, *&c.*, we find, if the whole orbit were divided into exceedingly many small arches, the angle *Sxz* to be a right angle, further on the angles of projection to decrease until we get to some place between *G* and *H*, where the angles are the smallest. From *H* towards *A* and *D* they increase and are largest in some place between *D* and *L*; from *L* the angles of projection perceptibly decrease again until we get round by way of *x* to the smallest angle between *G* and H. Besides the right angle at *x* we should find another right angle at *y*. We find also that where the smallest angle of projection is, there is also the greatest effect of acceleration produced, i. e. the velocity is increased fastest in equal times, viz: between *G* and *H*; and again, where the largest angle of projection is, there is the greatest effect of retardation produced, as between *D* and *L*. 4) Applying the rules as laid down in §420–430, with regard to storing up velocity-lineïts and the evolution of heat-lineïts, in bodies moving against the counteracting streams of gravitation-cosmolineæ, we find that soon after the aphelion *x* has been passed, *heat ceases* to be evolved and velocity-lineïts begin to be stored up. Between *G* and *H* most velocity-lineïts are gained in equal times; in *y* the storing up of velocity-lineïts ceases and the evolution of heat-lineïts begins; between *C* and *L* the *most heat*-lineïts are evolved in equal times. From thence less and less heat-lineïts are evolved until the planet has passed *x*, where no more heat is set free. With regard to our own planet, the greatest evolution of heat in the earth ought to take place during the months of March, April, May. But the evolution of heat begins already with the 21st of December and ends with the 21st of June. 5) The value of the centripetal force for the different places of the orbit decreases and increases from fortnight to fortnight in the ratio of the lines *Cc*, *Dd*, *Ee*, *&c.*

In the motion of a planet through its orbit we have another case verifying the mechanical law: "a body alternately accelerated and retarded, so as to be brought back to its original speed, performs work by means of its retardation," exactly equal in amount to the attached velocity-lineïts producing its acceleration, but here this work is rendered in the shape of *heat* evolved (424).

508. We find if we attentively consult fig. 6, that from aphelion to perihelion the resultants G H, gi, etc., have compared with the tangent, *gained* in length, hence here the velocity-lineïts have gone to increase the planet's speed. But from perihelion to aphelion the resultants CD, EF, etc., have, compared with the tangent, *lost* in length; thus as the planet's speed actually decreased, many velocity-lineïts of the tangent must have disengaged themselves, and they could only have appeared again in the shape of heat-lineïts. These in heat converted velocity-lineïts are only those that were during the *planet's* motion of nearing to the sun stored up, that is, during its orbitual fall or descent. The greater the eccentricity of the planet's orbit, the greater will be the amount of heat evolved by the atoms of the planet in its *ascending* career from perihelion to aphelion.

509. Besides the falling of the planet from the aphelion to the perihelion, fig. 6, which we may term the *orbitual* fall, there is a fall of another kind presented to our consideration, viz: the fall through all the different circumferencial angles of its orbit, which fall appertains alike to the circle as well as to the ellipsis, and which we may term the *tangential* fall. In fig. 6, we plainly see that there is along the whole orbit a continual falling from the tangent, for instance, d′ c′ of the equilateral triangle c′ d′ a. Yet by all this falling the planet, after having completed its annual course, shows not the least gain of tangential force or orbitual velocity from what it had a year ago; and as moreover the planet after all this falling during one year, did not get in its average distance any nearer the centre of attraction than it was one year ago, it follows that all the velocity-lineïts added to the tangential force of the planet by the fall of the latter, were immediately and instantly evolved again, because of the planet's course going during all that time somewhat against the gravitation-stream, that impels the planet towards the sun.* These evolved velocity-lineïts can re-appear only in the shape of heat (§352) in every monit or atom of the planet gradually and continually, but sometimes more, at other times less, if the orbit be an ellipsis. In a perfectly circular orbit the evolution of heat will be uniform throughout the whole circle, and the quantity of heat evolved through any arch of the circle will be to that evolved through the whole circle as the angle subtending the arch is to 360 degrees of an angular subtension.

510. If the same planet has its orbit at half the distance from S, (fig. 6,) the quantity of evolved heat in the planet during a complete circuit will be four times greater than in its first orbit, i. e. always inversely as the squares of the distances. This holds good both for circular as for elliptical orbits. For the latter, however, the heat of the *orbitual* and that of the

---

*If the centre of attraction could have gone along parallelly with the tangent of the planet's starting point, and kept equal pace with the motion of the planet, then the latter would have been obliged to draw continually nearer to the centre of attraction, or rather have an actual fall upon it, no matter how great the tangential force might be.

tangential fall must be taken separate. In a body coursing round the sun, very near the latter, the evolution of heat must be enormous.

511. Every particle of the whole earth, from centre to circumference, thus evolves heat of its own. How much the quantity of this heat amounts to with regard to our planet while going through its annual course, is not beyond the possibility of calculation, but such a calculation I will leave to others.

512. A CAUSE FOR THE ACTION OF EARTHQUAKES AND VOLCANOES. That portion of the heat which in the above manner is set free or evolved at a comparatively small distance below the earth's surface, is gradually conducted upwards and escapes into the atmosphere, or as radiant heat into free space. But the heat evolved at greater depths will be conducted away slower than it is being evolved, and hence it will accumulate and raise still higher the original enormous temperature already there existing, until attached to the molecules of steam or some other gaseous body, the latter forces a passage for itself through the earth's crust, carrying along molten lava and giving rise to earthquakes and volcanoes.

513. Besides the heat continually evolved during the earth's orbitual motion there is, no doubt, a great amount of the intense heat that originally, at the time of the agglomeration of the earth's particles into a sphere, was disengaged by the condensation of its matter, yet shut up in the earth's interior, and keeps the latter in an intensely heated liquid state.

514. The secular inequalities in the moon's motion compared with eclipses observed 2000 years ago, have proved that the length of time which the earth needs in revolving once around its axis, has within the last twenty centuries not decreased even by the one-hundredth part of a second. This proves that the velocity of the earth's rotation has not increased within the last 2000 years, which it certainly would have done, had the mean temperature of the earth perceptibly decreased; for in that case its volume would have contracted accordingly. We are therefore justified in believing that the mean temperature of the earth at present is *not less*, even by so small a quantity as $\frac{1}{170}$ of a degree Cent. than it was 2000 years ago.

515. On the other hand, history teaches that from time to time within the last 2000 years many eruptions of volcanoes have occurred, and in more recent times we find accounts of innumerable instances of steam of immense tension, hot gas, heated air, boiling water, and incandescent liquid masses of melted rock, having been issued from below the earth's surface in continuous streams for weeks and months together;—the *permanent* hot springs not to be forgotten, which with steady flow carry off heat incessantly. And we may well be astonished at the thought, how immensely great the amount of heat must have been, that forced its way through miles in thickness of solid layers of rock by making thousands of fissures and apertures on dry land and still more beneath the sea, during all this long period of twenty centuries.

516. It is not so much the great eruption of lava by the volcanoes, as it is chiefly the continued and incessant escape of *steam*, even from inactive craters and from innumerable fissures of the earth's crust that robs the interior of enormous amounts of heat; for we know that to form steam of 212° F. from water of the same temperature nearly a thousand degrees of heat are necessary. Every drop of water as it sinks down to the heated masses of the interior of the earth, is formed into steam [sometimes of immense tension] after having absorbed a very considerable amount of heat. This heat is lost forever to the interior of the earth as soon as the steam has reached the outside, and by just so much the earth's interior ought to have become cooler.

517. Now it may well be asked, if so much heat has been escaping from the depths of our planet, how is it that the mean temperature of the earth did not, in the least, decrease thereby? The answer is: the earth must have received, in some way or other, as much heat as it had lost. But how, or in what manner did the earth receive the above amount of heat? Certainly not from the sun, for his heat penetrates but to very inconsiderable depths, and may be said to radiate into celestial space again, so that it does not even raise the mean temperature of the earth's surface-crust permanently from year to year. The only answer we can find to the last proposed question is, that the earth receives its new heat by and through the planet's motion along its orbit, as explained in preceding paragraphs.

518. That the interior of the earth constantly receives new accessions of heat in some way or other, seems to be corroborated by a most remarkable phenomenon which has been observed near the island of San Miguel, one of the Azores or Western Islands, namely: the periodical lifting up of the bottom of the sea occurring at *regular intervals* of 80 *or* 90 *years* [June 1638, December 1719, June 1811,] as if thereby to show that it required just so many years to gather strength of heat wherewith to do the lifting.

519. It is by no means improbable, if the texture and cohesion of a planet's crust be so tenacious as not to allow the formation of apertures and fissures, that the gases generated under increasing temperature and shut up within the planet, may by constantly accumulated heat, be stimulated to such enormous tension as to break with most gigantic force the consolidated crust into pieces, either few or many, as may happen.

520. It needs only the simple condition of totally shutting off all exit of heat by the solid crust or shell, in order to make the latter burst and break at last. If the shutting off be complete, there is no power strong enough to avert the catastrophe; for new heat is here evolved, not only from beneath, but both from beneath and from *within* the solid shell, as well as from the planet's fiery core itself.

521. Nothing can stop this evolution of heat, which is *bound to go on* constantly, as long as the planet moves in its orbit. Century after century, day and night, yet more especially so through one-half of the year, the elastic fluids gather pushing strength with every second of time until liberated.

522. Hence there is nothing absurd or unnatural in the supposition, that the so-called *asteroids* between Mars and Jupiter are the fragments of a planet that once existed between these two planets.* Neither is it strange of being forced to the conviction, that eventually the bursting into fragments may be the fate of all such of the celestial spheres as are possessed of orbitual motion around a central primary and which at the same time are from the latter so far off, as to be allowed to form by cooling a stout and solid crust outside. More strongly yet is this conviction impressed upon us if we also take into consideration the important law (322): *If in a given compass of space the number of heat-lineïts be doubled, then their whirling energy and pressure outward will be four-fold, that is as the* SQUARES *of the number of heat-lineïts.*

523. It is also a significant fact, that nearly ⅞ of all the active volcanoes of the earth are to be found upon extensive fissures running along the litto-

---

* Judging from the shape and nature of their orbits, these fragments can never have originated from excessive centrifugal force of rotation, as assumed by some.

rals of the western coast of North and South America, and the eastern and southeastern coast of Asia, *forming a maximum circle nearly bisecting the globe.* The timely opening of its natural safety valves, which we find in the volcanoes distributed along this circle—very probably, at some time or other, saved the earth from being rent asunder. Let all the vents for subterranean heat be stopped at once, and the growing giant of pressure would not be long in executing its terrible work of explosion.

524. The many fearful earthquakes of the last few years, and especially the recent* simultaneous disturbances of the earth's crust in Japan, and in Oaxaca, Mexico, places situated upon the great fissure just spoken of, afford grounds for believing that there is pent up an agency throughout the interior of the earth *incessantly recuperating its force,* and is equal to its aim wholesale explosion of the crust that in vain tries to confine it.

525. Heat evolved by the moon. What has been said in the preceding chapters about the evolution of heat by the earth in its orbit around the sun, holds good also with regard to the earth's steady companion, the moon, in her annual path around the sun. Yet more than this, while the moon revolves once around the sun, she is at the same time forced to bend her course a little more than twelve times around the earth. Throughout this course the earth's gravitation makes the moon fall in a similar manner as the sun's gravitation makes the earth fall.

526. From this it follows that the moon evolves in proportion to her mass a great deal more heat than the earth does. And if the moon were surrounded by a heat-retaining atmosphere, the moon's heat would increase to an enormous degree. Another heat-ameliorating circumstance besides the absence of such an atmosphere upon the nearer hemisphere of the moon, we find in her numerous immense volcanic craters which serve as so many vents for the escape of heat.

527. And if, besides this, we take into consideration the fact [geometrically demonstrated] that the moon's centre of gravity is eight miles further off from us than her centre of circumference, or in other words: that the average level of the central surface part of that hemisphere of the moon which is exposed to our view, is sixteen miles higher than the remotest part of the other hemisphere, it appears still more astounding to behold at such a high level, gigantic mountains towering 2 or 3 miles higher still, topped with *volcanic vents* at these excessive heights. Now, if in such high places already so many apertures for the escape of heat exist, how many more of a lower class may there be expected to exist on the other side of the moon, where the general level of its middle surface is 16 miles lower, and where the obstructions to the heat's exit must necessarily be far less formidable. All these considerations tend to show that, in proportion to size of the two spheres, the upheaving forces must be vastly more energetic and violent in the moon than in the earth.

528. On account of the more abundant supply of heat from below, the remoter half of the moon may even during its protracted nights enjoy a comfortable temperature conducive to the well being and thriving existence of organized beings. And if an atmosphere of considerable density existed on the remoter hemisphere, the hottest and most uncomfortable region there during its protracted day, would be that part which is most remote from the earth; because this part being the nearest to the centre of gravity, i. e. the lowest, the atmosphere there would be densest, besides lying in the most vertical path of the sun. However, in this region we might expect to find an

* May 11th–13th, 1870.

extensive ocean [if there be, as is very probable, any water on that side of the moon's surface] from which an excessive evaporation is then bound to supply an abundance of rain clouds and rain to the concentric, more elevated rim of this great circular sea.

On this same exterior hemisphere, the wide and elevated lunar rim reaching with its outside margin as far as the visible circumference of the moon, may be supposed to have its inner concentric margin 3 miles, and its outer border at least 8 miles further off from the moon's centre of gravity than is the moon's lowest surface level from the same centre; the rim gradually rising from the shores of the thus supposed ocean to an elevation of five miles, the height of any existing mountains not taken into account.

From the extraordinary high position of our side of the moon above the moon's centre of gravity, it is evident that even if a lunar atmosphere, pressing upon the moon's more distant hemisphere, be as dense as the earth's, we can never expect to find any signs of this atmosphere on the only side of the moon ever presented to our view.

529. That a fluid nucleus and a hard consolidated crust embracing that nucleus, existed contemporaneously together in the moon in times past, and hence do so now, may be inferred from the very fact that the moon has its centre of gravity in its remoter hemisphere; for if the moon had always been in a solid state, the heavier matter which obviously has been carried by centrifugal force to where it is now, could never have got there. Originally the steadiness of the moon was the cause of her eccentricity of gravity, the latter is not necessarily the cause of the former.

530. Railroad train, and the most ultimate cause or power of its motion. In the first place we find the force to be in the expanding steam that is pushing the piston of the cylinder. But what drives apart the particles of steam? Answer: The whirling [Versatile Activity possessing] heat-lineïts that are set free in the burning of the wood or coal, set free in the combining process of the carbon of the fuel with the oxygen of the atmosphere.

531. But where did the carbon get the heat-lineïts from, which it held locked up so long? Answer: from the rays of heat emanating from the sun the heat-lineïts have been taken and shut up in the organs of vegetation under the influence of light and the parenchyma of the plant.

532. But where did the sun get the heat-lineïts from? Answer: from the heavy particles of solar matter that, first descending and afterwards ascending, rush in long trains from the centre of the sun to its circumference, having first fallen towards that centre from the sun's circumference on the side opposite to where they come up and *thereby acquired velocity-lineïts.* By retardation in the upward motion, velocity-lineïts were evolved and thus converted into heat-lineïts.

533. If the heavy particles of solar matter got their velocity-lineïts in consequence of their falling towards the sun's centre, what was it that caused them thus to fall? Answer: the gravitation-cosmolineæ which are constantly streaming towards that centre push them along, and from these same cosmolineæ the heavy particles took the velocity-lineïts. (268).

534. We have, however, not yet arrived at the ultimate *cause* or *causes* of the motion of the railroad train, for we may still ask: what makes the cosmolineæ move, and why do they flow in the direction of the sun's *centre?* The latter part of this question regarding the centre, is answered in §584–587. The first part of the question, what makes the cosmolineæ move? may be answered thus: 1st, the *striking aside* the foremost lineïts of the cosmolineæ by the rotary monits of the sun's matter, thereby producing gaps between the monit and the free end of the cosmolinea; 2d, the *uniting* effort in the ends of the lineïts of the cosmolinea to join endwise, as well as the same kind of Effort situate in the free end of the monit's radii, and thus to close again the gaps just previously produced,—make the cosmolinea move.

535. Here then, we have come to the end of our inquiries and find, that the ultimate causes of the motion of the rail-road train are the two primitive effort-exerting powers of *striking* off and of *joining*, that is, the power of **Versatile Activity** and that of **End-unition**,* which are at all times at work in the sun, the first in the sun's monit's (atoms), the second principally in the cosmolineæ, but also in the monit's radii. And in fact, these two powers are the ultimate two causes of all translatory as well as rotatory motion. And as there cannot be any further cause for the *most ultimate and simple* principle in nature, we need not seek for one.

536. Remarkable connection between distant phenomena. What a wondrous connection between distant phenomena do we find here. The sun's matter consists of monits, and these monits by *spinning about their respective axes*, and acting by means of a certain medium upon other monits,—by pulling invisible threads (the cosmolineæ), thus actually furnish the force which indirectly, and after having once been converted into heat, propels the long train of cars with thundering noise along the iron rails laid on the surface of the earth, in places over ninety million of miles from the sun.

537. And in most cases, the *spinning* that produced the motion of the cosmolineæ from which sprung the very heat that now moves the train, has ceased a fifty, a hundred, or even thousands of years ago,—the heat meanwhile having been kept locked up in the wood or in the coal, and man is invited to help himself from the rich stores thus laid up.

---

* The same two powers that are at the root of all the motions caused by gravitation. (v. 166).

SECTION XI.

MUSCULAR POWER.

538. Preliminary remarks. The organization of the animal body has for its object the accomplishment of two most important processes.

1st. To keep itself at a certain constant temperature independent of all caloric influences from without.

2d. To store up within itself a certain amount of energy or force, and by it to execute muscular motion.

539. In order to obtain object No. 1, the body has first to generate and then to distribute a certain amount of heat within itself. The process of generating this heat by oxydation, chiefly of the carbon derived from the animal's food, is accomplished in the blood; and the distribution of this heat throughout the body is done by the blood's circulation.

540. The following are the principal parts of the animal's body that are needed to co-operate in generating and distributing animal heat, viz: the organs of the lungs, the muscles of the chest for the alternate expansion and contraction of the chest, the heart, the blood, the blood-vessels, and all the organs for digesting food and preparing chyle.

541. In order to obtain object No. 2, (538,) the body has first to convert a part of the heat that was produced within the blood, into velocity-lineïts, called *muscular* energy when acting in the muscle. For this purpose, and for that of spending these velocity-lineïts (muscular energy) it requires the whole nervous as well as the muscular system.

542. The muscles together with the nervous system, including the brain and spinal marrow, may be said to be a contrivance or apparatus of the animal body for the conversion of heat-lineïts of the blood into *velocity*-lineïts, and for keeping the latter in store, subject to any call or requisition from the muscle, and perhaps, from the substance of the brain also.

543. In the boiler of a steam-engine, heat-lineïts are stored up to push outwardly in all directions the molecules of water, and to execute the requisite mechanical work whenever desired by the engineer to do so. The heat-lineïts, however, that are set free in the blood of a living body and carried to the muscle could not be applied directly as in the steam engine, nor in a similar manner, when needed, because a surplus of heat could not, without causing much suffering and even death to the body, be accumulated in sufficient great quantities, and stored away subject to the arbitrary orders of the will.

544. Even if it were possible that heat-lineïts could without injury to the animal body be stored up in the latter in quantities equivalent to all the mechanical work required, the unmodified heat-lineïts never could execute proper motion by means of the muscle, for the muscle's organization is wholly unfit for such a purpose. It is arranged and adapted to spend velocity-lineïts, and not heat-lineïts.

545. Velocity-lineits, representing muscular energy, can be accumulated in great quantities in the animal body without injury to the body, by being attached in any requisite number to the molecules circulating through the nervous filaments and thereby giving to the molecules merely an *increase of speed; and this superabundance of speed or motion then becomes the reservoir* from which muscular energy (velocity-lineïts of the muscle) may at any time be drawn in quantities to suit.

546. Fig. 10 may serve to make these operations more intelligible to the reader. Let *m* represent the substance of a muscle, *b* the substance of the brain, *t f* a filament of the nerve of motion, *g h* a filament of the nerve of sensation, *n* a blood vessel.

547. In the first place, there is incessantly flowing through the channel *f t* from *f* to *m*, a stream of ordinate cosmolineæ. The flow of the cosmolineæ towards *m* is caused by the rotary monits of the muscle *m*, in the same manner as gravitation-cosmolineæ are caused to flow towards a planet. The *detached* or *polarized* lineïts which are struck off from the cosmolineæ by the monits at *m*, take isolated their way through *g h* to *b*, where they are connected again into continuous cosmolineæ. These cosmolineæ consist of *ordinate* lineïts.

548. In the second place, the channels *f t* and *g h* are abundantly supplied with nervous molecules to be pushed along, which latter at the same time serve as vehicles of velocity-lineïts for the muscle. In their course from *f* to *t* these molecules receive their velocity-lineïts from the cosmolineæ flowing towards *m m*, and there in the muscle yield up more or less of these velocity-lineïts causing motion of muscle. The molecules, now possessing fewer velocity-lineïts, enter the channel *g h* more slowly.

549. In channel *g h*, however, there are no continuous cosmolineæ to push the molecules along, but instead of being pushed by cosmolineæ they are now pushed by the heat-lineïts, that come from the blood vessel *n* and go towards *h*. These heat-lineïts in moving the molecules, are at once attached to the latter and thereby converted into velocity-lineïts. Thus heat vanishes to manifest itself in quite another form, viz : that of velocity.

550. On both ways then, the nervous molecules receive velocity-lineïts, on their way from *g* to *h* and *b*, and from *b* to *t* and *m*,—but they receive them from two very different sources. In going from *g* to *b*, the molecules receive them from the newly introduced heat-lineïts of the blood ; in going from *b* to *m*, they receive them from the cosmolineæ of the nervous filament *f t*, as in the falling of bodies.

551. But those velocity-lineïts which the nervous molecules receive from *g* to *b*, are yielded up on the inside lining of the brain compartments as heat-lineïts, which are by Synduction instantaneously bereft of their rotary whirling motion by being made parallel, and then in the same manner as detached polarized lineïts annexed to the continuous cosmolineæ flowing from *f* to *t*, to which they in this way furnish a steady supply of lineïts, so much needed to restore their loss when the muscle is active.

552. The above process is necessary for the reinforcement of the cosmolineæ in *f t*, because those lineïts of the latter that have fallen out of the ranks, and in the shape of velocity-lineïts gone over to the moving nervous molecules, and afterwards have been spent by the muscle to perform mechanical work, are lost for ever to the cosmolineæ of *f t*, which thus are always in need of a steady supply.

553. The detached polarized lineïts which within the muscle are struck off from the nervous cosmolineæ *f t* that enter the muscle at *t*, go along *g h*, constituting what may be called the *magnetic* or *electric current*, which is likewise deprived of its vibrating motion and annexed to the nervous cosmolineæ *f t*, thus always adding to the latter at *f* just as much as they lose at *t*.

554. The muscle then is a machine not only for continually setting the nervous cosmolineæ in motion, but also for the proper stewardship of the very velocity-lineïts by the spending of which their (the lineït's) effect becomes manifest, in the performance of mechanical work.

555. Thus the nerves with the brain and muscle constitute the principal parts of a system nearly complete in itself, and together with the parts that furnish the heat they represent a world in miniature; for here we see the same operations carried out on a small scale, which (if we keep our mind's eye open) we see performed on a more simple, yet immensely more magnificent scale in what we may call the mechanism of the celestial system. The operations of the nervous system and its arrangements are, however, of a much higher order.

556. DIFFERENCE BETWEEN GRAVITATING COSMOLINEÆ AND NERVOUS COSMOLINEÆ. Towards the sun and other celestial and planetary orbs the cosmolinæ flow *converging* from all directions as gravitation cosmolineæ—towards the muscle the ordinate cosmolineæ flow *parallel* inside the ducts of nervous filaments, and thus become nervous cosmolineæ.

557. If necessity calls for vigorous movements of the muscle, then the velocity-bearing molecules of the nervous filaments in *f t* arriving at *m*, transmit freely and rapidly all their velocity-lineïts until they are more or less completely divested of them, and now accumulating, move very sluggishly at *g*, while at *h* there will be a scarcity of molecules and a lack of heat-lineïts. There may be cases in which the velocity-lineïts are not to be had in sufficient quantities even if the blood should furnish its *usual* quota of heat-lineïts. The blood in such cases is obliged to furnish more, and can do it by a more lively circulation, by increased respiration and a more complete digestion of food.

558. When the blood has been drained of its store of heat-lineïts it can, of course, give no supply to the nervous filaments, the latter then cannot furnish any more velocity-lineïts to muscle *m*, and thus one of the principal sources of motion in the muscle is cut off.

559. ON WHAT THE VIGOR OF THE MUSCLE DEPENDS. Each of the cosmolineœ in *f t* represents an efficient medium to dispense velocity-lineïts, and the more of such cosmolineæ there exist in the nervous filament, the greater will be the possibility for vigorous muscular action.

560. The more abundant and crowded the monits are in muscle *m*, that is, the more compact and heavier the muscle is, the more energetic may the cosmolineæ be made to flow from *b* by *f t* to *m*, provided the action of Synduction in *b* to be proportionally vigorous.

561. Hence the muscular vigor and its endurance depends:

1. On the number of rotary monits in the muscle, that is, the muscle ought to be large, compact and heavy.
2. On the number of cosmolineæ in the filaments of the nerve of motion *f t*, which are to be pulled upon by the rotary monits of the muscle.
3. On the number of nervous molecules to be sped along the channels of the nervous filaments by the cosmolineæ of the nerves.

4. On the number of heat-lineïts furnished by the blood to the nerves of sensation.

5. On the prompt action of Synduction in the brain.

562. No. 1 and No. 4 of the preceding conditions indicate that there necessarily ought to take place an augmentation, and occasionally a renewal of the monits of muscular tissue by nitrogenous substances derived from the blood ; as from the same source, viz : the blood, are also taken the heat-lineïts to make good the waste of velocity-lineïts. The blood therefore has to furnish not only the pulling monits but also, to a great extent the medium that is to be pulled.

563. The blood gets the monits for the muscle from the *nitrogenous* substances of assimilated food ; the lineïts for the nerves it receives in the shape of heat-lineïts from the oxydation of *non*-nitrogenous substances, such as starch, fat, sugar, &c., and not from the oxydation of the muscle, as has been asserted formerly. Experiments have proved that not all the heat developed in the blood of living man is expended in keeping up the normal temperature of his body, but that a great part of it is spent in producing mechanical effect, muscular work done.

564. VELOCITY-LINEÏTS LEAVING THE MUSCLE AS MUSCULAR ENERGY. The velocity-lineïts of the nervous molecules after having been yielded up to the muscles, say for instance, to those of the arm and hand, proceed from the latter to the object that is to be lifted, pulled, or pushed, and perform the intended mechanical work. In throwing a ball, the velocity-lineïts go from the hand that flings it to the ball.

But when a muscle is exerted and is contracted in vain to move an obstacle or weight, then the nerve velocity-lineïts, being unable to attach themselves to the obstacle or weight, are obliged to evolve as heat from *within the muscle.* Suppose a man, in trying to lift one end of a heavy beam from the ground up to a platform, works for three minutes with all his strength and at last succeeds by unusual exertion to lift it a couple of inches, when the beam suddenly slips from his hands. He goes at it again, and toils and exerts his strength for several minutes longer, when he succeeds to raise it once more to the height of an inch, but down the beam goes again, he still strives and exerts himself with no better success until he has spent so much of muscular force that he is completely exhausted. His force is gone, and he has to rest to get strength again in his muscles and nerves. Would you say, this man did not work because he did not succeed in his aim ? What has become of his muscular force thus employed in vain ; is it stored up in the beam? By no means. It was evolved inside the muscle as heat, and left the muscle either as latent heat with the moist vapor issuing from the skin, or otherwise as free radiant heat. That part of the muscular force which actually lifted the beam left as heat also, but by way of the beam as the latter ascended, while the beam in *falling* to the ground thereby acquired force from quite another source, viz : from gravitation, which force on being stopped by the ground was changed into heat likewise.

Ultimate agencies of all the mechanical, chemical, and structural phenomena.

565. Changes and modifications, severing and re-uniting, levelling to the dust and rearing heaven-ward again, are performances going on unceasingly, —and are constantly to be met with in nature's ever varying scenes.

Amid all these changes there are certain things which have been and shall remain eternally the same with regard to number and quantity. These are, 1st, the immaterial lineït, it being the ultimate *substance* of which every thing in the universe consists. 2d, the universe's three ultimate primary powers. to wit: End-unition, Synduction, and Versatile Activity.

566. A general review of the contents of these pages leads to the conclusion, that the primitive power of VERSATILE ACTIVITY possessed by heat-lineïts,* and by the lineïts of the *monits* (a *material* combination) together with the two other primitive powers END-UNITION and SYNDUCTION possessed by all the other remaining lineïts which are never constituents of monits, but on the contrary, are the constituents of *immaterial* combinations, viz: of the cosmolineæ, the cosmo-velo, and the central convolutions—these three combinations together making up what may be called the macrocosmic-soul—are at the foundation of all mechanical as well as chemical phenomena of the universe. Both parties, the vivacious power of the monits of matter and of heat, on the one hand, and the two powers of the *immaterial* combinations, on the other hand, are perpetually and incessantly busy. The one set, viz: Versatile Activity, violently breaks the *continuity*, and forcibly scatters the detached lineïts of the cosmolineæ,—the other, viz: Synduction, at the cosmo-velo silently and gently directs the irregularly dispersed lineïts into the proper track,—and the third, viz: End-unition joins them to the cosmolineæ and again restores continuity.

567. Monits and lineïts are small, yet they are many. By their immensity in number and minuteness they may well bewilder the human mind; but when these innumerable little activities act together in unison, and the effect resulting therefrom is viewed in its full power, as it scatters every thing before it, the mind is struck dumb with awe. In tracing any mechanical or chemical work that is performed anywhere, on earth as well as at the most distant verge of the universe, no matter how astonishingly great that work may be, it must after all be accredited: 1) to the for ever vivacious unruly power of Versatile Activity residing in the monits of matter [as well as in the heat-lineït and the polarized-lineït] and 2d) to the lineït's ever-busy End-unition and Synduction residing in the central convolution, in the cosmo-velo, and the cosmolineæ, all three together making up the macro-cosmic soul.

568. Is it the sun, or is it the vegetable cell of the leaves, that performs all the work in the following phenomena? has been a subject of dispute: We behold the deposits of rich alluvial soils. The meadows sprout, the herbs and grasses grow and blossom; the horses grazing there derive their strength from these. Using this strength they pull the mowing machine, cut down the tiny stalks, and gather the fodder for future use.—Crops of cereals and fruit of every kind, to serve as sustenance of muscular vigor for man and beast, are gathered from the teeming earth by labor's hardy sons. Hills and valleys are covered by forests, ready as fuel to yield up dynamic energy to drive machinery in a thousand different ways. Textile fibres are furnished by plants for the clothing of man, while trees yield timber for the structure of houses. By decomposition of carbonic acid gas, the atmosphere is made fit to be inhaled; we see even the climate of countries change with regard to distribution of moisture and heat.

569. In beholding all these and many more of the most important results in nature, some writers impute them to the action and workings of the vegetable leaf and say: "The *leaf* does it all." While one writer ascribes it all to the leaf, another says: "The *sun* does it all." But strictly speaking, neither the sun with all his marvellous power and splendor, nor the leaf with all its intricate and wonderful structure can do anything of the kind

* And it may be added: the polarized lineïts also.

without some deep-seated *powers* within them. By going into a more close and critical examination of the subject we shall find, that the leaf is but the apparatus, inside whose cells* the great operations for storing up heat and for manufacturing digestible substances are carried on by two sets of primitive Powers: Versatile Activity on the one hand, End-unition and Synduction on the other. These same eternal powers that do the work within the living cells of the leaf, are also acting perpetually in and through the monits and lineïts of which the sun, that effulgent centre of heat and light, is made up. The sun is but the grand and magnificent apparatus to which the cosmolineæ are streaming, in order to be worked up into light inciting heat-lineïts, to be sent abroad for the benefit of planets teeming with life, that otherwise would be for ever benighted and cold.

570. It is by virtue of the primitive powers End-unition and Synduction of the macrocosmic soul, by their Efforts, of joining again and directing into the channels of union what the power of Versatile Activity severed and scattered, that all the beneficial agencies of heat, light, and motion spring into existence;—that, so to speak, the world is stirred up from its lethargy into agitation and life and action, and that thus it continues to be what it is—a world of phenomena.

571. The functions of Versatile Activity are those of an attacking and demolishing power. Versatile Activity is distributed among innumerable myriads of monits and heat-lineïts. Though these power-portions are small, they are formidable in numbers, with no other aim but that of entire, complete, eternal destruction of every thing that springs from harmonious *unition*. Yet, by their very attacks, they furnish under the gentle rule of the macrocosmic soul's Synduction and End-unition, inexhaustible opportunities for a directing and re-arranging reaction of the All-Intelligent, and thus become of most essential service in spite of themselves.

572. Both sets of power—Synduction and End-unition of the macrocosmic soul, on the one hand, and Versatile Activity of the monits of matter and of heat- and polarized-lineïts, on the other hand—are equally necessary to the maintenance of a material *busy world*. Both claim our most profound attention. The vivacious, unruly, versatile one is in so far beneficial

---

* THE ORGANIC CELL. There are among the seaweeds (or Algæ) plants consisting of a single cell. With them the cell constitutes the entire plant, a true individual, complete in itself, performing all the functions essential to vegetation, imbibing its food through its permeable walls, assimilating this food in its interior, and converting the organizable products first into materials of its own growth, and finally into new cells which thus become its progeny.

Here then, we have in the young vitally *active cell* (fig. 11, plate 4) a system complete in itself which, it may be said, is an apparatus worked and kept in operation by means of the same space-traversing lineïts of the universal medium, and the same three ultimate primitive powers: Versatile Activity, End-unition, and Synduction—that keep the machinery of the nervous system in motion, yea, the same that propel the wheelwork of the great universe itself.

And if in the great concave sphere, the universe of *all* material as well as immaterial things, we recognize the macrocosm—in the diminutive, living, organic active *cell* we recognize the microcosm. Because what the cosmo-velo is to the former, the enveloping *cellulose* is to the cell; what the cosmic-core of the universe is to the universe, the *nucleus* (*or cytoblast*) is to the cell; and equally well do the *currents* that traverse the cell in various directions, and which appear to radiate from and return to the nucleus, and are not at all influenced in their movements by other cells from without, represent in miniature the system of streaming cosmolineæ of the great universe.

Thus the cytoblast, the cellulose, and the currents of the cell, together make up the *microcosmic soul*, just as the convolution, the cosmo-velo, and the cosmolineæ constitute the macrocosmic soul of the universe (131).

as it arouses by its tumultuous acts of destruction and disturbance a world that otherwise would lie dormant, into stir and bustle, and outward motion, and stimulates the macrocosmic soul's Synduction and End-unition into works of repairing, recomposing and reconstructing.

573. While Versatile Activities work hard to produce desolation, dismemberment and death—yet with Synduction and End-unition set against them—there is being silently modeled and shaped a world of creatures, and upheld, embraced and bound with invisible threads* the whole universe in regularity, order, and beauty.

574. Versatile Activities [both in the monits and in the heat-lineïts] are constantly engaged to destroy all continuity, to dissolve all association of matter as well as of force, to disintegrate all composition and structure, and to scatter even the very atoms and monits of what they destroy;—in short, they are working to counteract combination, union, and coherence of every kind.

575. Though all the Versatile Activities, which are constantly at work in innumerable myriads of monits and heat-lineïts, know no weariness nor rest, and never pause even for a moment, to muse over the wrecks strewn in their wake, yet they can never make dissolution prevail, for as long as Synduction and End-unition co-operate against them, and by means of meteoric streams our sun and other luminary spheres are enabled to produce light and heat, new forms arise from out the scattered particles of matter—and from countless millions of germs, as they give up their life in decomposition, new life and health expand.

576. Yet, in the course of untold ages to come, Versatile Activities will at last achieve—not the final dissolution and dispersion of all things—but the very opposite they aim at; they will achieve the universal consolidation of all matter, in pulling and gathering all bodies together, in causing all celestial orbs to sink and settle down around the cosmic-core, to make them stay there for ever. They will even succeed to put out the glorious light of sun and twinkling stars, and to "erect the standard there of ancient night"—yet, they can never bring stagnation into the macrocosmic soul's essential life, i. e. can never stop the circulating cosmolineæ, which they are themselves compelled† to pull—nor can they ever impair the sublime faculties of the All-Intelligent. Neither can Versatile Activity ever dissolve the ties‡ by which the monits are forced† to keep each other in bondage.

---

* Gravitation-cosmolineæ.

† By virtue of Versatile Activity's own nature.

‡ The gravitation-cosmolineæ.

SECTION XII.

Propositions with regard to gravitation.

577. Books on natural philosophy treat the subject of gravitation in a very brief and sometimes even in an erroneous manner. It was only after I had already finished this chapter on gravitation that I could get hold of Newton's *Principia.* All that I previously could gather from books about the laws of gravitation was :

1. That every particle of matter in the universe attracts every other particle.

2. That the energy of attraction is in proportion to the mass of the attracting body.

3. That the force of gravitation varies inversely as the squares of the distances.

4. A particle outside a homogeneous sphere is attracted the same as if all the matter of the sphere were collected in its centre.

578. Notwithstanding these drawbacks I was, simply by reflecting upon the properties of the cosmolineæ and those of the monits, enabled to announce the following twenty-four propositions :

579. PROP. 1. Every monit and molecule of matter does *incessantly* attract every other molecule and monit as well as any larger body at any given distance.*

580. PROP. 2. Every monit of matter is able to attract *simultaneously* in more than one direction with equal energy.—If a monit be surrounded by a number of other monits, all at the same distance from it, it attracts each of the surrounding monits with the same energy as it would if opposed to only one of them. Because every operative radius of the monit does, independent of all the other radii, its work of striking and pulling the cosmolineæ.

581. PROP. 3. The energy of a monit's [and molecule's] attraction at different distances from the monit [and molecule] is *inversely* as the squares of the distances. (v. §164).

582. PROP. 4. There is with regard to the energy of attraction, no difference between the individual monits; they all attract alike and with the same energy, (132).

583. PROP. 5. Hence the energy of attraction of any assemblage of monits, i. e., any mass of matter, is proportional to the number of monits of which that mass of matter consists (155, 156). Or : The attraction of gravitation of a body is proportional to the mass of its matter.

---

* This attraction, however, extending only indefinitely far, and not infinitely, because in nature there can be no power or force absolutely infinite.

584. In homogeneous spheres the attraction of gravitation is always directed towards the centre of the sphere. As every operative radius of the monit, in performing its work of striking the lineïts and pulling the cosmolineæ, does represent the whole strength of the monit in that very direction ; and as, moreover, in any spherical aggregation of monits one of the converging cosmolineæ for each monit has to pass through the centre of that sphere, it is clear that this centre will represent the whole number and pulling strength of all the monits contained in that sphere.

586. Hence to this central point will each traversing cosmolineæ, as it were, transfer and add the strain of its linea-gaps, and in proportion to the number of such traversing cosmolineæ augment and stimulate the effort for action of the power of End-unition in that very spot. There will, in other words, in every sphere in proportion to the number of its monits be a proportionate number of linea-gaps concentrated in the centre, and melted as it were, in one common intense desire for connecting lineït to lineït. To this central spot, as to a common distributing reservoir, will then converge equally the cosmolineæ from without, to be drawn upon by the sphere's individual monits from the same reservoir.

588. Propositions with regard to gravitation of spheres.*

Prop. 6. A particle of matter situated *outside* a sphere homogeneously filled with matter, is attracted as if all the monits of the whole sphere had their energies condensed in the sphere's centre, and from that single point exerted their combined attraction equally in all directions.

589. Because for each monit of the sphere there is *one* gravitation-cosmolinea being pulled to it from without the sphere, and *by way of the sphere's centre* (584–586) ; and to the full outside stream of the cosmolineæ, thus coming from all directions and flowing towards and into this centre, the aforesaid particle is incessantly exposed.

590. Prop. 6′. Two or more particles of matter situated around the same sphere in different places but at the same distance from the sphere's centre, are all attracted with *equal* energy, no matter on what side of the sphere they may be.

591. From fig. 5, plate 2, and from §586 it is clear that around a perfect sphere, all the streams of cosmolineæ going to supply the demand which is equally urgent in all directions at the centre, must in rushing towards the same exhibit *equal* energy everywhere at equal distance from that centre.

592. Prop. 7. Two or more particles of matter situated *outside* the same sphere, but at different distances from it, are attracted with energies, *inversely* proportional as the squares of the distances from the sphere's centre. [v. 164, and fig. 5, plate 2].

593. Prop. 8. Two or more particles of matter situated *within* a sphere homogeneously filled with matter are, when at different distances from its centre, attracted toward that centre with energies proportional to their distances from the centre.

594. Because a particle placed at b (fig. 13) within the solid sphere E will by the stream $a'c$ be pushed towards c with an energy equal to the whole attractive energy of E as being represented by radius $a'c$, from which, however, must be subtracted $a\,b$, the monits of which pull b towards a. Hence as $a'c$ is $= ac$,† and $ab = a'b$, we say : b will be attracted towards c with $a'c - ab$ or $a'c - a'b = bc$. In a similar way we find that d is attracted towards c with an energy equal to dc, therefore $b : d = bc : dc$.

---

* In some of these propositions we must be careful not to use promiscuously the words "body" and "particle" one for the other.

† The line $a\ c$ being in fact a straight line.

595. Prop. 9. [v. fig. 12]. A solid sphere's attraction upon a particle placed on the summit of an isolated steep protuberance of the sphere, is to the attraction upon the mean surface-level, inversely as the squares of distance of these two places from the sphere's centre, just as if the protuberance bp was void of matter.

596. Let $a\ a\ a$ (fig. 12) represent the mean surface-level of the sphere, then will ac very nearly express the common resultant energy with which centre c exerts its pulling influence equally all around at equal distances from it, and the cosmolineæ-stream that flows towards b will in itself be intrinsically no stronger than that which flows towards a, because the comparatively insignificant mass bp goes to make up the resultant of the whole; hence the only thing to be considered here is the *distance* of b from c, the matter between p and b is not to be taken into account at all. The result of attraction will be the same as if b were situated *apart* from and unconnected with the solid sphere as in Prop. 7, and hence we may with regard to the energy of gravitation exerted upon b as compared to that upon a say, attraction of b is to that of a as ac^2 is to bc^2.

597. Prop. 10. If, however, instead of a perfect sphere we have a flattened elliptical body, and instead of the steep protuberance of Prop. 9, we have the equatorial bulge of the ellipsoid (fig. 17), then the case will be very different; for here we have in the first place according to Prop. 9, $a : d = dc^2 : ac^2$. If ed be the shortest diameter, and the angle fcb as well as angle bcg right angles, then is the segment $fcba$ considerably greater in mass of matter than the segment $bcgd$; hence we have to conceive the attraction upon a greater, namely by $\frac{ak + dm}{4}$, and that upon d less, by a like quantity $\frac{ak + dm}{4}$; this will give us the proportion $a : d = (dc + \frac{ak + dm}{4})^2 : (ac - \frac{ak + dm}{4})^2$.

If now, for instance, the elliptical figure $p\ g\ d\ a\ f$ is to represent our own planet, the earth, a will indicate a point at the equator, and d one of the poles, the greatest semi-diameter ac according to Airy being 3962.8, the smallest $dc = 3949.5$,* and the difference between both (i. e. $ak + dm$) $= 13.24$ Engl. miles, then the proportion would stand thus:

$$a : d = (3949.5 + 3,3)^2 : (3962.8 - 3,3)^2$$

that is $a : d = 15624627.84 : 15677640.25$

and $15677640.25 - 15624627.84 = 53012.41$; $\frac{15624627.84}{53012.41} = 294\frac{39}{53}$.

This value of $\frac{1}{294\frac{39}{53}}$ being equally distributed over two equal cones bcg and fcp (fig. 21), it follows that owing to the elliptic form of the earth alone, and independent of the centrifugal force, the attraction on each of the two poles is greater than at any point of the equator by $\frac{1}{294\frac{39}{53}}$ divided by 2, hence $= \frac{1}{589\frac{25}{53}}$, or very near $\frac{1}{590}$, agreeing with the value given by Sir J. Herschel.

598. Prop. 11. (v. fig. 12). A solid sphere's attraction upon a particle placed on its surface-level, vertically *beneath* the summit of a steep protuberance, is to the attraction upon the mean surface level, as the sphere's radius *minus* the height of the protuberance is to the sphere's radius. So that in fig. 12, the sphere's attraction upon p compared with that upon a is, as $ac - bp$ is to ac.

---

* According to *Airy*.

599. Here both p and a are attracted with equal energy, because in the first place both are situated at the same distance from c, and secondly p is pulled upon by c with the same common resultant force as a is; but the monits situated in the vertical line bp having their vacui or lineæ-gaps fed through centre c by way of p, p is pushed towards b by the cosmolineæ supplying bp; and being thus also acted upon in an opposite direction by a force represented by bp, p is attracted towards c with $pc - bp$ or, which is the same, with $ac - bp$.

600. *Note.* The word hollow in the following propositions means *void of matter*. And by a hollow sphere we always understand that its inner surface is exactly *concentric* with its outer surface, and its solid shell homogeneous.

601. Prop. 12. A particle of matter situated *outside* of a hollow sphere is attracted as if all the monits of the whole material shell were collected in the centre of the sphere.

The reason for this is a similar one as in Prop. 6.

602. Prop. 13. (Fig 14.) A particle of matter situated *within* the empty space of a hollow sphere is in equilibrio at any point, wherever it may be placed.

603. For in fig. 14 p tends toward c with a force ad, which represents the mean attractive energy of the shell expressed by its thickness ad, at the same time p tends toward d with a force $= d's$, but as $ad = d's$, it is clear that the *in*going and *out*going streams of cosmolineæ striking the particle p are of equal strength, and hence keep p at rest, or in equilibrio.

604. Prop. 14. If, however, a section of the shell be removed, any particle within the hollow space can be in equilibrio in no point (except in the very centre) and will always be moved to the nearest point of the inner surface of the shell. If the particle happens to be between the centre and the removed section, then the particle will be moved toward the centre.—The greater or less velocity of this motion will depend upon the comparative size of the removed section of the shell. The greater the mass of matter thus removed, the greater will be the velocity of the moving particle.

605. For in fig. 14, if a section of the shell $m\ s\ a\ f$ be cut out, for instance, in f, then within the hollow space $d'c$ the centrewards flowing stream of cosmolineæ ac is in its average energy less than the outgoing stream cs, hence p will be attracted towards d'. If $s\ n$ be the removed section, and the particle p happens to be between d and c, in the straight line sc, then will p (nd being less than ad) be moved towards c, and by its momentum to the opposite side of the shell's inner surface beyond c.

606. Prop. 15. (fig. 15). And if we place within the hollow space of a hollow sphere a solid spherical body of measurably great diameter, instead of an inappreciably minute particle, the different parts of the spherical body will have to sustain different degrees of attraction, although the body itself will be in equilibrio with regard to the hollow sphere.

607. In fig. 15, t is attracted towards centre n with tn; again t is attracted towards h with $th = 2\ tn$; t therefore has to sustain a pressure from attraction of 3 tn in *one* direction; n the centre, has to sustain only an attraction of $1\ nh = 1\ tn$, and so has h to sustain the attraction of only $1\ hn = 1\ tn$.

608. And if body tn, fig. 15, be changed to a soft, yielding mass, it will flatten out and spread as much as possible, having its shortest diameter in the direction of the hollow sphere's radii, and settling upon h as its lower level. Any particle placed anywhere in the hollow space of this sphere will fall upon the nearest point of the spherical body th.

609. Although the section $b''a''$ of the solid shell is nearest to ht, yet ht does not draw nearer to a'' on that account; because ht acts equally energetic on its opposite sides, that is: the affected areas on the opposite inner surfaces of the shell are directly as the squares of the distances.

610. PROP. 16. If (fig. 16.) in a spherical shell with a solid spherical concentric nucleus separated by a hollow space, two particles are placed at different distances from the sphere's centre, one particle in the *hollow* space, the other on the surface of the nucleus, both will be attracted with equal energies towards the centre, and not in proportion to their distances;—neither will the particle in the hollow space be in equilibrio, but has to fall upon the nucleus.

611. For in fig. 16. if ab is the shell, dc nucleus, bd hollow space, we reason thus: x tends toward c with $ab + dc - ab = dc$.

and d tends toward c with $ab + dc - ab = dc$.

612. If, however, the particle moves in an orbit around the nucleus with centrifugal force sufficient to prevent its falling upon the nucleus, then will the motion around the latter be as undisturbed as if the material shell of the hollow sphere did not exist at all.

613. PROP. 17. (fig. 16.) If in a spherical shell with a solid spherical concentric nucleus separated by a hollow space, two particles are placed within the nucleus, but at different distances from its centre, they will be attracted towards that centre with energies proportional to their distances from the centre. In this proposition the results are the same as if the whole spherical shell were solid throughout, and also as if the shell ab did not exist at all.

614. For in fig. 16, if ab is the shell, dc nucleus, bd hollow space, we say: m tends toward c with $ab + dm + mc - (ab + dm) = mc$.

and d tends toward c with $ab + dc - ab = dc$.

therefore $m : d = mc : dc$.

615. PROP. 18. (fig. 16.) If in a spherical shell with a solid spherical concentric nucleus separated by a hollow space, two particles are placed at different distances from the sphere's centre, one particle in the hollow space, the other inside the nucleus, the attraction upon the latter compared with that upon the one in the hollow space, will be as the distance of the former from the centre is to the length of the radius of the nucleus.

616. For in fig. 16, if ab is the shell, dc nucleus, bd hollow space, we say:

x tends toward c with $ab + dc - ab = dc$

and m tends toward c with $ab + dm + mc - (ab + dm) = mc$;

therefore, $x : m = dc : mc$.

617. PROP. 19. (fig. 14.) If in the solid shell of a hollow sphere two particles are placed at different distances from the centre, they will be attracted in the direction of the centre with energies proportional to their radial distances from the *inner surface of the solid shell,* and not from the sphere's centre.

618. For in fig. 14, we say:

g tends toward c with $ag + gd - ag = gd$

and b tends toward c with $ab + bd - ab = bd$;

therefore $g : b = gd : bd$.(and not $g : b = gc : bc$)

619. COROLLARY. (Fig. 14). Although a particle placed within the hollow space is in equilibrio in any point in this space, and does not sink down to the centre, yet all the lower parts of the solid shell have to sustain (and do so by means of their *cohesion*) an immense pressure from the layers above. (We are speaking all this time of non-rotating spheres). And with the melting of the solid shell would its liquid matter fall towards the centre and fill up the hollow space.

620. It may seem paradoxical that a particle placed within the hollow space, close to the inner surface of the solid shell, and left to be in a state of perfect freedom to move, should not fall towards the centre, while on the other hand, the shell as soon as liquified should do so at once. But the pressure from the overlaying matter is doing it as soon as cohesion is taken away.

621. PROP. 20. (fig. 15). If from the inner surface of a spherical shell, steep protuberances, say in the shape of cones of different vertical extent, project centreward, and a particle be placed at each apex of these cones, then the said particles will be attracted towards the nearest points of the shell with forces proportional to the vertical extent of their respective protuberances.

622. In fig. 15, d tends toward c with $ab = a'b'$,
and d tends toward a' with $a'b' + a'd$ in an opposite direction, hence d towards a' with a force equal $a'd$.

In a similar manner we find this proportion to hold good with regard to all other protuberances.

623. PROP. 21. (fig. 15). If from the inner surface of a spherical shell, a steep protuberance in the shape of a cone project centreward, a particle situated at the base of the cone and in a vertical line drawn through the apex of the cone, will be in equilibrio with regard to gravitation, just the same as if the protuberance was not there at all. In fig. 15, a as well as a' tend toward c, with $ba = a'b'$;
and a' tends toward b', with $a'b'$;
hence a' in equilibrio.

624. PROP. 22. (fig. 15). But if there be an open tunnel leading from the apex of the protuberance vertically to the outside of the shell from d to b', and a heavy body be dropped into the centre of its exterior orifice b', this body will fall to a', and would remain there if it had no momentum. But as every falling body has acquired a certain amount of momentum, the body will leave a', ascend against gravitation and go beyond a', that is beyond the level of the inner surface of the shell, into the protuberance; and even far beyond the apex d towards centre c, if the shell be of sufficient thickness to give to the falling body the requisite momentum. The body will oscillate up and down, alternately below and above a, and finally, if there be a resisting medium in the tunnel, come to rest in a', similar to a body oscillating up and down a tunnel through the centre of a solid globe. This follows from Prop. 18, and its corollary.

625. PROP. 23. (fig. 14.) If there be an open vertical tunnel leading from the outside of the shell through gbd fig. 14, and a heavy body be dropped into the centre of its exterior mouth a, this body will fall as far as d, the inner surface of the shell, and then being unaffected by gravitation, on account of the opposite and equal streams of the latter, proceed solely by virtue of its acquired momentum to the opposite side of the hollow space until it strikes the solid shell, and there it will stay if perfectly non-elastic. It will not settle down into the centre, however near that may be.

626. COROL. In a solid sphere suppose a narrow *hollow* cone having its apex in the centre of the sphere, and its base in the circumference of the sphere. Two particles placed within the *hollow cone* at different distances from the centre of the sphere are attracted with energies inversely as the squares of the distances from the centre; while on the other hand, two particles placed within the *solid sphere* at different distances from the centre are attracted with energies directly as the simple distances from the centre. Two particles placed not far from the centre of the sphere may therefore be only a short distance apart from each other horizontally, the one in the solid sphere, the other in the axis of the hollow cone, and yet, although at equal distance from the centre, how very differently will they be attracted towards the centre, the one with an immense energy, the other scarcely at all.

627. PROP. 24. GRAVITATION OF RINGS. If inside a ring of solid matter and of equal width and thickness a particle be placed between the ring and its centre, the particle will be attracted towards the nearest point of the ring. This applies not only to a ring having its greatest width in its own plane, but also to those rings having their greatest width at right angles to the ring's plane.

628. In the ring the demand of the monits for cosmolineæ is, as in the sphere, also made upon the *centre* of the ring, and therefore these cosmolineæ will have to flow from the centre to the body of the ring, and can thus push along particles being in their way. But with the inflowing cosmolineæ that is, those streaming from the outside *towards* the centre, the case is quite different, for here the cosmolineæ in going centrewards are *not all* obliged to pass through the matter or body of the ring; they do come in from every other direction also, while the same total amount of cosmolineæ thus going in, has all to pass back again from the centre to the narrow rim of matter, and consequently being then much more concentrated. Hence any of the attenuated inflowing general streams that happen to pass through the body of the ring, must be very much inferior in strength to the more concentrated particular streams opposing them; and a particle placed between the body of the ring and its centre will necessarily be pushed to the nearest point of the ring.

629. OBSTACLE INTERPOSED BETWEEN TWO BODIES MUTUALLY ATTRACTING ONE ANOTHER. Newton says: "Suppose an obstacle is interposed to hinder the congress of any two bodies A, B, mutually attracting one another, then if either body, as A, is more attracted towards the other body B, than that other body B is towards the first body A, the obstacle will be more strongly urged by the pressure of the body A than by the pressure of the body B, and therefore will not remain in equilibrio." This as a general expression is true enough, but it does not hold good with regard to the attraction of gravitation, for which it is naturally supposed by the reader to apply likewise, from the wording of the whole sentence. If A is by gravitation more attracted towards B than B is towards A, it surely indicates that B contains more matter (i. e. more monits) than A, for according to Newton's own gravitation laws the attraction of gravitation of a body is directly proportional to its mass of matter. If, for instance, A contains four monits and B twenty monits, then will B pull upon each monit of A by means of five times as many cosmolineæ as A pulls upon each monit of B. Yet that side of the obstacle which is near B will be pressed by the 20 monits of B, each urged by four impulses = 80, and the side near A by the 4 monits of A, each urged by 20 impulses = 80. Both sides of the obstacle therefore have to support the same pressure, and the obstacle remains in equilibrio.

630. If, however, on the other hand, in the preceding case A and B are allowed to *fall freely* towards each other, then body A will fall with the same momentum that B falls, viz: 20 times 4 = 80; but A will fall five times as fast as B, and if the obstacle is placed at some distance midway between the two falling bodies, then will the obstacle be hit and moved *first* by the body of *less* matter, but all three, viz: body A, body B, and the obstacle be arrested and come into equilibrio as soon as they meet.

631. FURTHER REFLECTIONS ON THE GRAVITATION OF SPHERES. Sup-

pose a hollow sphere, its shell solid and to have a thickness of a thousand miles; the hollow part of the sphere to extend another thousand miles from the inside of the shell to the sphere's centre. A particle of matter introduced into any place of the hollow space will remain in equilibrio (Prop. 12).

632. But if there be placed at the centre *c* of the sphere a nucleus, even of the exceedingly small diameter of one foot, the particle which thus far had been in equilibrio, and, may be, only a few inches from the inner surface of the shell, is now forced to move a thousand miles towards *c* away from the ponderous shell untill it arrives at the diminute nucleus.

633. It may seem strange that the particle spoken of should be obliged to go to so small a mass of matter (one foot diameter) from which it is separated by a distance of a thousand miles, and not to be moved by the attraction of the enormous mass of the shell from which it is separated by a distance of only a few inches. But that it must be so is certain, for within the hollow sphere the outward going stream of cosmolineæ is balanced by the centre-wards flowing stream of cosmolineæ which latter is here augmented by the additional attraction of the nucleus.

NOTES APPENDED.

Ad §9(1). There are two words which are at present almost universally considered as synonyms, as expressing the same identical thing, but which always ought to be kept distinct to represent two widely distinct ideas or conceptions; the same word should invariably be used only for the same idea it is intended for. We allude to the words *power* and *force*. Both are capable of causing motion of matter, but the former, being innate constituent, and at the bottom of all,* moves matter *indirectly* by means of force in the shape of force-lineïts in motion, while the latter, viz: force, moves matter *directly* by virtue of indwelling active power.

Power is a primitive cause, force a secondary. Power is an active constituent principle, an indefatigable, uninterrupted activity, *dwelling* within the most ultimate minutest substantive entities of extension, the *lineïts*. Forces, on the other hand, are lineïts in motion, urged on by innate power. By forces we are not to understand any innate, interior, unextended principles; forces are extended entities of *one* dimension, they are lineïts in motion. One class of them may exteriorly be applied to matter, and is fit of being communicated or transferred from one body to another, and on that account they might be called *accessory* force-lineïts, to distinguish them from the other class which are the lineïts composing the monits, and called the *constituent* force-lineïts.

If we keep these distinctions always in view, we shall find it easy in all our investigations of nature, even in the most abstruse ones, to steer clear of the meshes of confusion, contradiction, and one-sidedness, in which so many philosophical systems are entangled. We can, for instance, clearly perceive 1st, what *Heraclitus* of *Ephesus* called the first principle of things, belongs to the category of power† and by no means to that of force; and 2d, what *Newton* calls *inert* matter, can justly be called "inert or inactive" only in case the innate *power* of matter be entirely ignored, and the *accessory* force to be assumed as the sole cause of motion existing. Without accessory force, a body or any of its atoms can not leave its place; and again, when partaking of this force, a body or any of its atoms cannot stop moving on its own account. Only in this sense, with regard to accessory

---

* *Primitive* powers are the ultimate causes of all physical action, and of these is Versatile Activity the ultimate source of all possible *changes* amongst the particles or materials of the universe.

† According to him Fire is the first principle, but this fire or heat is nothing material like the "caloric" once advocated by scientists, but a kind of rational power, working by necessity, is self-motive and never at rest.

force can matter be called inert, while as regards power, matter is at all times full of action, both versatile and pulling, and is never inactive or dead. Even if stripped of all its accessory force (translatory motion), the ultimate particles of matter would still be full of the two primitive active powers End-unition and Versatile Activity which in fact constitute its very essence. Hence the ancient Greek philosophers were in so far right that they conceived all nature alive with active matter; they knew nothing of, and could never have considered that idea [made by a more modern doctrine so familiar to us] of a so-called inert dead matter in contrast as opposed to the active principle of power, because they were unacquainted with the conception of *accessory* force, the existence of which becomes apparent enough in Newton's researches on motion, but its real existence, essence, and nature, was not even recognized by him. The doctrine of *inert* matter is of comparatively recent origin, first propounded by Newton. He, however, instead of leaving to matter its interior powers and of saying: matter is inert only with regard to *accessory force*, went so far as to deny to matter and its atoms all and every kind of activity,* thus sending down one valuable truth of the ancients while raising another truth, valuable in itself, though imperfectly announced.

Ad §9(2). In the quotation at the head of § 11, *Tyndall* justly calls the motion of the hands of a watch a "phenomenon" and not a force. Other authors mean by forces simply the "tendency of a body to pass from one place to another."

R. Mayer defines *forces* to be "whatever may be converted into motion." Here then, by the word "whatever" is indicated the existence of something else that is not motion, yet which may be converted into motion. This "whatever"—the force—is therefore asserted to be something independent of and distinct from motion, a reality capable of manifesting motion. Moreover he asserts in unequivocal terms: forces are indestructible, convertible, *imponderable objects.*

Many physicists take "force" to be identical with "motion," another kind of force is to them another kind of motion, and instead of calling a certain law the law of the convertibility of natural forces, it is thought more appropriate to call it the law of the convertibility of *motions.* To the quivering motion produced in molecules by their falling upon each other, they give the name of heat. According to their views, this quivering motion of the molecules is merely the redistribution of the straight translatory motion which the molecules lost in coming together. Now we may well ask, is it possible that by the mutual fall of the molecules of sulphur upon those of potassium, and of the molecules of carbon upon those of oxygen—which latter, moreover, consume some energy in being *pulled apart* from the molecules of the nitrogen and potassium in the saltpetre—all being already close together within a little lump of gunpowder, can the falling motion of these molecules through inconceivably short distances ever in any way be the equivalent to the motion of the ball propelled by the explosion, a ball many times heavier than the powder that was used for its lifting? The fall of all the molecules of the powder, in mutually combining, can do in the end no more than to lift them again to the distance from which they fell, which would be an inappreciably small distance, and the intermediate state of quivering does not in the least alter the result. How much less able are they by their fall to raise a mass many times heavier, to

* Nine years preceding his death, Newton declared most decidedly, that he by no means considered gravitation as an essential property of bodies.

the height of 60 or 70 feet. Consequently the assumption, that force is mere motion, must be an error.

"The word force," says Faraday, (1859), "is understood by many to mean simply the tendency of a body to pass from one place to another. What I mean by the word 'force' is the *cause* of the physical action," and "none of the separate forces can vary in its absolute amount."

Ad §**25**. Ever since the amount of scientific research has multiplied and grown into unwieldy proportions, the scholar, or rather the schoolman, spinning webs of ideality from out his own brain, will have nothing to do with physical science and experiments,—the experimentalist, on the other hand, steadily engaged in testing the realities offered solely by changing phenomena, will have nothing to do with speculative philosophy; "the student of mind ignores matter, the dissector of brain ignores mind;" neither takes any interest in the labor of the other, nor caring for the results of each other's inquiry, and both seem either unable or unwilling to scale the imaginary barrier (existing only in their prejudices) that separates them, and to examine the realms of their rival lying on the opposite side. The division of labor in science "seems indeed to narrow and dwarf the producer while it improves and multiplies the product."

Ad §**47**. It is quite plain that without a *persevering* exertion in the *primitive powers* not only to act, but to act persistently, always, and for ever, in a determined particular manner peculiar to itself, no reliance could be placed in any physical law whatever, no consistency in them could possibly be ascertained; nothing in physical science could ever be undertaken with the least assurance of success, and demonstration by experiment would be out of the question, because it could never be known what was going to happen in manipulating with matter and force, or how soon and unexpectedly, at any moment, from a thousand different directions, thousands of unforeseen impulses of far off acting forces might burst upon and influence the action of forces at hand. Nature under such conditions could never answer any of our interrogations addressed to her, not even with: "it can be so," or with "it cannot be so." Nothing but a most complete chaos of motion and uncertainty of results would then be prevailing, instead of assurance, and order, and physical laws.

Ad §**79** and **80**. That it is not a strange and unheard of assumption to treat on a subject such as here put forth in §66–79, viz: on the cosmolinea or immaterial physical line as a medium, will be apparent when we are made aware of, that even so extremely cautious a physicist as Faraday had a long and valuable paper published "On the Physical Character of the Lines of magnetic Force," in which he most ably advocates and urges the assumption of the existence of *physical lines of force*, identical in their nature, qualities and *amount* both within the magnet and outside the same. "I conceive that when a magnet is in free space, there is such a medium (magnetically speaking) around it." "What that outer magnetic medium, *deprived of all material substance*, may be, I cannot tell;" but "the curvature of the lines of magnetic force to me indicate their *physical existence*." "As magnets may be looked upon as the habitations of bundles of lines of force, they probably show us the tendencies of the physical lines of force as they also occur in the space around." And especially in his experiments on induced currents did he find these lines to be such faithful assistants, that he could not think without them, and in testing his views with regard to the physical lines of force, both by experiment and by a "close cross-examination in principle," never had he been made aware of any error involved in their use. Indeed, he admitted that they led him safely through all the intricacies of the most difficult questions he undertook to solve.

"Thus," says Tyndall, "the lines of magnetic force are continually before his eyes, by their aid he colligates his facts, and through the inspirations derived from them he vastly expands the boundaries of our experimental knowledge. The beauty and exactitude of the results of this investigation are extraordinary. I cannot help thinking while I dwell upon them, that this discovery of magneto-electricity is the greatest experimental result ever obtained by an investigator."

Yet, notwithstanding all such splendid results, no one else besides Faraday seems to have placed confidence in his *physical lines of force*, and availed himself of the mighty lever for research which they offered. Scientists heard the words of the great master, but either not willing or not able to appreciate them, they left this useful and fertile field untilled, and allowed to run to waste again the ground already broken.

If after all this there are some of my readers who think I have gone too far in my speculative and hypothetical tendencies by proposing the cosmolinea, assuming something of which nothing can be known, I would refer them to an article in the London, Edinburgh, and Dublin Philos. Magazine, May, 1873, in which Sir Wm. Thomson reviews a theory which assumes with regard to the constitution of heavy bodies: 1) "Their indivisible particles are cages—for example, empty cubes or octahedrons vacant of matter except along the twelve edges; 2) the diameters of the bars of the cages," etc. Does any one know of cages—empty cubes or octahedrons having bars of matter only along their edges, and which cages are the *indivisible* ultimate particles of matter? and yet an eminent man in science justly has not disdained to give this theory a fair hearing.

Ad §**91**. To raise in our minds the distinct physical images of the various objects and processes referred to in the preceding paragraphs on gravitation, the faculty of imagination had to be called into requisition, and now in recapitulating the above in a more summary manner, we again need its aid. Let us in the first place contrive in imagination such a *medium* or *web and weft* of *force-lines* crossing and intersecting space in every conceivable direction and in every place—more predominant when converging towards any of the centres of the great celestial bodies, and being of more intense array and strength when near them than when further off. Let us next fill up the compass of space occupied by each celestial body, with ultimate minute *spherules of matter called atoms or monits,* as defined in §100–106, spinning or rotating unremittingly around their axis and striking away from the aforesaid converging force- or gravitation-lines portion after portion, thus pulling briskly towards them these continued gravitation-lines, which in their rapid flow* strike and move along any loose material particle or mass that lies in their path, or merely press upon them if immovable. Let us consider more closely this universal medium of immaterial force-lines in connection with the material monits (atoms) and see what our deductions will lead us to. In any material sphere, for instance a planet, by far the greatest number of the force-lines pulled toward its monits (atoms), intersect at the centre of the sphere, and this very centre will therefore be the place, from out which the most force-lines are pulled for internal use, and towards which just as many force-lines in the shape of gravitation-lines

---

* La Place estimates the velocity of gravity at six millions of that of light.

have to flow from the outside of the sphere to make up the deficiency. Le- us manage the whole of this machinery "in accordance with strict mechant ical laws, let every step of our deduction" be made in conformity with the primary operations assumed and laid down in §124–131, carry the different propositions thus found, from the world of imagination to the world manifest to our senses, and see if not the result of these deductions is to bring about the very phenomena of gravitation which have been revealed to us by observation of astronomers and physicists. "And if," to use the words of Tyndall, "in all the multiplied varieties of these phenomena, including those of the most remote and entangled description, this *fundamental conception* always brings us face to face with the truth; if no contradiction to our deductions from it be found in external nature, but on all sides agreement and verification," if, moreover, besides confirming those propositions on gravitation already taught by Newton, it has actually suggested a number of new ones that can be demonstrated to be true, and if finally this same fundamental conception be able to reconcile the contradictions and disputes of contending opposite schools and parties of philosophers, in short, if it be "such a conception, which never disappoints us, but always lands us on the solid shores of fact, it must, we think, be something more than a mere figment of scientific fancy."

The thus conceived and above mentioned medium serves two purposes at the same time. It not only informs us—by being undulated upon in luminiferous waves—of the existence of myriads of other celestial bodies besides that of our sun, but it also performs all the functions of gravitation by darting in converging rays with immense speed towards the centres of celestial bodies.

Ad §**97** and **391**. Progressive undulations, according to Airy, in order to explain the phenomena of *diffraction*, must not be of the nature of radial shakes like those assumed by Faraday in his "lines of force," but they must be true waves, where the motion of a succeeding set of particles or other substantive units is determined by the relative motion of the preceding set, so that the motion of the substantive units may be origin of motion to other such units "extending round them through a very large solid angle." "It is absolutely necessary to admit in the theory explanatory of diffraction, that each disturbance produces a swell, which swell is propagated in all directions." *Airy.*—With Faraday's undivided, not of parts consisting, indefinite lines of force these requirements can never be fulfilled, but they can easily be satisfied in the undulation of our cosmolineal medium, where each ray consists of an almost infinite number of but slightly connected substantive units, namely the lineïts, most easily loosened so as to be capable of acting in sets upon succeeding sets, as well as being acted upon by preceding sets, producing a kind of swell in the medium (viz: the web and weft of the cosmolineæ) which swell is propagated in all directions through any solid angle required. From this it will be seen that Prof. Airy's objections to Faraday's theory can by no means apply to mine.

Ad §**108**. Although agreeing with Faraday about the *existence* of physical lines, yet his speculations about their functions and essential properties, as well as his views on matter and force, differ considerably from those of mine on the same subjects.

a) From a comparison of his views on atoms with those contained in these pages on monits (atoms) it will be found that he conceivés an atom to be a *centre of indefinite force-lines;* our monit, on the other hand, though consisting entirely of force and power, is not a mere "centre of force," but is *composed* of a number of radii each being a lineït, i. e. the possibly smallest *unit* of force-lines. These radii are with one of their ends united to a common centre, and with the other ends arranged equally apart from each other, turning around an axis, and thus forming a rotating least spherule that may be said to consist of radii, which radii being the ultimate units of force-lines. These minutest of spherules have consequently a definite form and are of a certain least size and volume, and may serve as the bearers of velocity-lineïts, thus enabled to give rise both to momentum and inertia. These monits are separated from one another by intervening space which, however, is no void, but filled with the web and weft of darting *immaterial* force-lines of indefinite extent, themselves composed of lineïts joined endwise. Monits (atoms) are in fact little bodies existing independent of the forces by which they are surround d, and capable of existing without the latter. Force-lineïts being a something substantive, an entity, exerting resistance only in *one* dimension, whereas monits (or atoms) of matter exert resistance in all *three* dimensions.

1st. As to Faraday's centres of force, the radii of each centre extend to infinity, or at least as far as "gravitation extends," and the size of his force-particles or atoms "may be considered as extending to any distance to which the lines of force of the particle extend: the particle indeed is supposed only *by* these forces, and where they are it is" (Faraday 1846). Thus matter and force is one and the same thing with him. Matter, according to his view, is everywhere present, and there are no intervening spaces unoccupied by it, in short, matter is *continuous* throughout, and "in gases the atoms touch each other just as truly as in solids." Matter with him is not only continuous but it "is mutually penetrable." The *centres* themselves of the force are separate and vary in their distances from each other, closer together in solids than in gases, the same as atoms are separate from each other, but that which is truly matter with him are the radii or lines of force which, however, are of infinite extension, or reach at least as far as gravitation extends. "The power arranged in and around the centre might be uniform in arrangement and intensity in every direction outward from that centre, and then the section of equal intensity of force through the radii would be a sphere."

In the *monit* these radii are of shortest possible length, i. e. the length of a lineït or ultimate force-unit, the whole monit revolving around its axis and pulling the indefinitely long force-lines in converging rays towards its own little body [as explained in §124–130].

In Faraday's theory the next view that is similar to mine is:

2d. That instead of the universal ether pervading all matter as well as all interstellar spaces, it is the lines of force which penetrate all, the interstellar as well as the spaces between the atoms of matter; that these spaces are filled with nothing "but forces and the lines in which they are exerted."

3d. That there are lines of gravitating force, and that these are "certainly extensive enough to answer in this respect any demand made upon them by radiant phenomena."

4th. Another main feature of Faraday's hypothesis that finds with some modification its counterpart in the present pages is his opinion, that it is possible that the vibrations which in certain theories are assumed to account for radiation and radiant phenomena, by means of an ether, may "occur in the lines of force which connect particles" of matter and their atoms, as set forth in the preceding (v. 1st), a motion which as far as it is admitted, will dispense at least with the universal luminous ether, which has hitherto been held as the medium in which the vibrations of light take place. In Faraday's hypothesis, it is supposed that the lines of force—extending through the whole planetary and stellar system as far as "the lines of gravitating force" extend—may be affected "in a manner which may be conceived as partaking of the nature of a shake or lateral vibration."

In Faraday's view "matter is not merely mutually penetrable, but each atom extends, so to say, throughout the whole solar system."

To the system of Faraday as he left it, there may be made several objections. For instance:

1) In reference to his views that matter and its ultimate elements are mutually penetrable, we may remark that impenetrability in all three dimensions must always be considered as the most essential property of the ultimate particles which constitute matter, and wherever resistance in all three dimensions is found, there we say is *matter* or *corporeal* substance, and where we meet with resistance in no more than *one* dimension, we say, there is *force* or *linear* substance [as in gravitation.]

2) The mind can never be satisfied with the assumption of mere centres of indefinite force-lines as a substitute for atoms (monits). A something definitely circumscribed with regard to these centres of force-lines is required, to which must be ascribed a *surface* over which the velocity-lineïts of a body that is to be set in motion, may be attached and distributed, and from which surface they under certain circumstances again may depart and, in so doing bring the body to rest. You must have *something to which the velocity-lineïts may cling to,* and by which they may be carried. A something that does not, without a certain consumption of time, yield at once to a change of motion whenever a force is applied to effect this change; in other words: that it must manifest those very phenomena erroneously laid to the so-called *inertia* thought to be a body's most essential property.

In propelling a ball weighing, say, $\frac{1}{20}$ of a pound, with a certain force, for instance a definite quantity of gunpowder, the ball will have a certain velocity v. If now a ball weighing five pounds, i. e. one hundred times the quantity of matter, be propelled with the same quantity and force of gunpowder, the velocity of the ball will be only $\frac{v}{100}$. From this we see that there is something in matter over which the velocity is equally distributed, so that in proportion as the ultimate particles, and consequently the atom-surfaces, are more numerous, the less velocity does each one of them receive; notwithstanding this, the whole quantity of velocity, i. e. the *momentum* of the five pound ball, is the same with that of the $\frac{1}{20}$ pound one. Momentum as well as inertia in matter point to *something definitely circumscribed* as the constituent, indivisible unit of matter.

Ad §**118.** Let us in imagination dissolve and dissever all the different groupings and compounds of matter in the universe, and they will yield monits; next let these monits be dissevered into their constituents, and we shall have nothing left but forces in the shape of *lineïts*, each one consisting of two power-points; so that after all there remains as the constituent primitive principle of the web and weft of the universe nothing but couplets of power-points. These couplets of power are the most ultimate *real* entities, the lineïts. The most ultimate of the principles underlying even the lineït, is the reactive power-point, which, however, as its name already indicates, can never exist by itself. And thus we have come to the result that mutually *reacting power-points*—uninterruptedly active power-points unconsciously exerting an effort for some most simple elementary end, are at the bottom of all.

Ad §**146.** *a*) Yet the *repelling* action of the molecule §145, 146, will most generally be more energetic from around some of the vertical plains of its surface than from other parts of the same surface, according to the peculiar state of grouping of the monits within the molecule.

b) In the molecules of non-volatile liquids, such as the fatty oils, etc., the repelling lineïts issue more *equally* and *evenly* from all the different parts of the molecule's surface than they do from the surface of the molecules of volatile liquids. In the latter, such as water, alcohol, sulphuric ether, the repelling lineïts issue more from around certain circumferential lines of the molecule, so as to give to the sphere of the molecule's repulsion a lenticular outline, instead of that of a regular sphere. In alcohol this outline of the lenticular sphere of repulsion we suppose to have a much more flattened shape than that of the repulsion in the molecules of water; and still more flattened in sulphuric ether than in alcohol.

c) Hence if the same amount of heat is added to each of the above named liquids, they will expand very unequally, because this heat can assist the molecule's repelling lineïts in the one liquid not with equally good success as it can in the other. But when in the gaseous state, the molecules have been far enough removed from each other, so as to render by distance the *peculiar molecular* repulsion inefficient, then will equal amounts of heat added to each of the above named three volatile substances: sulphuric ether, alcohol, and water, do their expansive work with equal success in all three, or in other words: *the gases of all volatile liquids will be expanded alike by the same quantity of heat.*

Ad §**169.** The new theory sets to rest all the uncertainties that may be and have been entertained in regard to the doctrine of attraction, whether attraction must be considered as dwelling in the particles of matter or not. In the new view taken by us there is 1) not needed any "*actio in distans,*" which is opposed alike to sound common sense as well as to the most refined philosophical reasoning. 2) There is a substantial continuum (linearium) filling all the universe, this substantial continuum, however, consisting not of a material but of an immaterial, i. e. a one-dimensioned substance, by which the monits or atoms of matter are on all sides surrounded, liable to be taken along in its streams produced by the activity of monits of bodies situated even at enormous great distances from the attracted matter.

Ad §**172.** Objecting in one of my letters to the doctrine of "potential energy" as most generally set forth as regards a weight, which when suspended is said already to *contain* stored-up potential energy, I received the following answer from a highly esteemed authority offering a true exposition. "If there were but two elastic molecules of matter in the universe at a considerable distance from each other, and these were permitted to move at a given instant, they would approach each other with an increasing velocity until they arrived at an intermediate point very near each other at which attraction would cease and repulsion begin." We may here say that by virtue of their momentum the molecules would go on to approach even after they had come to the point where repulsion begins; but let that pass. We see at once that the foregoing answer contains no explanation, it states only a supposed fact. If you then ask, what makes these two molecules, whether elastic or not, move towards each other with increasing velocity, and how can you conceive a thing to pull or act without a medium upon another *distant* thing in a place where the acting thing *is not?* the answer will be this: "It is true, we cannot conceive that a thing can pull at a distance without a medium, nor do we care, but we believe in the fact because it is so, and thus we are satisfied, we do not trouble ourselves about the cause." Just as any other mere empirist is apt to answer who "employs himself in poring over the dissection of the dead carcass of nature rather than to set himself to *ascertain* the powers of living nature." (*Bacon*). But the above answer is not philosophy, and is unbecoming the vocation of the physicist. In this way of treating the subject we never get to any simpler and more general laws of nature. And yet, to arrive at unity, simplicity, and the most general conceptions among the innumerable facts of nature, should ever be the highest aim of physical investigation. How in gravitation, velocity-lineïts (or energy of motion) are taken from the surrounding medium and stored up in *falling* bodies, we have endeavored to make clear in another place (131, 268, 407).

Ad **197.** Overwhelmed by the contemplation of such magnitude of the universe and its innumerable systems of worlds, the student of nature is apt to come to the conclusion that the being called "man" is so utterly insignificant as to amount next to nothing in the balances of heaven, to be overlooked and neglected like the merest worm which, as it crawls in dust to seek its scanty food, is by the wanderer's foot crushed down into destruction.

Now let him step aside from his giant telescope, take up a microscope and espy the wonders of organic structure. Here he shall find, in examining, for instance, the structure of any living plant, that his researches have at last carried him to the individual **cell,** a thing so minute in size that three millions of them need only one cubic inch of space.

But what is still more remarkable, each of these little cells is a veritable *microcosm*, a miniature universe of its own. For there are currents and streams of cosmolineæ converging and diverging, and going round and round from nucleus to circumference, driving before them orbs in the shape of little globules. How minute the smallest of them are in the plant-cell has not been ascertained. Through the nervous filaments of animals, globules are propelled of $\frac{1}{30,000}$ part of an inch diameter.

Here then, each of these living cells represents a miniature world of action; and no doubt, in time to come some gifted genius shall unveil within the living cell a mechanism as perfect and complete, yet more complicated in its nature than the mechanism of the grand cosmical motions. For in the cell, especially the vegetable, we have not only a *system of motion* but at ths same time, a most powerful laboratory for the manufacture of chemical compounds, as well as for building up tissues and structures most subtile, chiefly for the binding of heat-lineïts which are to be stored up in such a manner as to be available to man as well as to the inferior animals, who find in this their vegetable food, not only the requisite means for keeping up their bodies' temperature, but also a supply of muscular energy.

If now, after such reflections as these, the observer who found himself next to nothing in comparison with the universe, institutes again comparison, but this time between himself and the organic cell, he will be apt to regard a human being of some significance, and may perhaps say: if there is *method* and *order* in each of these little individualities, the cells, how much more must there be in the united structure of my own individuality which to subserve, millions upon millions of such little worlds called cells, are constantly in attendance. But above all, of what wonderful construction must be man's mind which is able to institute researches, to draw inferences and deductions, to weigh, and judge, and calculate, to unravel and to compute the laws of nature, to make its forces obedient to his will, to soar to heights unspeakably sublime, and even to invade the macrocosm's most awful inner depths.

Ad **200**. Our theory has led us to perceive that several of its points are agreeable with the philosophy of Parmenides, though in other respects our views do differ widely.

1) The universe includes *all* that really **is**.

2) The universe or the All is not infinite, but limited and " like to the bulk of a sphere well rounded on all sides, every where distant alike from the centre."

3) Although within the universe there may be and are immense spaces void of *matter*, yet there is not the least interspace *absolutely void;* there is, according to our lineïstic view, no place void of cosmolineæ. The whole universe is a continuum full of them. The All is full of the Existent. The cosmolineæ offer resistance only in *one* dimension, and are therefore penetrable in all but *one* direction, hence allow transit and unlimited free motion to every thing moving, except in the exact direction in which they have their extension.

4) This All, in as much as its most ultimate fundamental principles are concerned, is " birthless and deathless" and ever-enduring.

5) The universe considered as an entirety does not change its place nor its spherical shape. And with regard to its boundaries (the cosmo-velo) and to its centre, the All is moveless and steadfast.

6) As to the three primitive fundamental powers (§62) each of them is " self-similar alway." They do not change their nature and particular functions (v. §63[1]), nor are they convertible one into another. And as to the lineït, it too is always self-similar and unchangeable in its constituent existence; yet its functions undergo changes in so far as it becomes either possessed or deprived of Versatile Activity.

7) Although we must dissent from Parmenides as to the immovability of that with which the All is filled and " sated," for we conceive that the cosmolineæ are incessantly broken at one end and joined again at the other, and that they have motion—yet any interspace so produced, does by no means imply vacuity of *being*. It implies merely the interruption of cosmolineal connection, while at the same time millions of other cosmolineæ are crossing these interspaces in innumerable different directions.

Ad **238′**. See, how by these terms it is sought to lay shackles on the inquiring mind, and to avoid all efforts for any further research and meditation on the nature and essence of the one, universal, and most comprehensive of all the beings with which man's faculty of INTELLECT may occupy itself. If writers had merely intended to denote the *present* inability of our race to get at the conception of the All-Intelligent in conformity with scientific principles, they would certainly never have made use of the above names, and rather chosen the words " The Undetermined" for it.

Ad **243**. 1) Materialism defines itself in the following few sentences: Besides matter—i. e. substance that offers resistance in all *three* dimensions —there is no other substance different from matter, no immaterial substance, for instance, no substance that offers resistance in but *one* dimension, and hence there can be also nothing composed of such a one-dimensioned substance. Therefore that which is usually called the immaterial soul of animal and man, as well as that called the great soul of the universe, said to consist of immaterial substance, has no existence.

2) Though being thoroughly convinced of the existence of immaterial substance (as offering resistance in but *one* dimension) and firmly believing in such of its combinations called "souls" in general, and the great macrocosmic soul of the universe in particular, I must add that the *action* of this universal soul [acting as it does by means of darting rays, and under the influence of its intellectual faculties, that are seated in the centre of the universe] is, as well as the *action* of any other soul, *dependent* upon the existence of matter. And moreover, neither the reflecting, living universal soul of the All-Intelligent, nor the soul of man, nor that of animal, could ever have existed if the universe had *always* been bare of all matter though it had been full of immaterial substance, as it is now. It does not, however, follow from this that the soul of an organized being must necessarily dissolve with the dissolution of its material frame. For only in case that ALL existing matter were to dissolve or vanish, could that inference be just and admissible. Both, matter and the universal soul, together with its all-comprehensive intellect are coeval. Not so, however, are the souls of man and animal, they are still being produced as they shall be produced hereafter.

3) The soul of the living organized being consists of immaterial substance extending through the different parts of the body, but the principal portion of this substance being rolled up so as to form a definite system of convolutions, constituting in the case of man: the immaterial convolutions within the human brain; in the case of the All-Intelligent the principal portion of this immaterial substance constitutes the convolution around the centre of the universe: in the first case giving rise and serving as a substratum to what is called man's intellectual faculties of mind, in the second case to the intellectual faculties of of the All-Intelligent.

Ad **264.** To assume, as some have done, that atoms of matter are characterized by their inactivity and inertness, is nothing more than to assume negations, and the assertion (added to these negations) that an atom is solid, without explaining what is meant by solidity of a thing that is thus marked by nothing else but inaction, must be confessed to be very incomprehensible and against all reason; for what else can solidity consist in, if not in a *power of action* to prevent any exterior forces from making it unsolid. To make the inactivity of matter doubly sure, physicists went even so far as to ascribe, inherent to matter and its atoms, a primitive power they called **vis inertiæ**, which should cause matter to persevere in its state of rest if any extraneous power were going to move it, implying thereby that if no such attacks were made, the vis inertiæ was *inactive.* But primitive power can never be inactive. How then, could matter be considered as in itself inactive. To be still more inconsistent, if the physicist requires it, this same power of inertia must do something quite contrary to its essential work of holding matter at rest, it must also be able to *move from place to place* a body which received only one *momentary* impulse of motion, and to *move it incessantly* in a straight line for ever. It is as true as any thing can be, that a power is needed to do this, but this power can never be the power of inertiæ the peculiar tendency of which is: to do nothing. Now even reason may be persuaded to accede sometimes to erroneous opinions, but to contradictions and diametrically opposite assertions never.

These questions, viz: 1) by what cause motion was continued in a body that received but a momentary impulse; and whether it be a substance, quality, or something else that is actually proceeding from the moving body into another body, by which the latter gains just as much as the former loses and no more. 2) What is it that makes a body resist any sudden attacks which try to move it from its state of rest, or to change the body's motion into another direction; and many more questions hitherto deemed perplexing, may be consistently and satisfactorily solved and answered by applying the doctrine of the *active lineït*, the accessory vivacious velocity-lineït.

Ad **269**. There are two cases then, where lineïts are disjoined and withdrawn from the *gravitation*-cosmolineæ, the 1st case, where detached polarized lineïts are struck aside by the monit; the second case, where lineïts are detached in the shape of velocity-lineïts acquired by the falling of bodies. These two cases we find not only in the macrocosm, the great universe, but likewise in the innumerable myriads of microcosms, or the little worlds in miniature, the organic cells.

The isolation and absence of these lineïts from the gravitation-cosmolineæ, however, is not an everlasting one. For though in the shape of velocity-lineïts many of them, at times cling to monits, and are transferred from monit to monit, and from body to body, afterwards to be converted into heat-lineïts; and although the others may wander in circuitous routes through interstellar space, yet eventually, sooner or later, they all are, as soon as they reach the circumference of the universe, annexed to the gravitation-cosmolineæ to act again as an integral part of the latter.

In our planetary system it is the *sun* in which the gravitation-cosmolineæ lose lineïts in greatest abundance, yielding them up not only as velocity-lineïts to the descending or falling metallic particles of its chromospheric trains, but also in immense amounts of detached polarized-lineïts.

In our terrestrial globe we find polarized lineïts being detached and isolated from the gravitation-cosmolineæ in due proportion to the earth's mass or weight. But as regards velocity-lineïts, i. e. force-lineïts, or vis viva, these are rather sparingly abstracted from the gravitation-cosmolineæ, chiefly in the planet's motion through its annual orbit; also in organized beings capable of muscular motion, and endowed with a nervous system; likewise in the *falling* of all bodies, especially in the fall of rain, hail, snow, aerolites, and running streams of water, as well as in the fall of ocean-waves and tides; we find them in the gentle descent of atmospheric air and the slowly subsiding grain of dust as well as in the avalanche that comes thundering down the mountain's side, or in the cataract that precipitates itself in the gulph below.

Every drop of rain as it patters down upon the leaf, every falling leaf as it noiselessly touches the ground, is charged with some force-lineïts taken fresh from the gravitation-cosmolineæ. All these falling bodies when stopped, let go again their newly acquired dynamic energy or force-lineïts, which now appear in the shape of whirling heat-lineïts upon the surface that stops or retards the body's downward motion.

What a hallowed spot then must be the alpine precipitous glen along which comes hurrying down the majestic torrent fed by a hundred rivulets above. Whenever in the mountain solitudes we look upon the waters of the cataracts, as they leap, and plunge, and roll, and rush with deafening din from rock to rock, a kind of presentiment seems to tell us that some powerful unseen agencies are being unfettered in our presence incessantly. And although even the scientific traveller, as he approaches these sanctuaries of nature, may not be fully aware of how near he is to the wonderful workshops where mighty forces of motion [soon changing into heat] are being struck off by myriads of invisible little hands (by the monits); yet in common with the untutored son of the wilderness, a peculiar sensation of awe is coming over him, and he *feels* that something there is present to halt the wanderer's steps, and make him pause in solemnity of thought.

Hence the commendable usage among many of the religiously disposed tribes of Asia, who, in order to invigorate and elevate their minds by means of prayer and devotion in some lonely and romantic spot among the hills and higher mountains, wander forth from time to time to chose such glens where rushing streams abound, and seated at the foot beside some waterfall, they chant together in religious worship, and make the mountains ring with shouts of adoration and deep emotional hymns.

Ad **279.** The word "possible energy" or "potential energy" is only another term for unknown energy x. Physicists in making use of the same, clearly admit that they do not know anything further about their potential or possible energy than that there is some kind or other of force in a falling body. Yet they assure us that it is the very identical force, somewhat modified, that proceeded from the hand that threw the body upwards, because it was found that the heat evolved from that body on striking the ground, was an equivalent for the force applied in throwing the body aloft. So also in the condensing of a gas by the external application of mechanical force, scientists assumed, that the heat evolved thereby is an equivalent for the force spent in compressing the gas. This assertion of Mayer which he repeated in several of his writings has, however, been proved to be radically false.

Ad **287.** Only give to gravitation-lineïts a chance to attach themselves to the atoms (monits) of matter, and they will do so most readily, and give you as much *vis viva* as ever you need. Gravitation-lineïts require nothing else but the proper conditions which allow them to attach themselves to bodies, and these conditions are: that the bodies are not to be hindered by any obstacle from being pushed in the direction in which the stream of lineïts flows. Therefore, if you can only remove these obstacles, no matter in what way it be done, whether by hard lifting, or by a short jerk, or by mere cutting of a string, or tipping over into an abyss, all will have the same effect; the only work to be done is to bring about these necessary conditions, which when not assisted by the heat of the sun [producing fuel, wind-, and water-power, etc.,] has to be done by muscular or some other force, and then it will be found that we have to *lift against* the gravitation stream, and spend or lose muscular force in proportion to the height and weight raised. But this lost muscular force does not stay and is not stored up in the raised weight, it goes off as heat into the atmosphere. Whenever the weight has been raised and no obstacle interposed, then the condition for the attachment of gravitation-lineïts is given, and it is, only in the act of falling, that force-lineïts taken from the gravitation-streams are stored up in the falling weight.

That which *causes* the weight to fall to the earth is not to be sought in the action that lifted the weight, but in the action of gravitation-lineïts urging the weight on towards the earth's centre, and the longer this action is allowed to go on, that is: the longer the distance through which the weight falls, the greater will be the opportunity for gathering and storing up force-lineïts in the form of *vis-viva* (velocity-lineïts) which, when brought to a halt by an obstacle, manifest themselves as heat. All these force-lineïts existed previous to the fall of the weight in the streams of gravitation-rays from which they were detached during the fall and attached to the weight. Thus are gravitation-lineïts diminished in numbers, and would eventually all be worked up, if there was no chance offered for the numberless heat- and polarized-lineïts—continually streaming in all directions towards the circumference of the universe—to be converted back again into gravitation-lineïts by the power dwelling in the cosmo-velo. [v. 385–389].

Ad **391.** Vide Notes appended to §97.

INDEX.

The numbers refer to paragraphs and not to pages.

CORRECTIONS.

Page 10, line 1 and 6, for "inertia" read "inertiæ."
Page 11, Axiom VI for "[6(2)]" read "[6(1)]."
§51, line 4, omit "most."
Page 25, line 5, for "it" read "cosmolinea."
§101, line 1, after "power-points" insert "each."
§135, line 5, for "b" read "h."
§188, line 8, for "either" read "neither."
§197, at the end add "(v. Notes app)."
§215, line 1, for "213" read "214."
§230, foot note, line 9, for the first "a" in rejuvanated read "e."
§234, line 6, for "primite" read "primitive."
Page 62, line 8, add "(v. Notes app)."
§240, in lower part of diagram put "*.n*"
§245, line 5, for "inconscious" read "unconscious."
§258, line 7, for "univeral" read "universal."
§308, line 6, for "veocity" read "velocity."
Page 79, line 1, insert "," after "flinging."
§330, line 5, for ". These" read ", these."
Page 90, line 5, for "354" read "355."
Page 91, line 1, for "359" read "360."
§438, line 8, after "not" insert "immediately."
§532, line 6, for "evolved" read "set free."
§553, line 4, after "is" insert "by the power of Synduction on the inside linings of the brain."
§597, line 20, for "21" read "17."
§624, line 10, for "a" read "a′."

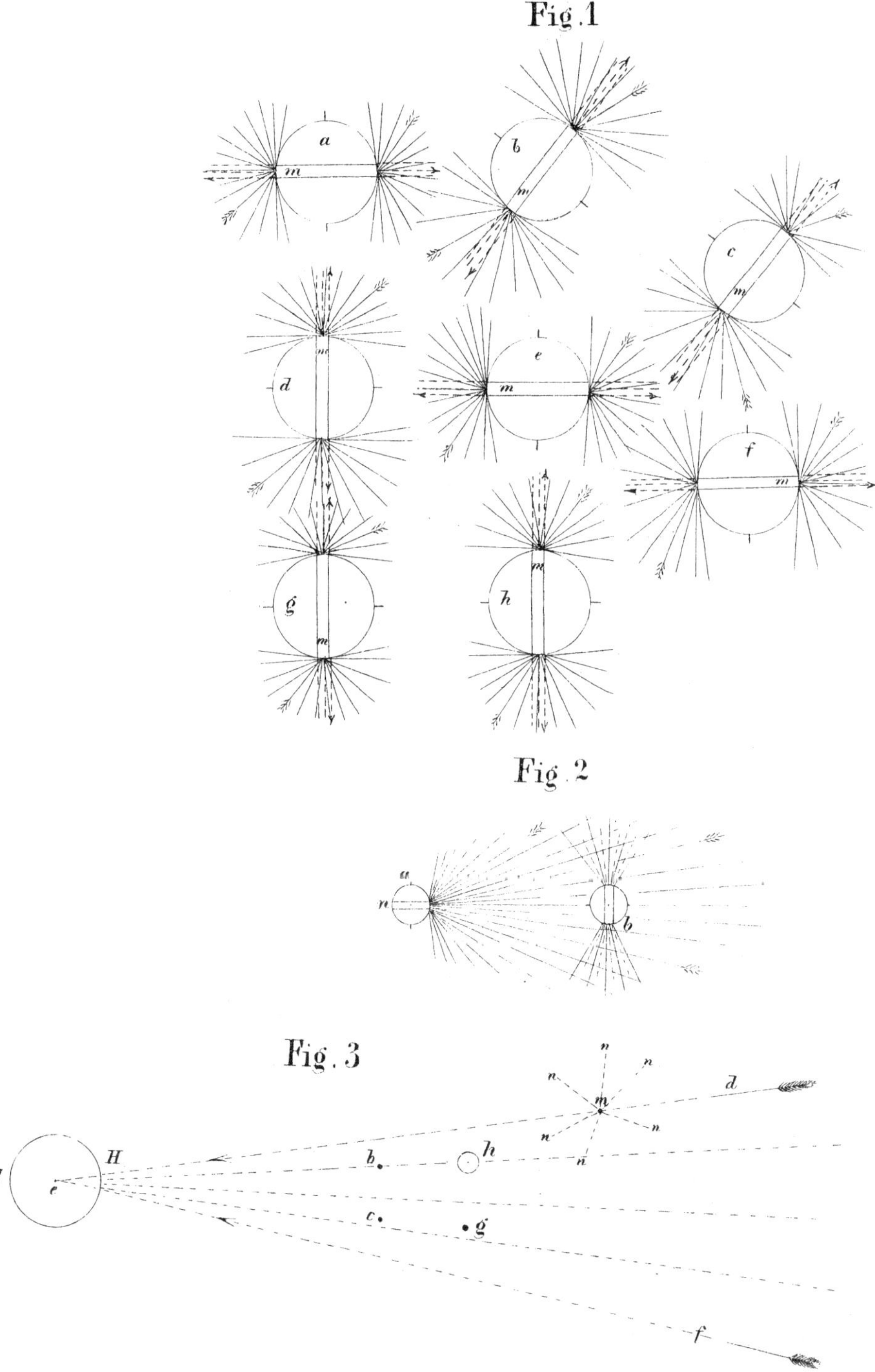
Fig. 1
a
m
b
m
c
m
d
m
e
m
f
m
g
m
h
m
Fig. 2
a
n
b
Fig. 3
E
e
H
b
h
c
g
m
n
d
f

Fig. 4.

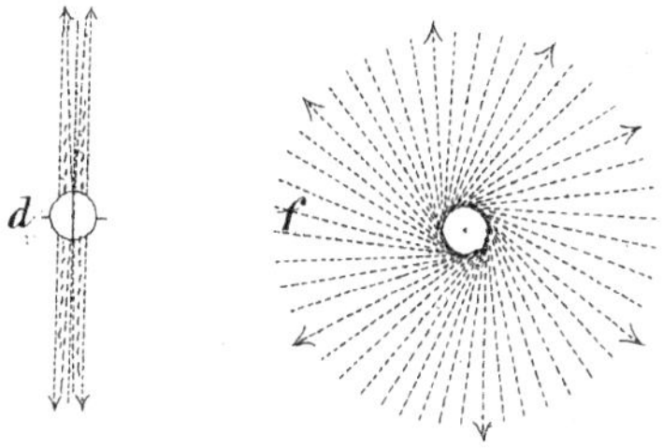

Fig 5.

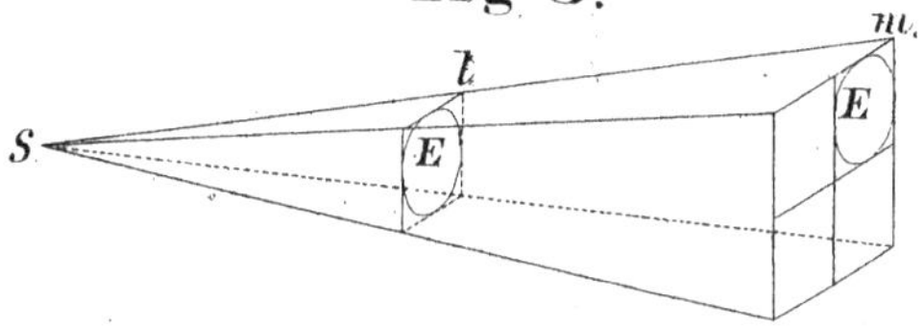

Fig. 6.

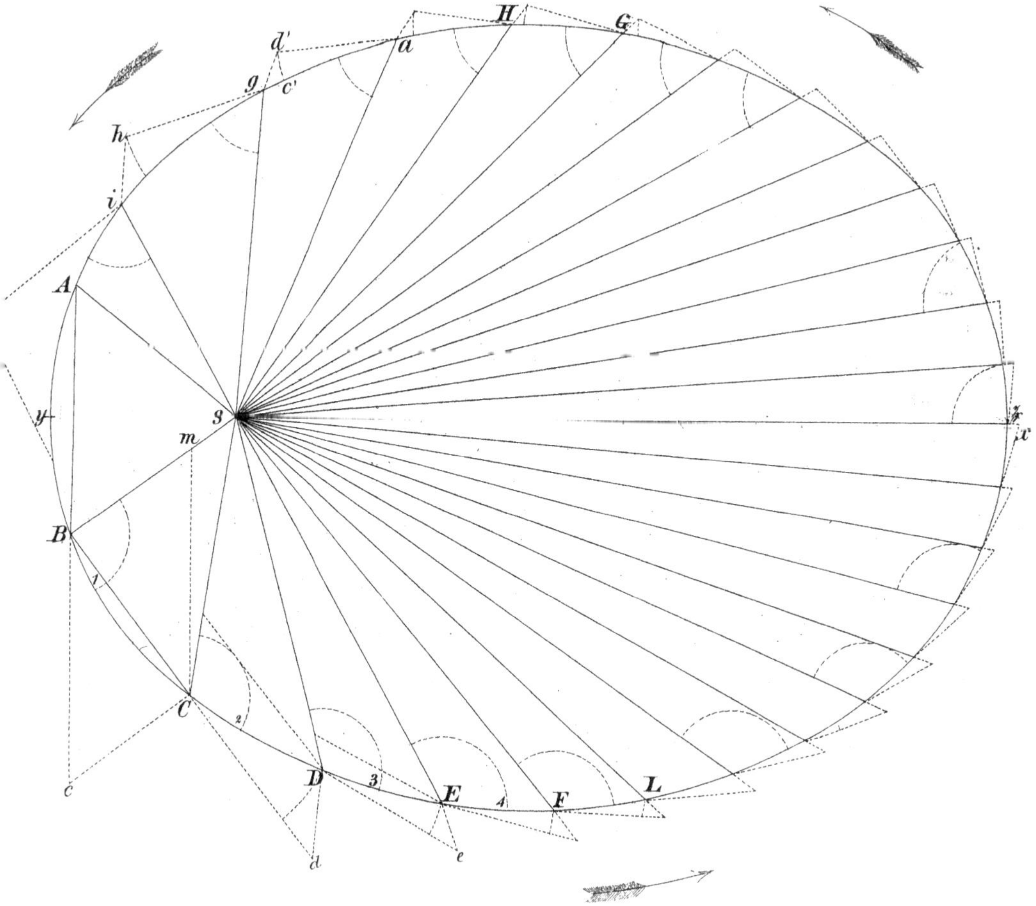

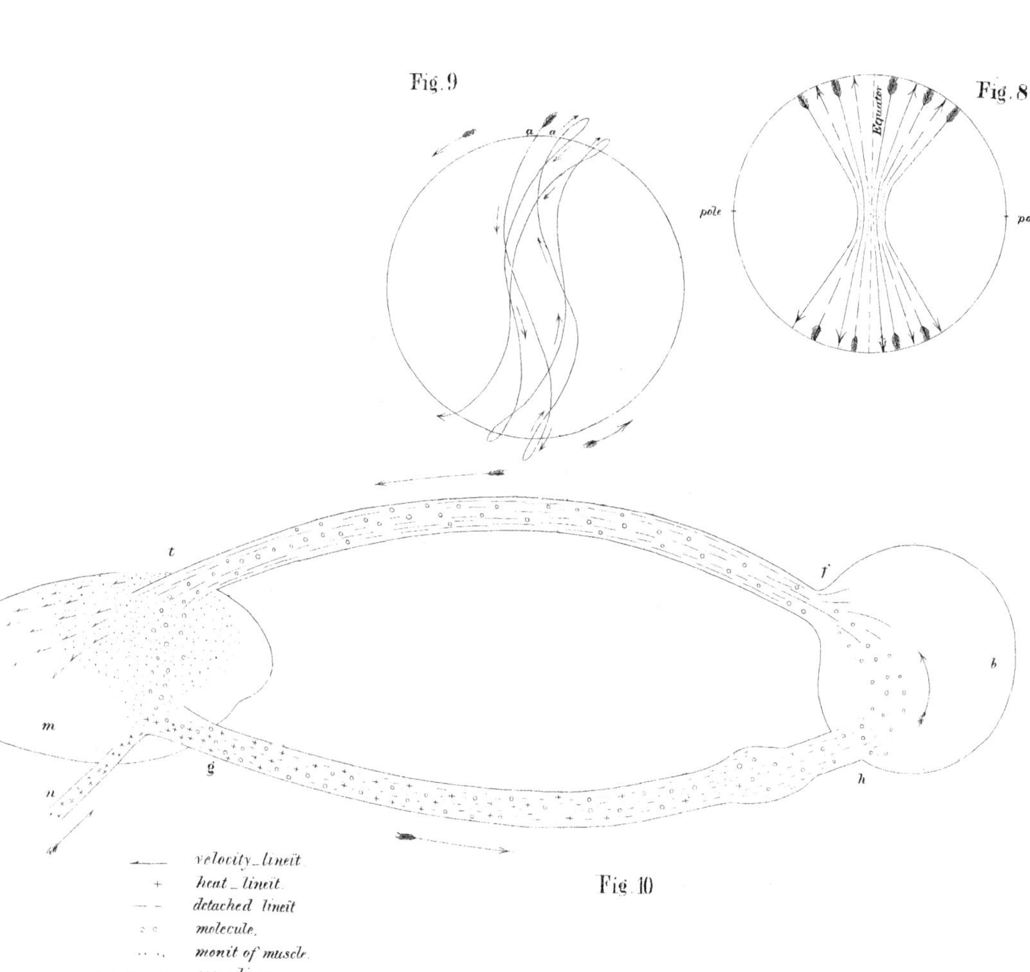

Fig. 9

Fig. 8

Fig. 10

Fig. 11

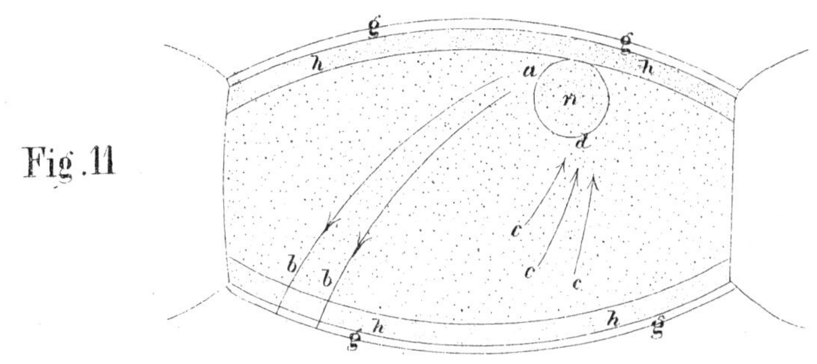

n nucleus or cytoblast.

g g permanent wall of the cell, Cellulose.

h h mucilaginous lining, protoplasm.

Fig. 13

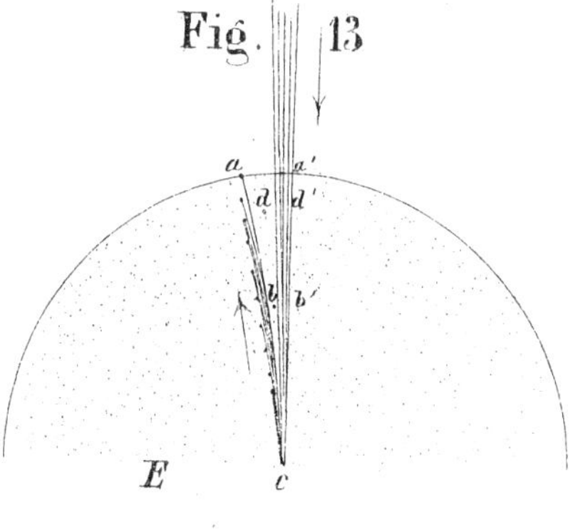

Fig. 12

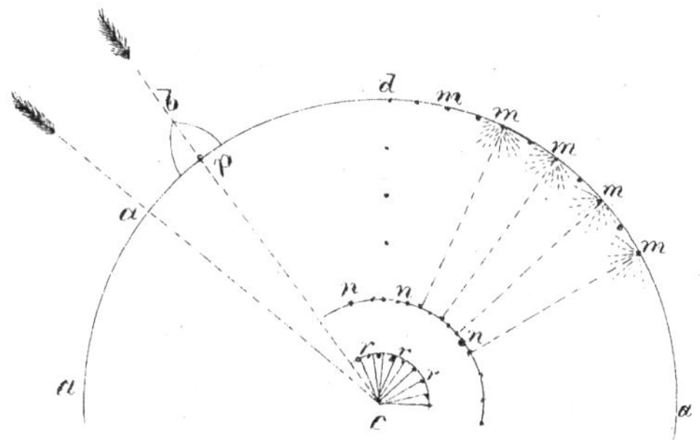

Fig. 15

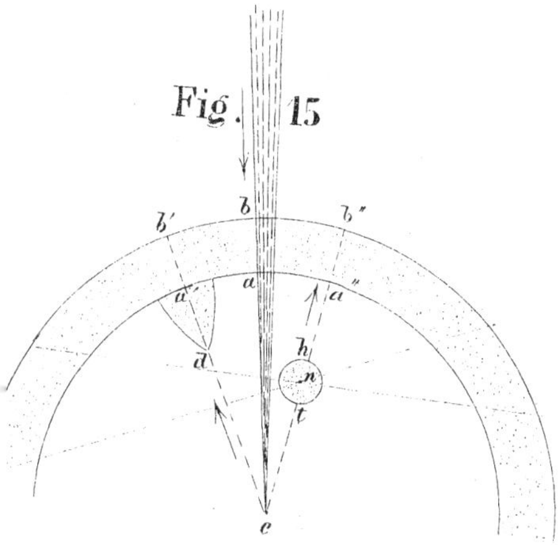

Fig. 14

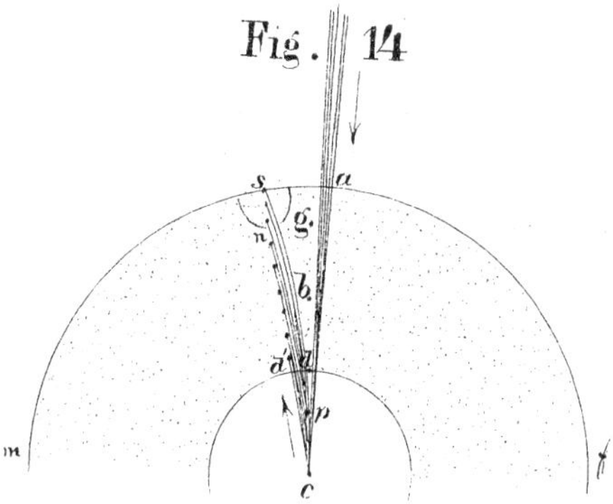

Fig 16

a
b
x
d
m
c

Fig 19

Equator

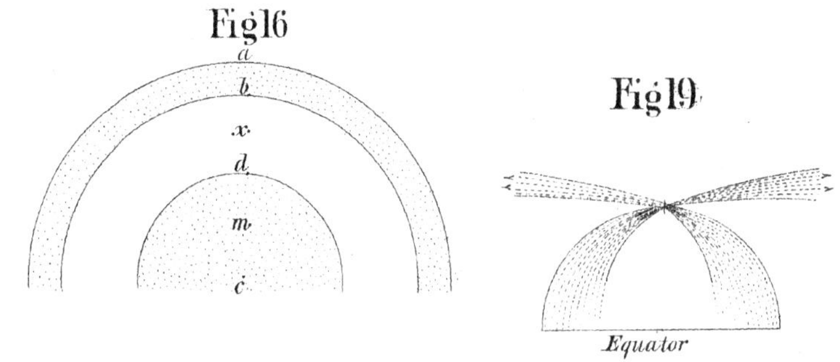

Fig 18

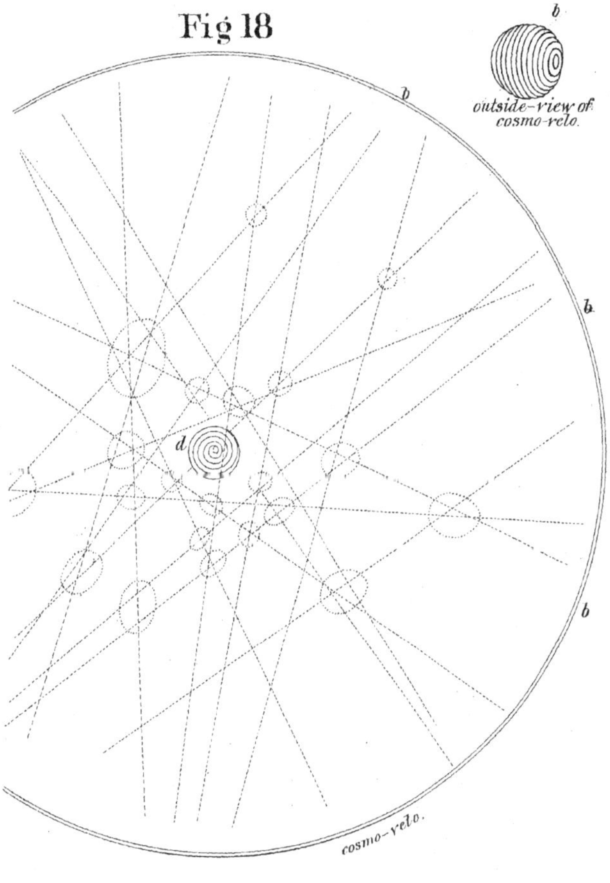

b
outside-view of cosmo-velo.
b
b
b
d
cosmo-velo.

Fig 17

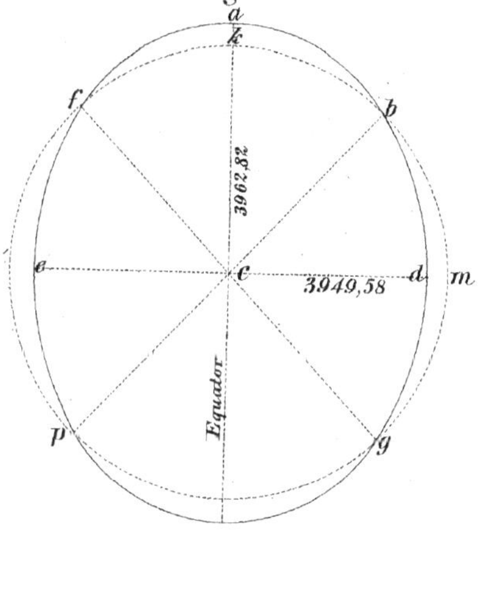

a
k
f
b
3962,82
e
c
3949,58
d
m
Equator
p
g

www.ingramcontent.com/pod-product-compliance
Lightning Source LLC
LaVergne TN
LVHW021359110826
845150LV00007B/1719

* 9 7 8 1 4 2 5 5 1 3 4 7 4 *